D0340760

Women in West Germany

BERG GERMAN STUDIES SERIES
General Editor: Eva Kolinsky

Volker Berghahn and Detlev Karsten, *Industrial Relations in West Germany* (cloth *and* paper editions available)
Peter J. Humphreys, *Media and Media Policy in West Germany*
Eva Kolinsky (ed.), *The Greens in West Germany: Organisation and Policy-Making*

In preparation

Josef Esser, *Industrial Policy in West Germany*
Richard Stoess, *Right-wing Extremism in West Germany*
Alan Kramer, *The West German Economy, 1945–55*
Gordon Smith, *The West German Party System*
Eckart Jesse, *Elections in West Germany*

GERMAN STUDIES SERIES

Women in West Germany
Life, Work and Politics

Eva Kolinsky

BERG

Oxford / New York / Munich

Distributed exclusively in the US and Canada by
St. Martin's Press, New York

First published in 19__ by
Berg Publishers Limi___.
Editorial offices:
77 Morrell Avenue, Oxford OX4 1NQ, UK
165 Taber Avenue, Providence R.I. 02906, USA
Westermühlstrasse 26, 8000 München 5, FRG

© Berg Publishers Limited 1989

British Library Cataloguing in Publication Data
British Library CIP data applied for

Library of Congress Cataloging-in-Publication Data

Kolinsky, Eva.
  Women in West Germany: life, work, and politics / Eva Kolinsky.
    p. cm.
  Includes bibliographies and index.
  ISBN 0–85496–238–7 : $43.75 (U.S.: est.)
  1. Women (West) I. Title.
HQ1623.K65 1989   89–31933
305.4′0943—dc20   CIP

Printed in Great Britain by Billing and Sons Ltd, Worcester

Contents

Tables, Figures and Appendices

Tables

To my mother

Acknowledgements

I would like to express my thanks to the Humboldt Foundation, and to Aston University for supporting research visits to the Federal Republic in preparation of this book. Special thanks are due to Dr Marita Estor (BMJFFG), Dr Wulf Schönbohm (CDU), Pia Wennigmann and Ruth Winkler (SPD), Eberhard Walde, Rita Werkmeister and Claudia Pinl (Greens), Otti Geschka (Frauenbeauftragte Hessen), Elvira Bickel (MdL Rhineland Palatinate), and Rotraud Hock (Frauenunion Rhineland Palatinate) for most informative interview sessions. Peter Munkelt and his colleagues from the SPD party archives have again provided extensive materials for my research, and endless cups of coffee. I have also been able to use the collections in the press archives of the Konrad Adenauer Foundation and the library of the West German Bundestag. Thanks are also due to Christel Lane, Catherine Hoskyns, Beate Hoecker, Melanie Sully, Helen Boak, Annette Kratz and many other colleagues and friends for useful discussions and comments. One of the most valuable resources in writing this book was the cheerful support I received from my husband and sons, their tolerance about meal times and their willing help with household chores. I would like to dedicate this book to my mother who has lived through all the changes and hardships and some of the opportunities of twentieth-century German women.

Introduction

In the course of the twentieth century and within living memory of anybody over the age of seventy, living conditions and political environments have changed dramatically. Given the emergence of advanced industrial societies in Western democracies, these changes are neither specifically German nor do they relate only to women. For the contemporary setting, Inglehart and others have shown how relative prosperity of lifestyle can shape value orientations, how educational qualifications can encourage political participation and how conventional institutional structures and processes have been challenged to adapt to new preferences, issues and personalised ways of doing things (Inglehart 1977; Barnes et al. 1979; Baker et al. 1981). These changes are broadly similar in advanced industrial democracies in the Western world, and in a global perspective of social and political change, a Western-type democratic citizen seems to be in the making.

For women, the emergent democratic citizenship includes visibly improved access to education, better opportunities of training and employment, equal rights to political participation and more scope to determine their personal lifestyle. Although each country continues to operate its own gender barriers or avenues of opportunity, the overall changes point in a similar direction: that of increased choice for women to create their own place in society, and to realise their potential and personality in the contemporary environment.

However, the German case and the situation of women in Germany are also special. Within living memory of older generations, Germany has experienced several political regimes, each with its own prescriptive doctrines and social values (Berg-Schlosser and Schissler 1987). The role individual citizens were expected or were permitted to play in the state, in the economy and in everyday life varied depending on the democratic or anti-democratic structures in the political system and the priorities of those in power. Until the foundation of the Federal

1

Republic in 1949, regime change dominated politics and forced adjustments of participation, party preferences and beliefs in people's lives. In addition, shock experiences such as the hyperinflation of the Twenties or the dislocations and deprivations suffered after the Second World War created personal living conditions in which choice seemed all but obliterated by circumstance, and the struggle for necessities (Conze and Lepsius 1983). In countries which experienced continuity of their political system, adjustments of social attitudes and the taking advantage of new opportunities of employment, political participation or social customs could emerge within a sheltering framework of established institutions and processes. In West Germany, which inherited the chequered legacy of conflicting regimes and anti-democratic political cultures, the framework, democratic practices and social values had to be created simultaneously and within a short period of time.

If all Germans had to learn democracy and develop a democratic political culture based on participation rather than obedience, women had to undergo the same transformation – only more so. German women had hardly tasted voting rights and the rights to a parliamentary voice during the Weimar Republic when National Socialism cancelled the democratic political process and tried to recast the role of women in terms of motherhood, subservience to the state and giving service rather than discovering and fulfilling their own potential. The beginnings of democratic government in the immediate post-war years found women ensnared in the tasks of physical survival and providing for their families (Kuhn 1984). The forty years since the foundation of the Federal Republic have provided the first opportunity in German history for all citizens to use their rights of social, economic and political participation over several decades and develop or consolidate democratic political attitudes. The general inauguration into democracy was all the more intense for women as inherited restrictions on their rights of equality and chances of participation in law, employment and political life were scaled down or abolished as democratic principles began to permeate social institutions. West German women gained full political rights of participation as they gained social opportunities and experienced a multiple transformation of conventional women's roles.

The different political backgrounds and social experiences which set generations of Germans apart from one another have been a core element in the fabric of West German society and politics (Fogt 1982). Among women, the differences between generations are large enough to speak of a recasting of the role of women during the lifetime of the Federal Republic. To give just one example: in 1969, Heinrich Böll, who had already achieved international recognition as one of the outstanding writers of the post-war era, used the weekly *Die Zeit* for an unusual cause – in an open letter addressed to 'A German Woman' he put it to his intended female readers that it was high time they should stop being obedient and start using their minds (*Die Zeit* 25 July 1969). His target was the established practice of most women – in particular Catholic women – always to vote for the Christian Democratic party as if there was no choice in German politics. The German word Böll chose to describe women's electoral record since 1949 was *Stimmvieh*, a herd of cattle manipulated by conventions and in the German case also by the political potency of Catholicism. Women, Böll implied, had failed to develop political candour; for them political participation consisted of obedience to the priest, their husbands, the government of the day; they had yet to discover the ability to make individual choices based on a personal assessment of issues, party competence and preferences.

Twenty years later, Böll's reprimand seems oddly dated. The derogatory notion of women as *Stimmvieh* may have been exaggerated in the Sixties; it is altogether wrong at a time when women of all ages, educational levels and occupational backgrounds have shown themselves to be an increasingly selective and discriminating electorate, and when no West German political party can rely on women's votes. Women's electoral choices are now based on personal preferences and, more specifically, on whether or not they consider the policies of a particular party relevant to women and likely to improve their social opportunities. There are generational limits to these changes, and older women have been less prepared to switch between parties than have younger women who grew up in a democratic environment. The younger generation of West German women, however, have developed a newly active role as voters, party members and contenders for leadership positions; they have

3

also established a newly active role for themselves in education, in seeking qualifications, and in using the scope for personal development an advanced industrial democracy has to offer.

With a special focus on women, this book traces the emergence of choice, equal chances and patterns of mobility in West Germany. On one level, it is an attempt to examine the social and economic foundations of West German political culture and the scope for participation in the contemporary political environment. On another level, the book is a monograph on the emergent participation of women and the obstacles which continue to separate women's expectations and the promises of equality from the real opportunities afforded in society. Based on largely empirical profiles of lifestyles, attitudes, and participation in education, in the labour market and in political life, the study of women in West Germany also charts the pace of change towards a democratic society: the displacement of pre-democratic legacies by democratic political behaviour or, to pick up Böll's impatient metaphor, the transformation of women from *Stimmvieh* to citizens for whom democracy matters and who matter to democracy.

Choice has been a major factor in this transformation. In West German political culture, the transition from being a subject, set to obey the rules of the day, to a citizen able and motivated to participate actively in democratic life began to take shape once economic conditions were such that people could exercise choices between political parties, between career paths, lifestyles, places of residence. West German women coped with unexpected tasks in wartime and in the post-war years, yet these tasks were not experienced as choices but as adverse circumstances which required the kind of unflinching service which women had been expected to render under National Socialism (Chapter 1). The cornerstone for creating socioeconomic choices in the post-war era was laid in the Basic Law and its commitment to equality of men and women, a commitment which future legislation applied to the private sphere of the family, to working conditions and career opportunities. Since the Seventies, European directives on equality acted as a catalyst of reducing inherited gender gaps and opening avenues for West German women in employment and training (Chapter 2). By that time, many of the restrictive conventions which conditioned girls and women to be homemakers whose life would centre around their husbands, children and families had faded sufficiently to create scope for choice. Families were smaller in size than in the past, domestic chores had been eased, although women continued to bear the main responsibility in this area, and an increasing number of married women with children have opted for paid employment (Chapter 3). In the Seventies and Eighties West German women reversed the age-old deficit of schooling and acquired better qualifications at secondary level than their male contemporaries. The educational motivation has also been evident at the vocational level, with an increasing number of girls and young women obtaining accredited qualifications for employment through apprenticeships and higher education (Chapter 4). For the younger generation of qualified and motivated women, however, employment opportunities have improved without closing the gender gap of socio-economic disadvantage. Women's employment tends to be punctuated by career breaks, bunched in a narrow field of occupations, frequently at lower levels of skill with fewer avenues for further training or advancement. Although there are signs that women have begun to diversify their career choices and move into fields where the demand for experts will be high in the future – management, technical specialism, computer analysis – equality of opportunities in employment, and choices which match women's expectations and qualifications, have yet to be accomplished (Chapter 5).

If there has ever been a truly man's world, politics comes close to it. Since their enfranchisement in 1918, German women have taken part as voters, but have had little say in parliaments, governments or in the party organisations. The few women who rose to elite positions preferred to concentrate on women's issues or were channelled in this direction; within the parties, women were expected to hold coffee mornings or help at election times, not bid for the leadership. These limitations of the political role of women no longer tally with the expectations and ambitions of West German women today, in particular those who are active enough to join political parties. They are determined to win their share of political influence. The gender gap in West German political life is on the verge of collapse as political parties are responding to electoral pressures and membership demands with a variety of schemes to give women equal access to party offices, parliamentary seats and positions of political leadership (Chapter 6). Women seem set to play a more visible role in the political life of the future with real chances of equal participation. These in turn should accelerate opportunities in employment, and the scope for choice in women's private lives.

Women in West Germany is designed as an introductory text, with case study chapters on each of the key areas: the post-war situation of women, legislation, lifestyles, education, employment and political participation. Each chapter also includes a selection of important empirical data or documents to make this a usable, pragmatic book, something of a reference compendium to disentangle the focus on women from its uncertain concern with women's nature and to concentrate instead on the bricks and mortar of women's social and personal environments past and present.

References

Baker, Kendall J., Russell Dalton and Kay Hildebrand, *Germany Transformed. Political Culture and the New Politics*, Cambridge, Mass.: Harvard University Press, 1981

Barnes, Samuel, Max Kaase et al. (eds), *Political Action. Mass Participation in Five Democracies*, Beverly Hills: Princeton University Press, 1979

Berg-Schlosser, Dirk and Jakob Schissler (eds), *Politische Kultur in Deutschland. Bilanz und Perspektiven der Forschung*, Opladen: Westdeutscher Verlag, 1987 (Politische Vierteljahresschrift Sonderheft 18)

Conze, Werner and Rainer M. Lepsius (eds), *Sozialgeschichte der Bundesrepublik Deutschland. Beiträge zum Kontinuitätsproblem*, Stuttgart: Klett Cotta, 1983

Fogt, Helmut, *Politische Generationen. Empirische Bedeutung und theoretisches Model*, Opladen: Westdeutscher Verlag, 1982

Inglehart, Ronald, *The Silent Revolution. Changing Values and Political Styles among Western Publics*, Princeton: Princeton University Press, 1977

Kuhn, Annette (ed.), *Frauen in der deutschen Nachkriegszeit* (2 vols), Düsseldorf: Schwann, 1984

1
Between Chores and Dreams: Social Situation and Personal Expectations of Women in the Immediate Post-War Years

Women carried a mixed legacy of expectations and opportunities into the post-war era. The bourgeois and socialist women's movements of the early part of the twentieth century both campaigned for women's rights but disagreed on the nature of these rights, and on women's place in society. In the Weimar Republic, women enjoyed equal rights of political participation although many did not endorse the democratic framework in which these rights were to be used. National Socialism, finally, tried to turn the clock back and prescribe motherhood as the major social role for women. When the immediate post-war years brought the emergence of West German democracy with new avenues for citizens' participation people's everyday lives lay as shattered as many of the cities, and women were too bound up in the practicalities of physical survival to extend their rights or rethink their social roles. Overwhelmed with chores, their dreams turned inward, towards the private world of family life and comfortable living. The bulk of this chapter examines post-war developments. A brief glance at some aspects of the past is, however, useful to place women's situation and attitudes in their historical context.

Women and the Modern World

In 1914, one of the 'mothers' of the bourgeois women's movement, Gertrud Bäumer, noted that industrial development and modernisation in Germany had altered the social environment of women so profoundly that they could enjoy the freedom of self-realisation for the first time in history. Domestic chores

which had dominated the lives of previous generations seemed
less daunting in the twentieth century:

> The move from a house of one's own with an orchard and a vegetable
> garden, an adjoining laundry, a chicken run and storage rooms to the
> one-floor apartment [*Etage*] signifies the disappearance of large areas
> of former domestic work which were time consuming and demanded
> special expertise. Through technological progress, heating, lighting,
> cleansing have been simplified. Through ready-made preserves,
> bakery goods and delicatessen the provision of food has received
> considerable external back-up. One does no longer have to pickle
> beans or cabbage, to smoke bacon, to dry fruit, to bake and store
> cakes, to salt meats, let alone to butcher at home. The urban means of
> transport make access to suppliers easier. And then – sewing. If we
> consider that our grandmothers had no access to a sewing machine
> and had to sew all linens or clothes by hand, mend them and
> produce new ones with unbelievable diligence and hard work, we
> can understand why Schiller let his praise of the housewife culminate
> in the phrase: and never rests. (Bäumer 1914: 35–6)

Modern living conditions, technical appliances and the first
signs of a consumers' society had eased the burdens of homemaking, and women seemed now free to play a more assertive
role in society. For Gertrud Bäumer and the bourgeois women's
movement which she inspired this did not mean that women
would compete in a man's world. Since men and women were
regarded as 'distinctly different in their physical and emotional
make-up' (ibid. p. 272; see also Greven-Aschoff 1981) women
would build their own realm of expertise and social influence in
education, social services and communal concerns.

Even within the bourgeois women's movements, the same
experiences of changing social environments were interpreted
by some in a more overtly political and competitive way. Helene
Lange, for instance, argued that family life and the lives of
women had become so intertwined with the public sphere that
women needed to play a public role: since women attended
schools, were employed – at least prior to marriage – and had to
rely on an increasing range of public services in their everyday
lives, they should also be allowed to influence the public sphere
and enjoy the right to vote:

> Through direct contact with society as a whole, the modern woman

has become a political being – *zoon politicon* – as views and elements of education have been incorporated into her personality . . . Bismarck said 'he who has no vote is politically dead'. As voting is gaining ground as a means of exercising political power and we are learning to relate to it, Bismarck's statement needs to be extended by a further piece of statesmanlike insight, namely that he who is politically dead is also placed on half-power in his attempts to exert cultural influences. (Lange 1908: 101, 104)

The most determined calls for the enfranchisement of women emanated from the socialist women's movement and the German Social Democratic Party, the SPD (Thönessen 1976). For them, industrial society held the promise of equal rights and opportunities in economic and political life for men and women: although the SPD and the women's movement affiliated to it were the first to demand voting rights for women, women were not regarded as a special group in need of special liberation or endowed with special capabilities. The right to vote, they argued, had to be extended to all adult men and women in society regardless of class, status or wealth (Quarteart 1979). While the bourgeois women's movements envisaged women as playing a separate role, equal in value to that of men, but different in its focus on the family, on education, on emotional or cultural values and on local themes, the socialist women's movement demanded equality for all and assumed that gender did not matter (Frevert 1989). With adjustments of emphasis and topical pitch, these two contrasting perspectives on equality for women have determined women's politics during the Weimar Republic and during National Socialism, and they continue to reverberate in the controversies about women and their rightful place in the West German society of the 1980s and beyond.

Weimar Experiences

It is one of the paradoxes of our time that wars seem to have been more powerful as agents of equal opportunities than have the social movements devoted to these opportunities. During the First World War women broke into previously male domains of the labour market in industry, trade and services, and consolidated their place in health care, nursing, or teaching (Marwick 1977; 1982; Stevenson 1984). In Germany, women were recruited into the wartime labour market between 1915 and 1918 to work in unskilled production jobs, nursing or communications (von Gersdorf 1969). Yet most of these war-induced advances proved temporary; women tended to lose their jobs as soon as the demobilised soldiers began looking for work. Some political and social gains were longer lasting than women's employment in the war industries and related services. In Germany, the economic and social contributions of women during the First World War resulted in better access for girls to schooling and to vocational qualifications in the Twenties. The most tangible effect of the First World War on the situation of women was their recognition as citizens with equal rights of political participation. In Germany, women won active and passive voting rights in 1918.

The Weimar Republic was the first period in German history wherein women could play a public and political role at the national level. Since 1918 women, as all adult German citizens, were enfranchised and women were represented in all German parliaments between 1918 and 1933. Women were somewhat hesitant about the uses of politics. The majority turned out to vote, and many of those who had played a prominent part in pre-war women's movements sought election to parliamentary seats and a more expansive political role. However, just as many lacked confidence in the political process to which the enfranchisement of women had contributed and in which women gained their first experiences of parliamentary politics. Gertrud Bäumer, for instance, had already been elected to serve in the National Assembly in 1919 when she confided to a friend:

> What passes as 'high politics' is nothing but a heap of improper, disreputable and mixed-up notions which could just make you ill. I have undergone a remarkable education. At first, the negotiations or negotiators are almost unintelligible. But just as soon as I began to realise that concrete self-interest underlies every single issue, then it all becomes as clear as day. And the leaders are so passive . . . Is there no place where we can get together with other women so we can purify our souls? (quoted in Koonz 1988: 33)

The notion of democratic politics as the epitome of self-interest was so widespread in the Twenties that the majority of Germans from the left and the right dismissed parliament as a talking shop whose activities could only undermine the common weal, not maintain and advance it. Women shared the sceptical appraisal of democracy. The new avenues of participation had not met the varied expectations about the effect women might have on the direction and the quality of political life. The socialist advocates of the enfranchisement of women were especially disappointed since the majority of women cast their vote for one of the parties on the right of the political spectrum. Had not women's votes in the early Twenties barred the SPD from leading the government and from recasting the post-war world in a truly democratic fashion with equality of opportunities for all? And, by the same token, had not the leanings of German women to the Catholic and national right in the closing years of the Weimar Republic and the attractions of National Socialism to Protestant women and to women who had not voted in the past helped to destroy democracy altogether, and also abolish the freedom to participate in the political life of their country which women had only just begun to taste? The right benefited politically from women's electoral support but viewed their place as separate and different, outside the fray of economic competition and political influence. National Socialism, whose rise to power in 1933 completed the destruction of the Weimar Republic, objected to women holding electoral political and parliamentary office. That women flocked to support a party which stressed that men and women were biologically and psychologically different and could not play equal roles in society, has been one of the enigmas of the twentieth century (Koonz 1988). German women of the Twenties remained distant from democracy. Their first opportunities of equal participation arose in a political environment whose democratic framework was widely disliked, and women shared these dislikes. The National Socialist regime encountered few obstacles when it abolished parliamentary government and only assembled the Reichstag to deliver preformulated messages to the nation. From our contemporary perspective we can conclude that the criminalisation of women's political activities at that time was little more than a facet of a criminalisation of parliamentary and democratic politics.

Post-War Challenges

The punctuated history of women's socio-economic and political participation meant that women after the Second World War had to regain the rights they held under the Weimar constitution, relearn using them, and in particular learn to accept them and the democratic process to which they belonged. At the same time, women had to cope with the devastations wrought by the war, the food shortages, housing shortages, with being refugees, with the collapse of the National Socialist regime into an apparent chaos of disorientation, and, of course, without the men who had been killed in the war or who were detained in prisoner of war camps. After 1945 women found themselves numerically in the majority and catapulted into a degree of self-reliance which was out of line with the restricted place they had occupied in National Socialist society. Politically weakened and inexperienced through over a decade of tutelage and consumed by everyday chores of survival and pulling through, women in the post-war years did not turn their numerical strength into an effective voice of innovation or take a leading role in the social and political life of the day.

The political recasting of post-war Germany all but by-passed women. After the military defeat of National Socialism, political control and the right to initiate reforms had been assumed by the Allied forces and their military governments. There was no resistance movement which – as in Italy or France – could have been a force of reform in the first hour. The victims of National Socialism who emerged from years of exile, persecution or incarceration, notably Social Democrats, trade unionists and communists, were not encouraged to take the leading role they had expected and to impress their priorities on the political realities of the day. In the Eastern zone, they acquiesced to a new regime masterminded by the Soviet Union; in the Western zones, each of the Allies initially pursued their own policies and chose their own German associates. In rebuilding a capitalist economy and establishing West German parliamentary democracy, equalisation across social classes, gender divides or employment opportunities remained secondary issues. The primary concern of the political parties and the policy makers of the first hour was directed at the nature of the political system, not at changing the fabric of society. All parties were conscious of the fact that women had acquired a sudden majority status with a numerical 'surplus' of seven million over men and that they constituted 70% of the electorate in the immediate post-war period. Here was a potential political force to be harnessed – as voters women could tip the balance and make or break governments. It was even suggested that in a party of their own, women might develop an alternative ideology to the male-dominated militarisms of the past.

> What use is all the male geniality, when men can do nothing better with it but destroy what they so wonderfully constructed? We have to save ourselves and men from such destruction in the future. . . . We can only achieve this goal if we succeed as women to work together with men in a way that the two approaches complement each other and thus allow progress towards humanity in the future. (Illing 1947)

In the early days of post-war politics, women were neither agents of political reorientation as leaders in parties, parliaments or public affairs nor were they targets of such reorientation with reforms, protective measures or similar initiatives designed to improve their living conditions and opportunities. Until the controversies surrounding the West German constitution and the paragraph devoted to equality (see Chapter 2), women remained in the background of post-war politics. A popular view at the time maintained that the National Socialist regime and the war had embodied male principles: 'in the history of political temptations of the German people through National Socialism, it was Adam who first ate the apple' (Bäumer in Schubert 1984a: 169). Female principles seemed to encompass the very opposite of National Socialism: women, therefore, needed neither special re-education towards democracy nor a new beginning. They had been 'completely absorbed in very useful tasks' and busy making practical contributions in a variety of areas. War and women did not appear to match. Looking back after forty years, one woman who had experienced the war and its aftermath summed up why women seemed neither implicated in nor especially activated by the events around them: 'women and war: these two terms do not harmonise together. The woman is the protector of all living things – war

13

the principle of destruction, the killing thing' (Mehling 1946: 3).

Such a socio-biological perspective on women avoided looking at the socio-economic realities of the time: how the immediate post-war conditions and the experience of National Socialism had influenced women in their opportunities and in their attitudes and how, after 1945, they were equipped for the practical tasks of survival and the political tasks of democratic involvement.

The Place of Women in National Socialist Society

Among the pre-eminent factors of post-war expectations and opportunities, the effects of National Socialism on the place of women in society is of particular importance since all adult and adolescent women had been exposed to its ideas and organisations, and many had known little else. From the ideological angle of National Socialism, things seemed simple enough: 'The woman has the task to be beautiful and to bear children. This is not as crude or old fashioned as it may sound. The female bird preens herself for the male, and hatches the eggs for him. In return, the male provides the food. Otherwise, he stands watch and drives away the enemy' (from Goebbels' novel *Michael*, quoted in Schüddekopf 1982: 13).

Motherhood was glorified, above all, as the contribution of women to the survival of the German people and was linked to the Nazi concepts of racial superiority and world domination. Legislation in the early Thirties, for instance, banned abortion and introduced child allowances for women who had been in employment, and a medal of honour (*Mutterorden*) was awarded to women who had four or more children. Nazi interest in motherhood was a corollary to racism and was geared to producing new generations who would fit the Nazi constructs of so-called racial purity (Schoenbaum 1966: 187f.). The creation in 1935 of an institution by the name of *Lebensborn* also reflects the Nazi disregard for people and the obsession with wayward notions of race. *Lebensborn* were breeding factories where specially selected German women should conceive biologically desirable (in Nazi terms) offspring from specially selected SS men. Women here were used – functionalised – as instruments

14

of national survival. The same dehumanising spirit is evident in a memorandum which was written in 1944 by Martin Bormann and which addresses itself to the problem of how the German nation could regain its strength after the war:

> The situation of our people [*volkliche Lage*] will be catastrophic after the war since our people experienced a second massive loss of blood within a period of thirty years. We are sure to win the war militarily but we will lose it in terms of people if we do not reach a decisive turn-about of conventional views and related attitudes. . . . Of course, the women who will not be married after this war, cannot conceive their children from the Holy Spirit but only from the still living German men. Increased male procreation – of course in the interest of the welfare of the people – is only desirable for some men. The decent, honest, physically and psychologically healthy men, but not the physically and intellectually unstable ones shall multiply and have more children. . . . Public education and information on this matter can only commence after the war. I want to mention only one reason for this: we cannot appeal to women today and tell them that their husbands will probably be killed in the war, and before starting our campaign we have to consider the soldiers. . . . Not every soldier will like it if his wife or fiancée will after his death bear a child from another man. . . . But we have to begin removing all the obstacles. We have to instruct the writers and poets of our times. New novels, stories and plays which present adultery as a problem in marriage, will be banned. The same goes for poems, writings and films which compare the illegitimate child unfavourably with the legitimate child. I have demanded for a long time already that the word 'illegitimate' [*unehelich*] has to be extirpated completely from our language. (quoted in Schüddekopf 1982: 17f.)

Motherhood and Service

Broadly speaking, National Socialist ideology envisaged a double role for women: like men, women should be unflinching servants of the state, and they should also function as child-bearing machines for national and racialist purposes. Ideologies are one thing, their effectiveness quite another. Let us look briefly at the success or failure of the two dimensions, women as mothers and women as obedient followers.

It was mentioned earlier that in addition to emotive appeals, the National Socialist government offered material incentives to

Table 1.1 Marriage cohorts and family sizes

Year of marriage	Number of children per 100 marriages					Children total
	0	1	2	3	4+	
1919–1921	16	23	24	15	21	234
1922–1925	18	24	24	15	20	222
1926–1930	17	23	25	15	20	223
1931–1935	16	22	27	17	18	218
1936–1940	14	25	31	17	14	205
1941–1945	13	25	31	17	14	205
1946–1950	13	26	30	17	14	207

Source: Wolfgang Kröllmann, 'Die Bevölkerungsentwicklung der Bundesrepublik', in W. Conze and R. Lepsius (eds), *Industrielle Welt*, Stuttgart: Klett Cotta, 1983: 112.

encourage childbirth. Since any effect of the Nazi ideology or policies could only be observed before the war, and a change in the pattern of birth rate would take several years to be visible, we have little evidence to prove or disprove a surge towards motherhood. Compared to the late Twenties, the birth rate rose in the Thirties, but during the Depression many couples had postponed starting a family until their economic situation had stabilised. Kröllmann argues that the Nazi message had some effect, however: it did not reverse the decline in the birth rate which had commenced early in the twentieth century but it slowed the decline down (Kröllmann 1983). Between 1938 and 1941 enough babies were born to keep the population figures stable. Once war broke out, the birth rate fell again. Table 1.1 shows changed family sizes for marriage cohorts. Couples who married between 1926 and 1935 had somewhat larger families than the overall decline would have suggested; this may be a repercussion of Nazi appeals to increase family sizes. The desired mass reversal to families with four or more children, however, never took off and remained a product of propagandist fancy.

Of the two roles for women, that of motherhood and that of loyal service to the state, the former had been a dimension of National Socialist aims from the outset (Hermand 1984). As focal points of the mass organisation of women motherhood and child-rearing were important to stake out the specifically female domain; decisive, however, was the concept of loyal service which allowed women to claim a public role in the Third Reich. In their detailed studies of the Nazi organisation of women Stephenson and Koonz have shown how the determination of women to win a slice of public power created an organisational structure in an ideological and political vacuum (Stephenson 1981; Koonz 1988). Originally, the Nazis had viewed women only as mothers who did not need an organisation of their own, nor, indeed, a share of the leadership. Those women who had joined the Nazi party with an eye to wielding influence were virtually left to their own devices and could build up their organisation and define its activities. The Federation of German Women (NS Frauenschaft), which replaced competing regional groups after 1933, was headed by Gertrud Scholz-Klink who followed a more ambitious ideological brief than motherhood alone: to incorporate women into the national community (*Volksgemeinschaft*) as members of equal value but different in nature from the male 'comrades of the people' (*Volksgenossen*). The Federation of German Women took charge of establishing a network of women's groups with an extensive network of office holders and functionaries. These groups masterminded the ideological integration of women into the National Socialist regime and provided essential support services such as second-hand clothes collections to fight poverty (*Winterhilfswerk*) and similar social ventures. In this way, women carved out a special area of activity which remained unchallenged within the Nazi state and could be used by it. This public role of the Federation of German Women as an agency of the national cause offered influence and material benefit to those women who were functionaries and office holders; for the average German women it did little more than draw on their sewing or knitting skills or similar 'female' specialisms, and extol passivity and obedience as public virtues.

The concept of unquestioning service – *Einsatz* – also dominated the mass organisation for girls and young women. The Federation of German Girls (Bund Deutscher Mädel – BDM) was created to mould the female half of German youth to the designs of the Nazi state, and create generations of physically fit, nationally devoted mothers. In practice, however, the Federation of German Girls resisted attempts to impose motherhood

or marriage as an educational or social goal which would dominate activities:

> We especially want to make our girls politically aware. This does not
> mean: women who later on will want to debate in a parliament, but
> girls and women who are fully briefed about the essential life-needs
> of the German people and act accordingly. We know that at all times
> the international enemy, no matter how he disguises himself, has
> tried to split the German people and set men against women, women
> against men. Women who were not politically aware became unwit-
> ting tools of our enemy. Marxism has claimed that men and women
> are socially equal and has attempted in this way to deprive women of
> their natural way of life and destroy the substance of our people.
> Another line of argument which originates in semitic traditions
> maintains that women are inferior. These ideas that women are
> socially equal or that they are inferior are alien to our race and not
> worthy of our people. . . . We have to free ourselves from these alien
> ideas and influences and refer back to the lives of our ancestors . . .
> when men and women were equal in value, standing side by side in
> equal responsibility they each did their duty towards their people
> according to their nature. (Jutta Rüdiger, 'Der BDM in der HJ, 1939';
> quoted in Klaus 1983: 113)

As with the women's organisation, that for girls opted for the
public dimension of women's role in Nazi society. The Bund
Deutscher Mädel chose to concentrate on paramilitary fitness,
on group activities, on helping with the harvest, and on running
leadership training schools and courses (Klaus 1983: 93). It saw
itself as the female equivalent of the Hitler Youth. Since membership for girls was compulsory from 1936 onwards, it played
an important part as a major socialising agent for a generation of
adolescent and young adult women in the Thirties and Forties.
BDM girls were conditioned to give their utmost at work and
play, and to step into the breach if and when men were not
available. Early grumbles by the Nazi leadership that girls might
be too militarised and insufficiently concerned with grace and
beauty show that ideology and reality did not always dovetail.
The younger generation of women and their leaders had little
inclination towards the motherhood cult advocated from the
top. The BDM aimed at carving out a distinctive period of female
life between childhood and motherhood where girls and women
could prove that they were of equal value to men, and indis-

pensable to Führer and state. Service and responsibility for girls also included 'womanly employment', which was advocated as one of the tenets of the National Socialist community. A compulsory 'year of service' for girls was introduced in 1938, and was normally spent in agriculture or domestic service. In the jargon of the time, it was called *hauswirtschaftliche Ertüchtigung*, training through domestic service. Even vocational training and regular, paid employment were incorporated into the myth of service to the nation: 'What matters in girls' employment today is not the income but the concept of service [*Dienstgedanke*] and the principle of optimal standards of performance at work which is as binding for young women as it is for young men. For girls, employment should not be regarded as just a temporary activity, but as a vocation, a calling in the true sense of the word' (*Das Deutsche Mädel. Zeitschrift des BDM*, December 1936: 11).

The ideology of service and achievement made the Federation of German Girls a ready tool for auxiliary war service after 1939. For many, the so-called youth activities consisted of assisting to evict Polish families from their homes and helping Germans to take over. One of the standard duties of the female servants in accordance with Nazi racial policies was to cook the equivalent of stew, *Eintopf*, for the Germans to whom Polish farms and houses had been allocated. Young German women had been organised and moulded into willing assistants of the National Socialist cause – albeit not into the child-bearing machines which were also envisaged in the Third Reich's ideological blueprint.

The Reluctant Labour Force

In more general terms, employment became the sector where German women were least responsive to the role prescriptions issued by the Nazi leadership. The Nazi image of women as mothers and homemakers did not tally easily with women's participation in the labour market. While the paid employment of single women or school leavers passed unchallenged, that of married women was initially discouraged and even discontinued. After 1933, married women were dismissed from civil and public service, and a vociferous campaign against so-called double earners (*Doppelverdiener*) accompanied the moves by employers and party to substitute male for female workers. The world economic crisis of the late Twenties and the unemployment it had generated in Germany had, in any case, hit men harder than women. In early 1933, male unemployment stood at 29%, female unemployment at 11% of the respective labour force. During the crisis, women increased their share of the overall labour force by 3% (Schoenbaum: 190; Mason 1975: 53). As skilled men were dismissed during the economic crisis of the late Twenties and early Thirties, women were kept on or even taken on instead of men. Employers, it seems, found women an easier labour force to hire and fire. Many were unskilled or worked part-time, their pay was lower than that for men and women were less likely to be members of trade unions and therefore more isolated and less protected by collective interests. Once the National Socialist regime had seized control, measures to implement the mother ideology remained indirect: it did not attempt to sack working mothers, but sweetened the pill by the compensatory social package of a 600 Reichsmark marriage loan which could be reduced by one-third with the birth of a child. Official estimates spoke of 800,000 women who were expected to leave the labour force and become full-time homemakers (Mason 1975: 51).

There are no reliable figures to show how many women really made way for unemployed men. What we do know is that the ideological juxtaposition of women and work conflicted with economic practicalities as soon as unemployment had eased (Winkler 1977). By 1936, war production had commenced and generated a booming economy. It brought with it a shortage of industrial labour which could not be satisfied by male able-bodied Germans. Contrary to the political glorification of motherhood, efforts were now intensified to recruit women as industrial labour, albeit at the bottom end: 'women must not be employed in tasks which demand special presence of mind, decisiveness and quick action. Women shall not normally be employed in tasks which require special technical understanding and technical know-how' (Mason 1977: 278–9).

Specific measures included an increase in industrial training places for girls; since the total number of places was very small, this was a gesture, not an effective reorientation. From October 1937, marriage loans were no longer conditional on the woman giving up her place of work. This measure was designed to persuade women to remain in employment even after marriage. German women, however, were unwilling recruits into the industrial labour force. Until the outbreak of the war, just 6% of industrial labour was female; during the war, it increased only slightly. Women who were in paid employment tended to work in agriculture, retailing, the small business sector, services and especially as helping members in their own family business. Between 1933 and 1939, the number of women in employment rose by about 2 million (Mason 1977: 277). Given the fact that it had become customary in the Twenties for young women to train or work before marriage and that some stayed in employment after marriage the modest influx of women into the labour market of the Thirties continued established trends, and was in line with the overall rise in employment after the economic depression (Willms 1980: 77). Nazi approaches to prescribe women's roles in society were essentially confused: they tried to recruit women into industry and at the same time to persuade them to become full-time mothers. On both counts, successes were limited.

That women were reluctant to work for the fatherland is clearly evident during the Second World War. Between September 1939 and the summer of 1940, the number of working women fell by 400,000. At the beginning of the war, the government had allocated especially generous payments to the so-called '*Kriegerfrauen*' whose husbands had been called up. The intention had been to boost the morale of the fighting forces and mollify any misgivings in the population about the war. That women would respond by withdrawing from the labour market had not been anticipated. They were slow to return, and female labour hardly rose throughout the war. Table 1.2 shows that 14.6 million women were in paid employment at the beginning of the war, and 14.9 million at its end. In industry, female labour remained around 2.6 million, again hardly changing throughout the war. The Nazis may have hoped that women would fill the gaps and replace men who were called up, but the party and the many competing institutions and agencies at the time never arrived at a unified policy which they dared to enforce. Statements about women's duty to work went unheeded by the majority of women, and unsupported by the kind of large-scale

Table 1.2 German and foreign labour in the war economy,[a] 1939–44 (in millions)

Year	German labour			Industrial labour		Foreign	Overall
	Men	Women	Total	Women	Total	labour	workforce
1939	24.5	14.6	39.1	2.6	10.4	0.3	39.4
1940	20.4	14.4	34.8	2.5	9.4	1.2	36.0
1941	19.0	14.1	33.1	2.6	9.0	3.0	36.1
1942	16.9	14.4	31.3	2.5	8.3	4.2	35.5
1943	15.5	14.8	30.3	2.8	8.0	6.3	36.6
1944	14.2	14.8	29.0	2.7	7.7	7.1	36.1
1944[b]	13.5	14.9	28.4	2.6	7.5	7.5	35.9

[a] for the German Reich, within the borders on 1 Sept. 1939.
[b] Data for September 1944; July 1944 for labour force/women in industry.
Adapted from: R. Wagenführ, *Die deutsche Industrie im Kriege 1939–1945*, Berlin: Colloquium 1963: 139; and Alan Milward, *The German Economy at War*, London: Athlone Press, 1965: 47.

coercion which characterised National Socialist policy styles in most other fields. Instead, the war economy was kept afloat through the conscription of forced labour who worked under slave-like conditions, and through the exploitation of concentration camp inmates as unpaid labourers.

Although Nazi thinking was directed at compulsory measures few were carried out or mobilised women in large enough numbers. Emotive appeals that women had a 'duty of thanks to those fighting at the front to protect their children' also passed unheeded. (Goebbels spoke of *Dankespflicht* in his Sportpalast speech in 1943; Wiggershaus 1984: 27.) Girls over sixteen and those applying to study at universities had, of course, been conscripted in 1938 into the so-called 'work service', and the early war years saw the introduction of a compulsory year in agriculture or domestic service. All these measures were riddled with exceptions and loopholes for avoiding employment, whether compulsory or not. Even after the government had established a compulsory employment register and empowered itself to restrict women's mobility between regions and places of residence, and conscript them into the labour force, these powers remained virtually unused. More specifically, they were used only against women from less advantaged social groups who were less able to command support in the Nazi hierarchy and to resist their call-up to employment. From January 1943, women who had 'always been at work' or who worked in industry in the past were obligated to work in prescribed industries and localities. The numerical pay-off was small (Table 1.2) and the measure was unpopular. Wives of Nazi activists seem to have had ready access to medical exemption certificates and women of middle-class backgrounds who had not been in industrial employment could escape the presumed duties to the father-land. The recruitment drive was also disliked by many men at the front who wanted their wives to be homemakers, and resented that the heavy hand of state interfered in their private sphere. In 1941, a confidential report by the National Socialist Security Service summed up the dilemma:

> The whole mobilisation of women happens in such a way that only the wives of workers and ordinary people [*kleine Leute*] are called up. Although the women in well-to-do circles appear to have plenty of time at their hands which could be utilised for work, the labour administration proceeds in a completely one-sided fashion and picks out the poorer women, since they have neither excuses nor connections. It is high time to utilise the women who have as yet done nothing for the common good, and who are too wealthy to know how to kill their time from day to day. The notion of a people's community is a good one, and it is therefore necessary that the authorities extend the concept of a people's community to all social circles also at the employment front. (Sicherheitsdienst Report no. 224, 29 Sept. 1941; quoted in von Gersdorf, 1969: 58)

National Socialist labour policies produced two classes of women – those in paid employment and the privileged who could stay at home. The National Socialists themselves tried to camouflage their patchy recruitment of women by pointing to Hitler's 'very deep concern for the health of our German women and girls and therefore the mothers of our people in the present and in the future' (Sauckel, quoted in von Gersdorf 1969: 54). The reality was less rosy since those women who were employed or were forced to work faced long hours, low wages and the multiple burdens of being a single working parent, and they often suffered from exhaustion and poor health. Throughout the National Socialist period, and regardless of the turnabouts in ideological priorities, the status attached to women's employment remained low and women were employed in those sectors of the economy where conditions and prospects were poor: in agriculture, domestic work, retail sales, general office work and – more important for the war economy – industrial labour, but here again at unskilled or semi-skilled levels (Müller 1983: 35, 47). Against this background, going out to work was widely perceived by women as a sign of hardship and not-working glamorised as a sign of affluence. Summing up the impact of the National Socialist years on women's attitudes in the post-war years, it seems that women had been hesitant to embrace the cult of motherhood but had not rejected it; young women in particular had embraced the doctrine of giving unflinching service, but women in general had resisted attempts to shunt them as labour drudges into the war economy. As a powerful legacy for the post-war years, non-working and a life centred on the private sphere were strong currents in women's dreams of normalisation and prosperity.

Nothing But Survival: Women in Occupied Germany

The war and its after-effects left hardly anyone untouched in Germany. The women who had stayed behind when the men volunteered for the front or were drafted saw their livelihood devastated through bomb damage, or in fleeing from the Soviet sphere of influence. In the closing years of the war, large numbers of women and children were evacuated from urban areas to escape from the bombings into the relative safety of the countryside. In 1944, the first wave of refugees arrived in the Reich. Most of them were women, children and old people who had followed the Nazi call to leave nothing but scorched earth for the oncoming Red Army. The so-called expellees were to follow in 1945 and 1946 after the Potsdam Agreement decreed that the territories to the East of the rivers Oder and Neiße should be handed over to Poland. Some 12 million in all fled to the Western zones of occupation and had to be accommodated in refugee camps or in the rural areas where housing was still available (Bauer 1987). It has been estimated that one in three Germans lost their belongings and homes through bomb damage or as refugees (Braun 1978: 286); overall, half the population were dislocated from their habitual social environment through war and the events which followed. The burdens of adjustment had to be borne mainly by women since in the absence of men, women were in charge of their families and women administered the chores of everyday living. The war created a large cohort of single women or single parents. In 1946, women outnumbered men by seven million (Castell 1985). Some 2.5 million women were widowed through the war and many more did not know the whereabouts of their husbands (Kuhn 1984: 172). By March 1947, an official report spoke of 2.3 million men remaining prisoners of war (Mehnert and Schulte 1949: 268). In July 1952, the whereabouts of 1.3 million former soldiers were still unknown. In 1955, the Soviet Union released the last fifty thousand or so prisoners of war to be reunited with their families. If we look at the life story of the average woman between 1939 and the early Fifties, even those whose husbands did return from the war might have spent a decade or more coping on their own.

The end of the Second World War on 8 May 1945 has been called the zero hour, but for the average German there was no excitement about a new beginning. From studies of oral history we have some information on how women experienced the onset of post-war living (Hoerning 1985). In the first weeks, the majority were terrified of being raped, and rapes appear to have been particularly frequent in the areas occupied by the Soviets (Meyer and Schulze 1988). Even those who were not threatened did not feel liberated. There was the 'nonsense of denazification' (*Entnazifizierungsquatsch*; Möding 1985: 277), the widespread distrust of the military governments and, of course, there were the shortages and hardships of everyday life. The shortages, and the concern to limit or alleviate them, were the overriding theme of the time, more potent than the destruction of the Nazi regime or the promise of democratic reconstruction. For Germans, physical survival was the core issue between 1945 and the late Forties, when conditions began to stabilise.

Before looking at the individual contribution of women to this survival culture, some of the broader political aspects are worth noting. During the First World War, Germans had experienced hunger; during the Second they experienced rationing and shortages but little physical hardship. The extensive use of forced labour in agriculture kept agricultural production going throughout the war, albeit at a much reduced level. Distribution of produce was controlled and enforced by the state; shops could not rely on a regular supply of goods, but they could rely on some supplies. In addition, the National Socialist government had hoarded large amounts of foodstuffs to forestall mass starvation. In fact, during the war starvation was never a real threat since Germany extracted all she could from the territories under her occupation. Regardless of the needs of indigenous populations, Germans took not only foodstuffs but anything from luxury goods to raw material to provide for the fatherland. The clothes and belongings of concentration camp victims appeared in German shops; soap and other consumer items were manufactured from parts of human bodies and supplied to the Reich. The technically efficient exploitation of occupied regions and human victims kept everyday hardship in Germany comparatively low during the war. In the circumstances, the shortages of goods after the war came as a shock to the population, who had never cared to ask where their soap, their shoes or their wheat came from. Germans interpreted the shortages as punishments they did not deserve and blamed the occupying powers for attempting to starve them. When the British stepped up rationing in their own country in order to divert food supplies to their zone of occupation, the measure went unnoticed among the German population (Marshall 1980: 655). German farmers who had willingly complied with Nazi orders now refused to cooperate with the Allies and make their produce available for central distribution. Hostilities were ripe against the occupying forces who seemed to requisition the best accommodation and suffer no shortages; hostilities, however, were particularly strong against former concentration camp victims and slave labourers who had been freed at the end of the war, and whose uncertain status as so-called displaced persons entitled them to receive better food rations than the German population.

There is no doubt that food, heating materials, clothing, household goods and other everyday necessities were in extremely short supply in the immediate post-war years, and that many Germans lived close to starvation levels. In 1946 and 1947, hunger led to a number of protest marches and strikes. The struggle for physical survival seemed to blot out the interest of most Germans in events of the present and it also blocked out all references to the past as people felt harangued and ill-treated. For stability they looked to the private sphere, home, family, enough food, furniture, comfort, not to the political changes towards parliamentary government and party democracy which were happening all around them (Kolinsky 1989). In these immediate post-war years, political culture as the impact of contemporary political processes and institutions on attitudes seemed suspended and substituted by a culture of physical survival from day to day.

Women were 'in the forefront of the fight for survival against hunger and want of all types' (Schubert 1984b: 235). On a practical level, life without electricity, water, heating or transport catapulted women back into pre-industrial times where family and household fulfilled major reproductive tasks in the economy. Families became the main refuge for those who had been dislocated and lost their possessions. In many households, all adult members were women as mothers, grandmothers, daughters, sisters, aunts and their dependants shared the scarce accommodation that could be had, and shared the tasks of obtaining food. The life story of two Berlin sisters, one of them widowed with a small child, is one of many similar ones and characteristic of its time. After their flat had been destroyed by bombs they had fled to the country, and returned on foot to Berlin – a landscape of ruins – at the end of May 1945. They had hoped to move in with an aunt, but her flat had also been destroyed and the family had disappeared; luckily, they could turn to their grandmother in another district whose home had withstood the war:

> We then lived in this two-and-a-half room flat, my grandmother, we two and little Jack. My mother was still in the Black Forest with her sister, but we had her officially registered as occupant of the flat. In this way we did not have to take in refugees even though my mother was not yet living with us. She joined us as soon as she was able to get through. And then, the whole struggle for survival began. The main problem was getting food for the baby. The four of us just had to help together, everyone as best as she could. We four adults each held ration cards grade five for housewives, we called them 'ascension cards' at the time. The baby was entitled to grade two rations.

But it was virtually impossible to survive on the rations alone. . . . The worst thing was that we never had enough to eat. My mother always dreamt that one could buy bread rolls again. And then she would cover the bread roll with smoked bacon which would be big enough to hang down the sides. Such a roll with a bacon-border, this is what she wished for. (Erna and Frieda Eschenburg in Meyer and Schulze 1988: 76–7)

The conditioning which women had received under National Socialism, that they should give service and be prepared for self-sacrifice in support of their children, nation, or whatever the prescribed cause may have been, appears to have served German women well after 1945. A 'new type of women' had been produced, resourceful, good at organisation and improvisation who had 'learned to make something from nothing' and manage somehow (Möding 1985: 257, 279). The corollary of this private resourcefulness was the emphasis on the private sphere and on the task of physical survival.

Many autobiographical accounts give the impression that the cramped conditions which existed in the bomb cellars of the Third Reich produced a spirit of communality; after 1945, everyday life seemed harsher. To supplement the meagre food supplies, women or young boys travelled in vastly overcrowded trains into the countryside to barter possessions for farm produce; the Germans called it *hamstern*. Judging from autobiographical accounts, the biggest challenge was to protect one's rucksack from thieves during the return journey – these also were mostly women and young boys. Animosities in everyday living were intense as refugees and other homeless Germans were compulsorily accommodated in those flats or houses which were still available, provided the families did not require the room themselves. From autobiographical accounts we know that sharing a kitchen between several families, sharing bathrooms and laundry facilities often caused severe friction. Overcrowded living, primitive modes of food preparation without ingredients, utensils and frequently without energy supplies seemed to have thrown everyday living back to pre-industrial times and cancelled the promise of liberty which had inspired Gertrud Bäumer and other protagonists of the women's movements half a century earlier.

Women and Family Living

In this harsh and uncertain environment, the family was perceived as a cornerstone of stability in troubled times. Some
conservative observers had hoped or predicted that a new age of
the family had begun, a rejuvenation of a kinship network
which seemed to have lost so many of its functions in modern
times (overview in Preuss-Lausitz 1983: 31f.). The centrality of
the family in post-war Germany was short lived and the kinship
networks of several generations broke up as soon as adequate
housing became available and material living conditions improved. A number of empirical studies have shown that women
in the Forties tended to play a dominant role as organisers of
day-to-day affairs, as advisers in personal and emotional difficulties and as mediators of conflicts (Wurzbacher 1952). For the
majority of women, looking after a family meant twelve or more
hours of housework regardless of whether or not they were in
paid employment. Help was more likely to be given by their
children than by their husbands (Thurnwald 1948: 36). Many
men had come back from the war dispirited, unable or unwilling
to make the practical adjustments necessary to cope with survival which the women had already begun to make during the
war. The domestic and organisational competence of women
and their increasingly equal status within the home had, in
some cases, produced women who expected their new-found
confidence to carry over into everyday life and change the
traditional male and female roles in their personal environment.
In many cases, however, women did not question these traditional roles but tried to fulfil them at high emotional and
physical cost. In 1948, Walther von Hollander used the popular
women's magazine *Constanze* to highlight the contemporary
dilemma of men's and women's places in post-war society:

> I know a great many women who try everything in their power to
> make sure that their husband does not notice the helpless and
> humiliating position in which he finds himself. In addition to the
> worries where the daily bread will come from and to the efforts of
> providing something resembling civilised living, women find the
> strength to encourage their husbands and to put up with his passivity
> and weakness. But the situation really becomes intolerable when the
> helpless man then acts like a domestic tyrant. A powerless tyrant – a

29

disgusting type. And however many excuses one may find for his behaviour in the adverse circumstances of our times, his demands simply are too much for the woman who is already stretched beyond her physical and emotional strength. (*Constanze* 15, 1948: 7)

Women, it seems, had not learned to focus on self-realisation despite years of self-reliance and resourceful survival. Men, on the other hand, had never been tempted, or indeed forced, to change their attitudes or expectations. In a satirical piece *Constanze* again pleads for change and also sheds some light on the personal and social climate at the end of the Forties:

The hunt for a man has assumed unprecedented proportions: 'a kingdom for a man' – regardless of how he is! Every other woman becomes a dangerous rival in the fight for the man. Therefore, grab him with all means of seduction even if it should cost one's comfortable home or even one's personality . . . And the man? Well, as the sought-after object he sits on his throne and has the best offers presented to him. It goes without saying that his character will not improve with all the uncritical and exaggerated pampering he receives. He used to woo, and is now being wooed. Who knows how it will affect him in the long run to be spoilt only to be conquered? One thing is clear: the situation is bad for both sides, the women who panic to land themselves a man, and the men who turn into real Good-For-Nothings [*Paschas*]. (Helga Prolius in *Constanze* 7, 1949: 3)

Clearly, personal lifestyles were destroyed or severely strained in the aftermath of the Second World War. The material deprivations which have been outlined in this chapter were all too apparent to people who lived through them. The clashes of attitudes and expectations were less apparent. Was it true that men had merely retained their values and the authoritarian behaviour that went with them, and stepped from the command structure of the armed forces into employment where, it has been claimed, similar structures prevailed? Or is it true that these attitudes were now out of line with the changes experienced by their wives and families (Thurnwald 1948)? Perhaps men and women had developed new egalitarian attitudes which could supersede traditional differences in gender roles (Wurzbacher 1952)? Or could it be argued that men would have gladly let go of the traditional authoritarian patterns but were held back by women looking for an ersatz father – and expected men to behave in a traditional mode in the private sphere while their working environment and the country as a whole had left authoritarianism behind (Adorno 1954: 7)?

Despite their new social prominence, and their role in the fight for survival, the place of women had only been disrupted, not transformed in the immediate post-war years. They had little impact on the social conventions that governed the private lives of men and women. After the zero hour deprivations, normality meant sufficient food, consumer goods, a comfortable home and a level of economic prosperity which could cushion the private sphere from the pressures of the world, and allow women to be homemakers and carers within that sphere if they wanted to. Coping in the immediate post-war years, as women had done, had been a required service. By itself, it did not generate new participatory styles in society. If anything, it gave the private sphere, its conventions and traditions a new aura of desirability.

Women at Work in Occupied Germany

While popular myth has it that Allied bombs turned German industry into rubble, the economic realities of the 'zero hour' were quite different. Even after bomb damage, German industry boasted significantly more capital stock than in 1936; what was left tended to be modern plant after a period of intense investment into National Socialist war industries (Abelshauser 1983: 20). Although branches of the economy with little relevance to the war effort were weak, occupied Germany as a whole and its Western zones in particular were potentially strong and ready for take-off. The National Socialists had even stockpiled essential raw materials and these were used until after the currency reform in 1948 to restart industrial production. Despite the restrictions imposed by the Allies in their attempt to curb German industrial potential and ban the production of raw materials, German industry experienced such a rapid recovery that the distribution and transport system could not cope. Abelshauser has shown convincingly that the apparent economic crisis of 1947 was in fact a crisis of distribution. Goods were produced and stockpiled because the heavily damaged railway network could not meet the transport demand (Abelshauser 1975). If anything, German industry in the immediate post-war period experienced over-production, not a zero-point.

A second myth, that Allied dismantling had deprived German industry of the few bits of plant which had survived the war, is similarly far removed from reality, at least for the Western zones of occupation. Dismantling had been agreed upon and some was carried out (Benz 1976: 77f.), but it had little effect on the overall economic performance. Locally some factories failed to reopen since they were earmarked for dismantling, and some closed to await dismantling, but most fears at the time were fears that all this *might* happen. The programme of dismantling was limited and patchily implemented but heartily resented by employers and workforce alike.

Labour Shortages and Employment for Women

The years until the currency reform were characterised by a labour shortage. In 1945, the liberation from forced labour of the foreigners and camp inmates, on which the Nazi economy had come to rely, had created several million vacancies. Manpower was also needed to compensate for shortfalls in technology and for clearing and repair work. Although nearly 10 million refugees had entered the British and American zones of occupation by late 1946, and the potential labour force had expanded by 14% (Abelshauser 1983: 23), many of the new arrivals were housed in rural areas, while labour was needed in the former conurbations where housing was not available. An additional difficulty arose from the fact that most of the refugees of working age were women. Recruiting labour also had to involve changing the gender balance of employment and opening fields or positions to women which had in the past been filled by men.

Compared with pre-war levels, the overall number of people in employment fell by at least one in four to about 26 million in 1946, with different rates of decline in various industrial branches (Stolper 1966: 236). The proportion of women in the workforce had declined to 28% on average from 35% during the last years of the Third Reich. The drop has been explained with reference to the higher number of women in the population and to the low wages, which were a disincentive for women to seek employment (*Gleichheit* 2, 1950). We shall come back to the question of wages later in this discussion. At this point it is worth noting that the vacancies in the labour market were not taken up voluntarily by men or women, and measures had to be introduced to recruit labour by decree. In July 1945, the German administration of the Rhineland introduced a compulsory labour register: 'in order to ensure our food supply, the reconstruction of our houses and the reorganisation of the economic and social life of our people, we have to draw on all our manpower reserves which can be used for reconstruction' (Schubert 1984a). With some regional and zonal variations, the 'new duty to work' affected men between the ages of fourteen and sixty-five and women between sixteen and forty-five, provided they did not have children under fourteen living at home or were not caring for other dependent relatives. Conscription to work could last between six and twelve months. The major incentive to enlist was linked to the core theme of physical survival. Going to work meant an improved entitlement to food through ration cards. Housewives received the minimum food ration, while women on work programmes received a more generous allocation. This lifeline via ration cards was enough to persuade many women, including many over the age of forty-five or with young children, to register for work. In July 1946, the Allied Control Council consolidated the regional decrees and ordered work conscription for all zones of occupation; this was followed in October 1946 by specific regulations about the type of work women could be expected to undertake. Moves to introduce a compulsory year of domestic service for girls, which had to be completed before an apprenticeship or paid employment could commence, were abandoned in the face of trade union and SPD opposition.

Although the Western Allies defined the legal framework for the recruitment of additional labour, its implementation was left to the German local and regional labour exchange offices. Their priorities and employment policies determined the involvement of women in the labour market, their wages or occupational mobility. To start with the broad conclusion: women derived no lasting benefits from their contribution to everyday life and work in the immediate post-war years. Not dissimilar to the practices under National Socialism, women were utilised as stop-gap labour in unskilled or semi-skilled work without career prospects and without the expectations that they should or would remain in these positions permanently.

Demand for additional labour was highest in agriculture and in the construction industry. In agriculture, women had traditionally found employment, with 93% working at the lowest level of *Magd* or casual labourer (*Gleichheit* 6, 1950: 241). Post-war recruitment into agriculture followed the established pattern and women tended to perform menial tasks. In 1946, they constituted 45% of the agricultural workforce; in 1949 they even outnumbered men with 54%. After the currency reform, many farmers could no longer afford to pay the wages for additional labour and unemployment of women in agriculture rose to about 10%, the majority of them refugees.

The Stop-Gap Syndrome

Another major area of employment for women was clearing the debris, and sorting the bricks ready for reconstruction. Apart from clerical work, women had not traditionally worked in the building or construction industries. In 1946, the restrictions were lifted although the reservations remained:

> The employment of women in the construction industry has now been authorised by the military government in the face of the massive task of clearing debris and reconstruction which has to be undertaken and because male workers cannot be found in sufficient numbers. Even if the employment of women cannot be avoided in the present adverse circumstances, it remains true that the employment of women in construction is new to Germany and is in principle undesirable because the work demands a high degree of physical strength and holds the danger of psychological coarseness; it can only be justified because of the current labour shortage and because it can be expected to speed up reconstruction and help to improve general living conditions. Using women in the construction industry can only remain a temporary measure. (From a circular issued by the Office for Employment, Westfalen-Lippe, 5 June 1946)

Working regulations took more trouble to protect women from the presumed dangers of rough language to their femininity than to advise on working processes or safety requirements. A letter from the President of the Rhine Province, Lehr, to the Industrial Supervisory Office in Dortmund links the issue of women in construction with assumptions about their different, inferior biological make-up. Although women were expected to perform equal functions, views and attitudes had not changed sufficiently to grant them equality of person and potential:

> I have fundamental reservations against using [*einsetzen*] women on scaffolding and ladders in construction, since there is a high risk of falling off. One must consider when using women for work, that the female physical constitution is completely different from that of the male. Women have a lower number of red blood cells and a smaller heart. It is possible and therefore probable that hard physical work can – also during the monthly period – lead more frequently to dizziness than it would among men. In the light of these considerations I do not regard it as useful to employ women in construction or other enterprises where there is a high risk of falling [*Absturzgefahr*]. (Quoted in Schubert 1984a: 282)

Those women who were employed in this controversial and supposedly male field were confined to auxiliary tasks, were prevented from obtaining the status of qualified workers, and only a handful were taken on for semi-skilled work such as shaping stones or heading work gangs. Although the public was keenly aware that gender boundaries had been modified, and although the so-called *Trümmerfrauen* – the rubble-women – acquired a hero-like status in the myths surrounding the founding of the Federal Republic, they remained in fact the lowest paid type of worker, with prospects neither of promotion nor of permanent employment. As soon as men became available, women in the building industry lost their jobs. Protests were muted since the work was backbreaking and underpaid, many women earning barely enough to pay for their transport to and from work every day. In construction, the utilisation of women was short lived and employment prospects dwindled once men became available and unemployment began to rise in the late Forties.

Unemployment in 1948, as a contemporary source pointed out, had a certain artificial character. People – men in particular – who had not registered for work at a time when they feared political reprisals or denazification, enlisted with the labour exchange after the currency reform. In the British zone alone, 39,000 such people came forward in 1948 (*Genossin* 4, May 1949: 99). Some women protested against losing their jobs, and against preferential employment for men, but many regarded their own paid employment as a stop-gap measure on the way to normalisation. The return of 'their' men into the labour market relieved many women from the necessity to seek employment. That the multiple pressures of low-paid, physically demanding work, the struggle for survival and the practical improvisations of day-to-day living did not generate tangible improvements in the situation of women at work or in society, made paid employment appear as a chore which would best be avoided.

Beginnings of social policy during the occupation period had not been encouraging for women: a day for housework had been demanded since 1948 and became official trade union policy in 1949. Although it seems to have been granted in certain areas and in some industries, women who made use of it reported difficulties with their employers and sometimes dismissals (Schubert 1984a: 294ff.). At about the same time, attempts were made to dilute the protective legislation which granted maternity leave as a right to pregnant women. The legislation had in fact been introduced by the National Socialists in 1942 to protect the unborn child, not the mother; in the post-war climate of rising unemployment and demand for work after 1948, the protective clauses were to be removed to enable employers to dismiss pregnant women and avoid having to grant maternity leave (*Genossin* 5, June 1949: 150–1; *Genossin* 7, August 1949: 217–18). Moves to change the career structure of public service were carried through to the detriment of women. In 1948, the category of white-collar employee was abolished. People in public employment were henceforth classified as either civil servants or workers; most women fell into the latter category and faced a loss in status and security (*Genossin* 4, May 1949: 110).

Women's experiences with rates of pay were not much better. On average, women received 60% of men's pay in occupied Germany, with variations between types of employment and industry. Although equal pay had been stipulated by the Control Council in its Directive No. 14, and had been accepted in principle, it did not become an early reality. A report on wage negotiations for a district of Northern Bavaria in 1948/49, for instance, highlights the range of practices, and the failure of negotiated wage settlements to include equal pay for women:

> Exemplary is the wage agreement for the wholesale and retail trade. It has the same rates for men and for women workers and for white collar employees. . . . A fair number of agreements for white collar employees, however, have remained retrogressive. In the textile, metal and chemical industries women employees will have 10% deducted from their wages. . . . Some agreements have even lower wages for women, especially those where women are strongly represented. Thus, women's wages are only 80% in glass making, 75% or 70% of men's pay in shoe manufacturing. (*Genossin* 4, May 1949: 111)

A trade union survey showed in 1950 that 75% of the workforce received less than DM230 take-home pay per month; for half of them, wages were low enough to border on welfare payments; full-time women workers frequently earned less than DM200 a month with hourly pay lower than that for men through all industrial regions and branches (*Gleichheit* 7, 1950: 339–43).

In the post-war years, women's employment did not receive the social and economic recognition one might have expected, given the contribution of women to rebuilding the country, their role in the family and their utilisation as additional labour force in times of crisis. The ready retreat of West German women into the private sphere has to be seen in this context. It was a retreat from the experience of unrewarded chores to a lifestyle which promised to offer more: the dream of normality, stability and personal status in the family world. That female employment in 1950 amounted to only 8.5 million and had reached its lowest level since the First World War would suggest that women's post-war involvement had no lasting impact on their social role. A drive to define the situation and potential of women more expansively as bridging the private and the public worlds of family, work or indeed politics had yet to emerge in West Germany (Moser 1984: 32).

References

Abelshauser, Werner, *Wirtschaft in Westdeutschland 1945–1948. Rekonstruktion und Wirtschaftsbedingungen in der amerikanischen und britischen Zone*, Stuttgart: Deutsche Verlagsanstalt, 1975

——, *Wirtschaftsgeschichte der Bundesrepublik Deutschland 1945–1980*, Frankfurt: Suhrkamp, 1983

Adorno, Theodor W., 'Vorwort', in Gerhart Baumert, *Deutsche Familien nach dem Kriege*, Darmstadt: Wissenschaftliche Buchgesellschaft, 1954

Bauer, Franz J., 'Zwischen "Wunder" und Strukturzwang. Zur Integration der Flüchtlinge und Vertriebenen in der Bundesrepublik', *Aus Politik und Zeitgeschichte* B32, 1987

Bäumer, Gertrud, *Die Frau in Volkswirtschaft und Staatsleben der Gegenwart*, Stuttgart: Deutsche Verlagsanstalt, 1914

Baumert, Gerhart, *Deutsche Familien nach dem Kriege*, Darmstadt: Wissenschaftliche Buchgesellschaft, 1954

Benz, Wolfgang, 'Wirtschaftspolitik zwischen Demontage und Währungsreform', in *Westdeutschlands Weg zur Bundesrepublik 1945–1949*, Munich: Beck, 1976

Braun, Hans 'Das Streben nach "Sicherheit" in den 50er Jahren', *Archiv für Sozialgeschichte* XVIII, 1978

Castell, Adelheid zu, 'Die demographischen Konsequenzen des Ersten und Zweiten Weltkrieges für das Deutsche Reich, die Deutsche Demokratische Republik und die Bundesrepublik Deutschland', in Waclav Dlugorski (ed.), *Zweiter Weltkrieg und sozialer Wandel*, Göttingen: Vandenhoeck und Ruprecht, 1985

Freier, Anna-Elisabeth and Annette Kuhn (eds), *Frauen in der Geschichte* vol. V, Düsseldorf: Schwann, 1984

Frevert, Ute, *Women in German History: From Bourgeois Emancipation to Sexual Liberation*, trans. by Stuart McKinnon-Evans, Terry Bond, Barbara Norden, Oxford: Berg, 1989

Genossin (SPD Informationsblatt für Funktionärinnen). Redaktion Herta Gotthelf, Hanover, 1946ff.

Gersdorf, Ursula von, *Frauen im Kriegsdienst 1914–1945*, Stuttgart: Deutsche Verlagsanstalt, 1969

Gleichheit (Das Blatt der arbeitenden Frau). Redaktion Herta Gotthelf, Bonn, 1950ff.

Greven-Aschoff, Barbara, *Die bürgerliche Frauenbewegung in Deutschland 1894–1933*, Göttingen: Vandenhoeck und Ruprecht, 1981

Hermand, Jost, 'All Power to the Women: Nazi Concepts of Matriarchy', *Journal of Contemporary History* 19 (4), 1984

Hoerning, Erika M., 'Frauen als Kriegsbeute', in Lutz Niethammer and August von Plato (eds), *Wir kriegen jetzt andere Zeiten* (pp. 327–44), Bonn: Dietz, 1985

Illing, Ulla, 'Das neue Thema', *Silberstreifen* 6, 1947

Klaus, Martin, *Mädchen im Dritten Reich. Der Bund Deutscher Mädel (BDM)*, Cologne: Pahl Rugenstein, 1983

Kolinsky, Eva, 'Socioeconomic Change and Political Culture', in J. Gaffney and E. Kolinsky (eds), *Political Culture in France and Germany – Contemporary Perspectives*, London: Routledge, 1989

Koonz, Claudia, *Mothers in the Fatherland. Women, the Family and Nazi Politics*, London: Methuen, 1988

Kröllmann, Wolfgang, 'Die Bevölkerungsentwicklung der Bundesrepublik', in Werner Conze and M. Rainer Lepsius (eds), *Industrielle Welt. Sozialgeschichte der Bundesrepublik Deutschland. Beiträge zum Kontinuitätsproblem*, Stuttgart: Klett Cotta, 1983

Kuhn, Annette, 'Die vergessene Frauenarbeit', in Anna-Elisabeth Freier and Annette Kuhn (eds), *Frauen in der Geschichte* vol. V. (pp. 170–201), Düsseldorf: Schwann, 1984

Lange, Helene, *Die Frauenbewegung in ihren modernen Problemen*, Leipzig: Quelle & Meyer, 1908

Marshall, Barbara, 'German Attitudes to British Military Government 1945–1947', *Journal of Contemporary History* 5, 1980

Marwick, Arthur, *Women at War 1914–1918*, London: Croom Helm, 1977

——, *British Society since 1945*, Harmondsworth: Penguin, 1982

Mason, Timothy W., *Arbeiterklasse und Volksgemeinschaft. Dokumente und Materialien zur deutschen Arbeiterpolitik 1936–1939*, Opladen: Westdeutscher Verlag, 1975

——, *Sozialpolitik im Dritten Reich. Arbeiterklasse und Volksgemeinschaft*, Opladen: Westdeutscher Verlag, 1977

Mehling, Elisabeth, 'Die Frau und der Krieg', *Frauenwelt* vol. 1/2, 1946

Mehnert, Klaus and Heinrich Schulte, *Deutschland-Jahrbuch 1949*, Essen, 1949

Meyer, Sybille and Eva Schulze, *Wie wir das alles geschafft haben. Alleinstehende Frauen berichten über ihr Leben nach 1945*, Munich: dtv, 1988

Milward, Alan S., *The German Economy at War*, London: Athlone Press, 1965

Möding, Nora, 'Ich muß irgendwo engagiert sein', in Lutz Niethammer and August von Plato (eds), *Wir kriegen jetzt andere Zeiten* (pp. 256–303), Bonn: Dietz, 1985

Moser, Josef, *Arbeiterleben in Deutschland 1900–1970*, Frankfurt: Suhrkamp, 1984

Müller, Walter, Angelika Willms and Johann Handl, *Strukturwandel der Frauenarbeit 1880–1980*, Frankfurt: Campus, 1983

Niethammer, Lutz and August von Plato (eds), *Wir kriegen jetzt andere Zeiten. Auf der Suche nach den Erfahrungen des Volkes in nachfaschistischen Ländern*, Bonn: Dietz, 1985

Preuss-Lausitz, Ulf, *Kriegskinder, Konsumkinder, Krisenkinder*, Weinheim: Beltz, 1983

Quarteart, Jean H., *Reluctant Feminists in German Social Democracy 1885–1917*, Princeton: Princeton University Press, 1979

Schoenbaum, David, *Hitler's Social Revolution: Class and Status in Nazi Germany 1933–1939*, London: Weidenfeld and Nicolson, 1966

Schubert, Doris, *Frauenarbeit 1945–1949*, Vol. I of Annette Kuhn (ed.) *Frauen in der deutschen Nachkriegszeit*, Düsseldorf: Schwann, 1984(a)

——, '"Frauenmehrheit verpflichtet" – Überlegungen zum Zusammenhang von erweiterter Frauenarbeit und kapitalistischem Wiederaufbau in Westdeutschland', in Anna-Elisabeth Freier and Annette Kuhn (eds), *Frauen in der Geschichte* vol. V (pp. 231–65), Düsseldorf: Schwann, 1984(b)

Schüddekopf, Charles (ed.), *Der alltägliche Faschismus. Frauen im Dritten Reich*, Bonn: Dietz Nachf., 1982

Stephenson, Jill, *The Nazi Organisation of Women*, London: Croom Helm, 1981

Stevenson, John, *British Society 1914–1945*, Harmondsworth: Penguin, 1984

Stolper, Gustav, *Deutsche Wirtschaft seit 1870*, Tübingen: Mohr, 1966 (2nd edn with Karl Häuser and Knut Borchardt)

Thönessen, Werner, *The Emancipation of Women in Germany*, London: Pluto, 1976

Thurnwald, Hilde, *Gegenwartsprobleme Berliner Familien. Eine soziologische Untersuchung*, Berlin: Colloquium, 1948

Wagenführ, Rolf, *Die deutsche Industrie im Kriege, 1939–1945*, Berlin: Colloquium, 1963

Wiggershaus, Renate, *Frauen unterm Nationalsozialismus*, Wuppertal: Hammer, 1984

Willms, Angelika, *Die Entwicklung der Frauenerwerbstätigkeit im Deutschen Reich*, Bundesanstalt für Arbeit Beitr. AB 50, Nuremberg, 1980

Winkler, Dörte, *Frauenarbeit im 'Dritten Reich'*, Hamburg: Hoffmann & Campe, 1977

Wurzbacher, Gerhardt, *Leitbilder gegenwärtigen deutschen Familienlebens*, Stuttgart: Enke, 1952

2
Equal Rights for Women: A Profile of Legislative Change

One of the principles which has been enshrined in the West German constitution and which determined the nature of legislative change since 1949 is the principle of equality for women. In post-war democracy, the old conflict as to whether women should occupy a separate sphere which allegedly carried equal value, or whether they should hold their own in society and enjoy social recognition and equal rights at work and in political life, seemed to have lost its punch when the Parliamentary Council voted in 1948 to include equality among the human rights on which the new polity should be based. However, the reality has been more complex. The intentions of the constitution have set in motion a process of legislative change to create equal rights for women. The emergence of women's equality in law is the theme of this chapter.

The Constitutional Promise

West Germany is a country in which the constitution is arguably the most important component of the polity. Given the course of twentieth-century German history, the prominent place of the constitution signifies an emphatic detachment from the unconstitutional and undemocratic conditions which preceded the Federal Republic. Its elevated status can be traced back further to the struggle of the German middle classes in the eighteenth and nineteenth centuries to win rights of economic and political participation in a country which was carved up into hundreds of feudal states, each run by its own king, duke or count. In these contexts, constitutions have served as important means of breaking feudal structures of government and of placing the relationship between citizens and state on a rational footing of defined responsibilities and rights. The constitution sets out

41

criteria with which the political process, its institutions and actors have to comply, and it uses the written word to define those criteria. The wording of a constitution governs the social and political process and spells out the principles to which reality should conform (Dyson 1980). To measure and match political realities against constitutional norms is the backbone of German democracy. To judge whether or not institutions, legislation and political decisions comply with the intentions of the constitution is the specific function of the Constitutional Court; it has also become a strong tradition of German academic analysis and debate to argue that the political realities of the day are out of line with the spirit contained in the wording of the constitution (Abendroth 1975). Constitutions have been credited with formulating a corporate consensus, a framework for the respective polity, which is non-individual, non-partisan and above party.

The constitution for the Federal Republic was formulated by the Parliamentary Council, an assembly of elected delegates from the *Länder* (federal states) and completed in May 1949. To this day it is called a provisional constitution to underline that a final binding constitution could apply only to a unified Germany, not to its Western part alone. Officially, the Federal Republic does not have a constitution but a Basic Law which serves that function. In practice, however, the Basic Law has set the norms for the polity and has been used as a fully fledged, non-provisional constitution (Seifert 1983). For women, it has been of central importance. Among the human rights to which the Basic Law makes explicit reference as cornerstones of democracy is the right of equality between men and women:

Article 3 (Principle of Equality)
1. All men [*Menschen*] are equal before the law.
2. Men and women have equal rights.
3. No one may be prejudiced or privileged because of his sex, his descent, his race, his language, his homeland and origin, his faith or his religion and political opinions.[1]

In retrospect, it may seem only right and proper to expect that

1. Quoted in the English translation by Peter H. Merkl, *The Origin of the West German Republic*, New York: Oxford University Press, 1963: 214.

women should enjoy equal rights with men since democracy is based on the notion that all citizens should be equal. The wording, however, went further than previous constitutional provisions for equality, in particular those of the Weimar Republic. The constitution of 1919 had made explicit reference to equality for women but it had restricted equality to the political sphere; social and economic life continued to be governed by the Civil Code (*Bürgerliches Gesetzbuch* – BGB) which had been in force since the early years of the century. The Civil Code was based on the assumption that clear biological and social differences existed between men and women which the law had to define and regulate. Two requirements in particular restricted the social choices of married women: a wife was required to look after her family and could only seek employment if her husband agreed to it (§1356); she was, however, obliged to support her husband by spending her inheritance or by going out to work if he failed to make the sort of living to which *he* was accustomed (§1360). With minor modifications the Civil Code was still in force when the Basic Law was passed; the constitutional promise of equality in all walks of life has to be seen as a direct challenge to the second-class status of women, which informed the Civil Code. It took eight years until the Civil Code was revised in 1957, and nearly twenty and a further revision before the intentions of the Basic Law had reshaped the legislation on the place of women in society.

Equality as an Issue in Recasting Post-War Germany

When the Parliamentary Council agreed in January 1949 to the unconditional wording of Article 3, 'men and women have equal rights', it expanded women's equality beyond rights of political participation and recognised the need to revise the German Civil Code (Reich-Hilweg 1979). Article 117 addressed itself to the process of legal reform and ordered the incoming government to complete the relevant revision by 31 March 1953 (Seifert 1983: 109). Suggestions to suspend the German Civil Code immediately and thus quicken the pace of change were rejected by members of the Parliamentary Council who argued that such a step would invite 'legal chaos' with one set of legislation suspended before the new laws were in place (*Neue*

Zeitung 13 Jan. 1949). Behind the apparently legal reasoning lay strong political reservations: with the exception of the two communist delegates who were in favour of full equality for all classes and both sexes, the delegates of other parties held a variety of reservations. In fact, the Parliamentary Council had not intended to exceed the wording of the Weimar constitution and grant women more than political equality. None of the parties had decided how women should combine family duties, child care and employment, and which balance between them should be envisaged in the constitution and through it in the legislation of the country. The *Länder* constitutions which were drawn up between 1946 and 1947 in the Western zones of occupation had been more audacious and promised specific measures to pave the way towards equal participation in society: all advocated equal pay for equal work. Special rates for women's work or percentage deductions from women's wages were to be discontinued. The constitutions of Hesse, Bavaria, Bremen and the three states in the Württemberg and Baden regions promised more rights for women inside marriage. Bremen and Hesse intended to create state-administered child-care facilities to make it easier for mothers to go out to work. That so many different plans were formulated shows that the issue was seen as an important one at the time. All, however, continued to regard motherhood and housework as normal female domains, and other activities as exceptions to the rule.

When the Parliamentary Council came to address the issue of equality the zeal of the first hour to transform the face of German society had already subsided; the focus was now on stability, not change. With regard to women, the Christian Democrats were closely linked to the Catholic Church at the time and attempted to design a constitutional framework in which the home was confirmed as the natural place for women; the Social Democrats seemed determined to make the Weimar model work and educate German women in the correct use of their political equality before expanding it any further. The Centre Party and the Free Democratic Party (FDP) who were also represented in the Parliamentary Council looked towards a similar reinstatement of Weimar practices, not towards innovation (Späth 1984).

The mood changed, and full equality was hastily accepted by

all parties after Elisabeth Selbert, one of the representatives for the SPD and a veteran of the socialist women's movement, had mobilised public opinion. In her view, women were about to lose out again despite having shouldered all the burdens during and after the war. The German public, and women in particular, shared her dismay, and feelings ran high enough to bring in baskets full of protest mail for the fathers of the constitution and gasps of disbelief in the press. Women, it was felt, had earned equality as a reward for their endurance. Elisabeth Selbert could draw on the support of former women's movements activists, and on public interest in the women's issue to win her constitutional case. If one examines her own views, the meaning of equality is more ambiguous than the clear bid for equal rights in the Basic Law would suggest. To her, men and women were not so much equal as of equal value. Equality should mean that men and women pursue different activities in society and perform different social roles. Not the roles, but their recognition should change. To the mother of women's equality in the German constitution, motherhood remained the major and natural task for women and housework as valuable as paid employment:

> Our demand for this type of equal rights does not originate in feminist tendencies. In the thirty years I have spent in politics, I have never been and never will be a feminist. On the contrary, I believe that even the participation of women in politics should be based on their specific character and qualities. Only a synthesis of male and female qualities will bring progress in politics, in the state, in human issues. (Parliamentary Council Reports, 18 Jan. 1949: 540.)

Elisabeth Selbert's views highlight the ambivalent approach to women and their equal opportunities which existed at the threshold of West German democratic development. Yet the success of her bid for equality meant that the Federal Republic had committed herself in her constitution to act within four years and align the Civil Code with the spirit of equality. The process of legislative change as adjustment to the constitutional promise had been set in motion.

Wife, Mother or Partner?

The 'constitutional command' (Münder et al. 1984: 31) to incorporate the principle of equality into existing legislation was not obeyed as swiftly as the Basic Law had stipulated. The first West German government, a coalition of Christian Democrats, Liberals and the German Party, were hesitant to move on an issue which their members had tried to forestall in the constitutional debate itself. In addition, the Catholic Church had voiced misgivings that equality legislation might undermine the stability of the family, and the place of women as mothers and homemakers within it. In January 1953, the Fulda Conference of Catholic Bishops appealed to the government to 'protect marriage and family as institutions in the new legislation', and to 'express clearly in the forthcoming legislation, in accordance with the natural image of marriage and family, that the prime task of the wife and mother consists of homemaking for the common good of all members of the family' (*Informationsdienst* 2, 1953).

When the government presented draft legislation in the summer of 1952 to revise the Civil Code, in particular the sections relating to parental rights and the economic and social scope of women inside the family, not much appeared to have changed. Rather than extending the rights of women, the legislative proposal reduced them by abolishing preferential treatments, such as dowry rights for girls or legal entitlements to maintenance after a divorce. The association of female lawyers and economists commented at the time:

> While the draft legislation in practice retains the regulations which place women in a position of inferiority, it eliminates without qualms all previous regulations which gave women certain advantages . . . this is not the way to do it. Either, one has to grant women equal rights, and then one might as well include among the legal requirements their contribution to family maintenance which, in practical terms, women have been making anyway. But if one does not grant them genuine equal rights, if a patriarchal structure is retained, one might as well confirm the legal obligation of the husband to be solely or mainly responsible for the maintenance of the family. (Quoted in Vogel 1983: 71)

The intention to reinstate Weimar conditions, and ignore the 'constitutional command' to move towards equal rights for women, dominated the first legislative period of the new West German state. In 1950, for example, the revised Civil Service Law retained the discrimination against married women which had existed before and during National Socialism:

> A female civil servant can be dismissed if he [*sic!*] marries. He has to be dismissed on application. Without application he can only be dismissed if his economic situation in accordance with his family income appears to be permanently secured. The economic situation is deemed secure if the husband is employed in the civil service, and has pension entitlement. (§63/1)

Apart from the fact that the male personal pronoun was used to describe female civil servants, the law also assumed that women should only be employed if the husband could not provide adequate economic security. That married women, even civil servants married to civil servants, could have a right to their own economic status, career, security, did not enter the legislators' minds in the founding days of the Federal Republic.

Even where the constitutional norm of equal rights was explicitly accepted, the underlying notion of social and economic roles in an orderly and stable world saw women as homemakers and men as breadwinners. In December 1953, for instance, the Federal Constitutional Court passed an important ruling on the question of equality. The function of the Federal Constitutional Court is linked to the elevated status of the constitution referred to earlier. In order to ensure that the spirit of the constitution does not get lost in the hurly-burly of political decision making or party political rivalry, citizens, political institutions or other public bodies can bring a case before the court to determine whether or not the principles of the constitution have been adhered to in a specific matter. Basing its verdict on the wording of the constitution, the court interprets its meaning and often develops it through detailed reasons attached to the verdict itself (Säcker 1977). In the matter of women's equality, the court did two things. It underpinned the validity of Article 3 by stressing that it was a 'genuine legal norm' not a programmatic political point. But it also explained that the principle of equality could not mean that conventional role divisions had lost their validity: 'regulations for the protection of the mother will be permissible and the fact should be taken into account that the man will normally serve the family by employment outside the home, and by making monetary provisions, while the women will serve the family by looking after the household and caring for the children' (18 Dec. 1953). Despite this recourse to traditional role patterns as accepted social practice, the Constitutional Court confirmed the commitment of the Basic Law to full equality and in doing so highlighted the need for change (Reich-Hilweg 1979).

The interim situation developed its own momentum. The government did not keep the constitutional deadline of March 1953 to incorporate the principle of equal rights into the Civil Code. From April 1953 until June 1958, when the new legislation finally came on to the statute books, the sections of the Civil Code which related to women, the family, and marital and parental rights were suspended. But far from generating 'legal chaos' the conditions of temporary lawlessness allowed changes in the social and economic scope of women to emerge without legal strictures. For instance, a woman could now enter into employment or leave it without seeking permission from her husband, as she would have had to do in the past. She could, in the case of divorce or a second marriage, retain parental control of her children. The lower courts began to apply criteria in their day-to-day jurisdiction which were closer to the constitutional norm of equality than to the traditional Civil Code. 'The failure of the legislator was matched by the increased power of the judge. It was he who made the principle of equal rights more concrete in the next few years until the legislation of 1957 ended this state of the law' (Schumann 1982: 137).

Equality through Legislation: The Reforms of 1957

The package of amendments to the Civil Code was agreed on 18 July 1957 and became law one year later. Although they took a decade to prepare, the changes ramained strongly indebted to their predecessors. The public debate on equality or social developments which had already taken place did not lead to rethinking the substance of legislation on equal rights: 'The corrections which were inserted into the Civil Code by means of the equality legislation of 1957 had left the core of the patriarchal model of the family untouched' (Helwig 1982: 48).

The most apparent focus on equal rights in the legislation relates to matters of family, marriage and parenthood where the interests of men and women meet directly. For women, especially married women and mothers, the role of homemaker remained the norm, employment outside the home the exception:

> The woman runs the household in her own responsibility. She is entitled to take on paid employment, as far as this can be combined with her duties in marriage and family. (§1356)

> Should the husband be unable to make an adequate living, the wife is obliged to seek paid employment in addition to her regular housework duties. (§1360a)

The major improvement in the situation of women concerned the economic evaluation of marriage: the property and possessions which a husband and wife achieve during their married life had in the past been regarded as the property of the husband; they were now declared joint property and, in the case of widowhood or divorce, the wife had a right to her share irrespective of whether she had contributed to the family income by being a housewife or in paid employment. Overall, the 1958 legislation advocated the 'housewife-marriage' which legal experts continued to expound as the type 'most suitable for marriage' – *ehegerecht* (Münder et al. 1984: 27).

From Housewife-Marriage to Partnership: The 1977 Divorce Law

In 1959, the Federal Constitutional Court modified the preferential treatment of men in the equality legislation somewhat and ruled that it was unconstitutional to grant fathers sole rights over a couple's children; rights, including custody and decisions concerning the welfare of children, were decreed to be joint rights. The verdict spoke of equal rank – *Gleichordnung* – of men and women within the family.[2] In this form the legislation

2. See the Constitutional Court Judgements, Bundesverfassungsgericht 10: 59ff. relating to the Civil Code §1629/1 and §1628.

remained in force until 1977, when the SPD/FDP government of the day relinquished the concept of 'housewife-marriage' and based the legislation pertaining to marriage, family and parenthood on the concept of partnership with equal rights and responsibilities of men and women in society.

> The partners [*Ehegatten*] agree on the running of the household. If the household is left to one of the partners, then this partner runs the household in sole responsibility. (§1356/1)
>
> Both partners have the right to take on paid employment. (§1356/2)
>
> Each partner is entitled to enter into business agreements linked to the needs of the family also on behalf of the other partner. (§1357/1)
>
> Both partners are obliged to support the family adequately by working or using their financial means. If one partner runs the household, the obligation to contribute to keeping the family through employment is normally met through running the household. (§1360)
> (*Unser Recht* 1982)

In the two decades since the 'constitutional command' to secure equal rights in German law had first been adhered to, women's participation in society and their expectations about the nature of equality had changed sufficiently to warrant a major review. The confidence of the Fifties and Sixties that 'full equal rights between men and women in the Federal Republic of Germany had at least been granted on paper' (Naumann Stiftung 1978: 2) or that 'through the Basic Law and with the legislative adjustments by the Federal Constitutional Court . . . the discrimination against women in German law has nearly been stamped out' (Erna Scheffler, a judge at the Federal Constitutional Court, in *Informationsdienst* 9, 1964: 4), had collapsed.

The 1977 legislation on marital reform has to be understood as one of a number of liberalising measures introduced by the social–liberal coalition with the intention of strengthening the participatory elements in social life and organisation. This does not mean that the concept of participation and the new scope for women which it seemed to open were accepted throughout society. If the legislative spirit had been retrospective in 1958, it was ahead of its time in 1977. The comments published in 1978 in a legal guide for non-lawyers show how persistent conventional role patterns for women were. They also show that the legal experts who compiled the guide hoped to shift the burden of restraint to women's consciences and sense of propriety after husbands had, of course, lost their age-old prerogative to allow or forbid their wives' employment. The example cases tend to stress women's obligation to homemaking despite the new rights of employment choice:

> J. and his wife have both worked during the first years of marriage. She was, in fact, obliged to do so. But when things went from good to better, the young couple liked it that she would keep the house immaculately clean and have prepared everything nicely when he came home for dinner. After some time, however, she no longer felt satisfied with doing only the housework and wanted to take on part-time employment. When she told him, he said: 'I don't like it at all that my wife works elsewhere and earns money from strangers, and you will also be always tired when I come home in the evening.' But part-time employment, which she intends to take up, can be combined with her childless marriage. It is an honourable activity, which will leave her sufficient time for her marital duties. (From *Knaurs Hausjurist*; Jochimsen 1978: 94–5)

It is not surprising that the same legal commentary for the general public recommended that women should give up work when expecting their first child in order to be 'available the whole day for the child and still have time for the husband' (ibid. p. 95), or that if a woman really had to work for financial reasons, she should take on work in the home, which could be done without neglecting the household.

In fact, the 1977 reform of the legislation governing families and marriages distanced itself from prescribed male or female roles and decreed that couples themselves should decide how they would organise their affairs. The distribution of household chores was left to their discretion, as was the commitment to paid employment of one or both partners. The major change affecting the status of women and their chances to make use of their constitutional right to equality occurred with regard to divorce. In the past, divorce in West Germany had been based on the principle of guilt. After the equality legislation of 1958 with its provision that both partners should be entitled to an

51

Table 2.1 Divorce in West Germany since 1950

Year	Total	Per 1,000	Year	Total	Per 1,000
1950	86,341	1.7	1976	108,363	1.8
1955	48,860	0.9	1977	74,719	1.2
1960	19,325	0.9	1978	32,578	0.5
1965	59,039	1.0	1979	79,602	1.3
1970	76,711	1.3	1980	96,351	1.6
1974	98,600	1.6	1981	109,520	1.8
1975	106,932	1.7	1985	128,121	2.1
			1986	122,443	2.9

Source: Statistisches Jahrbuch (1988) für die Bundesrepublik Deutschland, Stuttgart: Kohlhammer, 1988: 78.

equal share of the additional wealth created during the marriage, divorce was less likely to leave women without financial means, and had become more accessible. In addition, legislative practice in divorce cases had toned down the meaning of 'guilt' and no longer linked it to questions of custody or of maintenance payments. West Germans and the legal profession regarded divorces as amicable separations, with one partner agreeing to be named as the guilty party. The stigma which used to be attached to the 'guilt' component in divorce cases had begun to lose its sting by the late Fifties, and divorce began to rise. Since 1977, the legislation has allowed for divorce on the basis of marital breakdown without a 'guilty' sentence for either party, provided that a couple had lived apart for at least one year. In the past, this condition of separation would have deterred women since they would lose all claims to the marital home if they left it. Now, this no longer mattered, and women's rights to their share in the family possessions remained unimpaired even if they 'walked out'. Table 2.1 shows that change in legislation did not lead to a massive surge or a run on the divorce courts. The decline in the mid-Seventies can be explained as a consequence of the new laws: divorce proceedings tended to be withheld until the change of legislation had been completed. After that, it took until the mid-Eighties for divorce rates to surpass those reached in the past.

When the new divorce law was introduced, many observers felt that it favoured women and discriminated against men. An analysis of its effects in the weekly magazine *Der Spiegel*, for instance, noted:

> At the beginning of the reform discussion, the question was asked whether women were being punished, but now men are asking themselves whether they are 'in for it'. Since July 1st, the case of cases is no longer a mere vision: after 20 years of marriage, the full-time housewife . . . packs her suitcases and leaves her husband . . . and her children . . . because 'she is fed-up with the patriarchal behaviour of the man-of-the-house'. She is entitled to half the house, which she has just left. She receives half of the pension entitlement which he has earned. For the duration of her retraining as an X-ray assistant he has to pay 700 Deutschmark maintenance per month. Only her claim to have custody of her two sons is rejected by the family court. The children should be cared for by the father. All this may not happen too often, but it is not a caricature. That a women who so far had been forced to keep up an empty and irritating marriage for economic reasons only, simply gets rid of this burden, is condoned by the law. In the past, she would not even have been allowed to move out, without risking being declared the guilty partner on the grounds of 'maliciously abandoning' and she would not have been entitled to a single penny. (*Der Spiegel* 27, 1977: 46)

In reality, the demise of the 'housewife-marriage' has not been as rapid as the wording of the legislation and interpretations of the first hour would indicate. For instance, in explaining the implications of §1356, which rules that each spouse has to take due regard of the situation of the family when accepting employment, the government referred back to the well-worn notion of a woman's role: 'The rule does not suggest a schematically equal treatment of man and woman. The wife has . . . to take particular regard of the needs of the family, for example when children have to be cared for and brought up' (*Bundestagsdrucksache* 7/650: 98). Subsequent judgements and legal commentaries elaborated that young children needed a full-time person to care for them, and that this was usually the mother (Dorpfel 1978). Divorce also seemed more tied to acceptable behaviour than the letter of the law would appear to indicate. Women, for example, were refused maintenance payments and their share in the increase of wealth during marriage if they had moved in with another man on leaving their husband, an act which a Hamburg court called 'an arbitrary breaking-out from a long-lasting, perfectly average marriage' (*Zeitschrift für das gesamte Familienrecht* 1978: 118). A similar verdict by a court in Düsseldorf decreed that the woman had acted 'without any exterior cause from pure wilfulness' (*Zeitschrift für das gesamte Familienrecht* 1980: 779f.). The power of the courts to grant or to refuse maintenance in divorce cases appears to have been used to perpetuate traditional role patterns for women. The refusal of post-marital maintenance became a device to force women of today to remain 'little women' and homemakers. As one critic put it, 'patriarchy in the judges' robes' has prevented the equalising intentions of the legal reforms from taking their full effect (Derleder 1982: 20).

Women at Work Between Special Protection and Equality

The constitutional norm of equal rights has not been readily translated into working life and the collective bargaining agreements which govern it. On the one hand, the Basic Law itself is contradictory. While Article 3 guarantees equal rights, Article 9 guarantees the autonomy of the two sides of industry and their right to agree amongst themselves the conditions of work and pay. This principal freedom to determine the contents of any agreement according to the issues and circumstances at the time, and without preformulated strictures, has been interpreted by the trade unions and by the employers' associations as the freedom to set women's and men's pay and working conditions at different levels. This practice was corroborated by the existence of special legislative measures which pertained only to women. Restrictions on working time, for instance, were based on regulations which had first been formulated in 1938, and which remained in force until the Eighties (*Unser Recht* 1982: 78–9). Protection of women at work was detailed in legislation from the Weimar years, which had been reactivated in the Federal Republic. It stipulated special measures during pregnancy and in the first months after confinement such as a ban on overtime and on night and Sunday working. The work was governed by certain medical restrictions to ensure the health of mother and child (overview in Adamy and Steffen

1985: 108ff.).

If special treatment of women had only pertained to pregnancy and childbirth it would be hard to link it with inequality. However, these protective measures were only one type among others whose origins were more dubious and whose effects were less beneficial to women. One such area concerns pay. Until 1955, negotiated wage settlements assumed reduced rates for women with a standard percentage deduction within an industry. This practice was declared unconstitutional by the Federal Labour Court in 1955 after a woman who was employed as an unskilled labourer in a department store appealed to the court for equal pay with her male colleagues who performed the same work alongside her. The court outlawed differential rates with reference to Article 3 of the Basic Law which, it was argued, had implied that pay for men and women should be equal. In explaining the judgement, the court also suggested that wage groups should be specified in detail, and pay awarded accordingly. This had the immediate effect that the majority of posts held by women in manufacturing and service industries were classified as belonging to the lower wage groups, so-called *Leichtlohngruppen*. Men in these groups would, of course, be paid the same as women, thus complying with the law, but men's work would normally be assigned to a higher wage group. In other words, the constitutional norm of equality was adhered to on paper, but not in practice. This reluctance of German legislators to tackle equality at work came to an end only in August 1980 when the Bundestag responded to European policy initiatives with the law on 'Equal Treatment of Men and Women at Work' (*EG Anpassungsgesetz*), a number of adjustments slotted into the relevant sections of the Civil Code.

Before explaining the origins, the content and the impact of this legislation, we have to sketch the political and legal state of equality at work and opportunities for women in West Germany since the abolition of a separate pay structure in the mid-Fifties. With industrial relations focused on co-determination and on the autonomy of the two sides of industry, governments and legislators chose to endorse the law which had been in force before 1933, and allow the labour courts to innovate in individual cases. Although West Germany's legal system does not abide by precedence but is based on codified, written laws, the labour courts have played an important role in modernising and updating legal practice and in modifying inequalities in the world of work.

Employment Promotion – A Promise Unmet

The so-called Employment Promotion Law in 1969 has been a major step forward towards equal opportunities in the world of work. It was introduced on 25 June 1969 while a grand coalition of Christian Democrats and Social Democrats were in power, and administered by the coalition government of SPD and FDP which was formed after the elections in September 1969. On the surface, the legislation intends to facilitate the reintegration of the unemployed into the labour market, a problem which had surfaced in the mid-Sixties and seemed to have disappeared by the time the Employment Promotion Act was passed. The act bore the hallmarks of reform and was pledged to broaden choice through special state-funded training programmes, educational initiatives and provisions for the unemployed. Women were explicitly named as the priority group which should benefit from the new approach: 'women who are difficult to place under normal labour market conditions because they are married or because they have currently or had in the past other domestic obligations, shall be integrated into the labour market' (*Unser Recht* 33 §2/5). To enable women to return to the labour market and update their skills or acquire new ones, the law envisaged regular pay, refund of expenses for child-minding and transport, and reimbursement of additional costs for food or accommodation. In short, housewives without an income of their own and young mothers should be helped to qualify and re-enter the labour market.

Things did not go fully to plan. When the Employment Promotion Act was formulated, the West German economy had just recovered from a minor slump. The recovery had been faster than had appeared possible during the shock of unemployment in the mid-Sixties. Not only was full employment restored within a year; at the end of the Sixties, the West German economy was as buoyant as ever during the high time of the economic miracle a decade before. Between 1968 and the early Seventies, a combination of crisis management, full employment and rapid technological innovation had created a climate of optimism. Economic stability seemed within reach as long as government and the two sides of industry would coordinate their approaches and agree on objectives and their implementation. Broadening the employment and training opportunities for those who had missed out was a facet in a grand design for a society of equal opportunities and second chances.

The Employment Promotion Act has to be seen in this context of economic confidence at the manageability of economic recession and the role of government to enhance avenues of equality in society. The training measures offered in the new legislation were to be administered and financed by the Federal Labour Office (Bundesanstalt für Arbeit; BfA). The prime source of revenue for the BfA has been National Insurance contributions, i.e. its financial situation is best at times of full employment. When the legislation was passed unemployment had just been mastered and was not regarded as a problem which could recur for any length of time. With unemployment no more than a hiccup in a presumed era of lasting prosperity, the arrangement to fund the training and retraining measures through the Federal Labour Office seemed straightforward enough. The situation has changed drastically since the oil shock in 1973. Not only did the extent of the recession which commenced in the early Seventies defy the stabilisation tactics devised by the West German government, it also smashed the intended equilibrium of full employment as the normal state of affairs, and unemployment as a minor and temporary, albeit undesirable, interruption. However, since the oil shock and the recession it set in motion in the early Seventies, mass unemployment in West Germany has never been far removed from people's working environments, and from the agenda of everyday social and economic policy. Many of the good intentions of the Employment Promotion Act became victims of circumstance. As payments to the unemployed and a fall in revenue from National Insurance contributions emptied the coffers of the BfA the resources which should have supported the Act became increasingly scarce (Adamy and Steffen 1985). The BfA reduced expenditure on courses, retraining and occupational innovation and the government imposed more stringent preconditions of acceptance to any of these programmes.

Between 1969 and 1987, several amendments to the legislation restricted eligibility for training or retraining measures. Many of the incentives for women were reduced or rescinded. The original legislation had stipulated that within three years after the birth of the youngest child women could retrain and receive monthly payments plus costs. Subsequent amendments reduced the financial provisions, especially the monthly stipend. To qualify for retraining, women had to undertake to be employed and pay National Insurance contributions within four years of training (Hellmich 1986: 230). After 1981, women were only admitted to courses if they could convince the authorities that their domestic duties would not impair their ability to work at least twenty hours per week; no such conditions were imposed on men:

> In the case of men, the intention to seek employment is assumed as a matter of principle, in the case of women, the obligations of housework and family are regarded as 'personal circumstances' which draw in doubt the intention to seek employment. Women, therefore, have to provide a special written declaration which has to be assessed, in addition, by the relevant official at the labour exchange as to its credibility. . . . (*Amtliche Nachrichten der Bundesanstalt für Arbeit* 9, 1981: 1029)

The same modification reintroduced an assessment of women's economic and personal situation with reference to that of their husbands: 'The intention of a married woman to return to employment is only supported by the Employment Promotion Act, if her economic upkeep by the husband is not guaranteed . . . Support for the occupational plans of a married woman is thus dependent on the employment status of her husband' (ibid.).

In 1982, the legislation was amended further (this was now called the Act to Consolidate the Employment Promotion Act) to abolish subsistence payments for women 'after the family phase', i.e. for women who had brought up their children and intended to retrain prior to employment. Only women with young children or invalid family members retained an entitlement; the remainder could claim only the costs directly related to the course (Hellmich 1986: 232; *Arbeitsförderungskonsolidierungsgesetz*, 1 Jan. 1982). In short, the commitment to advancing the opportunities of women in the labour market which had been a core intention of the 1969 legislation fell victim to the pressures of unemployment. In her study of the effectiveness of training and retraining programmes for women, Andrea Hellmich lists a number of shortcomings: women who receive unemployment benefit are not entitled to take part in retraining measures; women whose husbands are unemployed are forced to look for immediate employment to make ends meet since the remuneration paid for retraining is too low to support a family. The payment of course fees and related expenses, however, has made it easier for women who qualify to make use of the retraining on offer and improve their opportunities in the labour market (Hellmich 1986: 166ff.).

That the federal government failed to review the funding basis of its employment administration meant that the intention of the law could only have been realised if the economy had been booming. As soon as the bulk of BfA income had to be used to support the unemployed, the tasks of creating new opportunities and shifting the balance of opportunities in the workforce had to take a back seat. Since the BfA is required to apply for special government funding to cover shortfalls in its finances, labour market policies have come increasingly under the direct influence of government. From the vantage point of the government, women were not the hardest hit by unemployment, and not the most likely group to generate socially or politically adverse effects if they remained unemployed. Priorities shifted towards the young and their integration into training, and through employment into society. This priority focus on the young was particularly evident after the Christian Democratic Union and the Christian Social Union (CDU/CSU) headed a new government from October 1982. Among its first measures were appeals to industry and the small business sector to provide more apprenticeships. It also passed legislation which removed some of the protective measures concerning working times and conditions for young people. These, it was argued, had deterred employers from taking them on.

Women, however, have not been altogether bypassed in the new legislative climate since 1982. In May 1985, the government launched an Employment Promotion Act (*Beschäftigungsförderungsgesetz*) which included further amendments to the 1969 legislation, and some new measures relating to women at work. Some of these measures broadened women's opportunities and rights. For instance, the entitlement to financial support for retraining and special employment programmes was expanded to include women who had left their previous employment up to five years earlier to raise a family. Previously, entitlements had ceased after three years. Other measures were more ambiguous. Thus, contractual conditions and legal safeguards of part-time employment were strengthened, especially concerning protection from dismissal in job-sharing arrangements. The legislation also underwrote capacity-linked, variable working time (*Kapovaz*) but required employers to give some advance notification of the working time required. This was not a women's law but women constituted the largest group in this type of employment. The regulations on part-time employment were most advantageous to employers who did not wish to take on permanent staff and who could increase or decrease their labour force quickly through job sharing or tailoring working hours of part-time staff to varying demand. From the perspective of equal rights and opportunities, little was gained. The Act set out to promote non-permanent patterns of employment; it may even have persuaded employers to recruit more temporary and part-time staff. With the power to hire and fire or to step up or reduce weekly working hours solely in employers' hands, the traditional drawbacks of part-time work – economic uncertainties and a lack of advancement – remained untouched (see Chapter 5). Since the main 'users' of part-time employment have been women, the 1985 legislation can be regarded as a dubious step on the road to full equality (useful synoptic overview in *Frauen in der Bundesrepublik* 1986: 70–1).

Equal Opportunities and the European Context

Until the late Seventies, West German legislation and the measures adopted to implement the 'constitutional command' of equality had been inspired and masterminded by the government of the day, the Bundestag, the parliamentary parties on both sides of the house, the Bundesrat as the voice of the regions in the political process and of interest groups such as trade unions, employers or women's associations (Schenk 1981).

Formulating legislation and designing modes to improve the fabric of society and the structure of opportunities, or deciding instead to prioritise economic efficiency, stability and sectoral employment had been internal West German affairs. Since the mid-Seventies, the European Community has taken on an active role in promoting certain modes of social and political change. Equality for women and improvements in their situation in the labour market have featured high among them. In the women's issue, West Germany can no longer follow her own political preferences or perceived economic constraints, but has come under the influence and control of the European Commission and the European Parliament, monitored and at times nudged by the European Court of Justice (ECJ). Policies on equality have ceased to be national policies, and have assumed an international, supranational dimension (Pfarr and Bertelsmann 1985; Bulmer and Paterson 1987).

The European Community (EC) of today with its eleven member states emerged from the European Economic Community of the original six, France, West Germany, Italy, Holland, Belgium and Luxembourg. The founding document, the Treaty of Rome, came into effect on 25 March 1957. As a quasi-constitution for the new cooperative venture it set out the principles and aims the member states were to pursue, among them a pledge to ensure equality of women at work, in particular equal pay. Article 119 of the Treaty of Rome spells out that women are to receive the same rates of pay as men and that pay should be linked to the place and type of work, not to gender (*Frauen Europas* 1983; English edition *Women in Europe* X/318/83, 1983: 1).

For two decades, Article 119 of the Treaty of Rome led a shadowy existence. The issue of women's equal pay was pushed into the background by the more pressing challenge to create the community and to intensify cooperation in the economic and political spheres. In the Seventies, the question of political unison gained new salience as new members joined and as socially, economically and politically diverse polities now shared the European umbrella. The renewed focus on women was partly a concern to curtail inequalities across Europe and partly an attempt to prepare the ground for more effective political integration by creating an improved and congruent social fabric across EC member states. This also meant that the situation of women in EC member states should be governed by the same principles offering similar access to equal opportunities and equal treatment.

Between February 1975 and December 1978, the European Commission published three directives on women's equality. On 10 February 1975 the Commission advised member states to revise their legislation to guarantee equal pay to men and women in all countries. One year later, on 9 February 1976, the Commission requested member states to put the principle of equal treatment into practice and ensure that men and women enjoyed equal access to employment, training and promotion, and that working conditions were the same for both sexes. The third and last of the guidelines, issued on 19 December 1978, ordered member states to commence the legislative process needed to ensure that men and women were treated equally in all aspects of social security, notably insurance cover and pensions. These guidelines served two major purposes: to unify diverse national laws and practices, and also to provide the Commission with a lever with which to put pressure on member states which were reluctant to legislate on equality and change their social and economic practices accordingly. Focusing on equal pay, on equal access and treatment of men and women at work, and on equal social security provisions, the guidelines attempted to define discrimination and curtail it across Europe. Similar to the West German Federal Constitutional Court, the European Court of Justice has played a major role in interpreting the European Commission guidelines, and in assessing whether or not states have complied. The Commission has used the European Court of Justice to bring cases against national governments in an attempt to generate compliance with its directives. Since no specific sanctions have been attached to non-compliance, change has been slow and legislation on equal rights and conditions for men and women remains diverse in EC member countries. The court has, however, sharpened the meaning of equality in two important areas and set new standards for social reforms. Firstly, in prescribing equal pay for equal work the court defined the latter as work of equal value. For the comparison of positions and pay associated with them, this encouraged an assessment within the context of the employment, and one not merely geared to looking for identical tasks, qualifications or localities. The principle of equal pay for work of equal value has been an important step towards abolishing special categories for women's work and the pay scales linked to it, and has prepared the ground for equal treatment of women in employment. The second principle emphasised by the European Court of Justice concerns discrimination in the working environment. Although overt discrimination, such as the percentage deductions from women's wages which had existed in West Germany into the Fifties, have been outlawed in most European countries, the court stressed that indirect discrimination continued to be applied, and impaired equal opportunities and equal treatment of women. One example where the court banned indirect discrimination was the practice to pay different hourly rates to part-time and full-time employees engaged in the same kind of work (ECJ Judgement 61/81: 104, quoted in *Frauen Europas*, Nachtrag zu 12: 7).

West German Responses

Since the mid-Seventies, West German legislation on employment and on the situation of women at work had to relate to the criteria and guidelines formulated by the European Commission and by the European Court of Justice. Initially, all parties, legal experts and interest groups were convinced that West German legislation needed no adaptations to the newly outspoken directives on equality. While the employers feared that equal rights legislation would increase their costs and restrict their freedom of contract, the trade unions also felt that their bargaining rights and their position as the dominant voice of the labour force would be threatened if the women's issue received a special emphasis, and in particular if bodies were created to monitor equality, a duty and privilege which the trade unions claimed to have performed adequately since their inception. The legal profession defended the scope of existing laws, while feminists rejected the notion of equality of women with men in law and at work, and pleaded for legislation and employment norms geared to women and based on women's special abilities and wishes (Hoskyns 1986: 11ff.).

With so little enthusiasm across German society and among

opinion leaders to implement the directives on women's equality, the government remained inactive until the European Commission intervened. On 10 May 1979 it opened proceedings in the ECJ against the West German government for breach of treaty. Simultaneously, the Commission sent a formal letter to the West German government, requiring information about steps which had been taken to bring West German legislation into line with the European directives. In August 1980, the West German government responded with a legislative package called the Labour Law to Comply with the European Community Provisions (*EG Anpassungsgesetz*). The low-key name clearly indicates that the West German parliament neither saw a need for this law, nor took pride in it as a further step towards achieving equality in substance (Pfarr and Eitel 1984). It is not an independent piece of legislation but consists of paragraphs which have been slotted into the Civil Code to accommodate the new focus on equality.

In our context, three main sections are of interest: the first concerns equal treatment (§611a) of men and women. This has become obligatory for all aspects of appointment, promotion and dismissal; should a dispute arise, the employer has to prove that discrimination has not taken place while the employee enjoys a right to equal treatment. The second innovation relates to recruitment. All positions have to be open to men and women, and all advertising of posts has to remain gender-neutral (§611b). The third (§612b) prescribes equal pay for men and women and finally incorporates the intentions of the Treaty of Rome into West German legislation. However, the move towards equality has been half-hearted and the amended legislation makes special mention of 'exceptions for technical and other non-personal reasons'. Since these exceptions remain unspecified, they are open to interpretation, and the *Anpassungsgesetz* appears to have fewer teeth and more loopholes than the European Commission had intended. Compensation for discriminatory treatment also remains unsatisfactory. The law stipulates that compensation should not reflect a potential loss of earnings. A complainant who had expected to be promoted and whose expectations remained unfulfilled because of discriminatory practices, does not have a right to receive compensation for lost opportunities. Where court cases have been brought with reference to this section of the Civil Code, compensation payments, if they were awarded at all, were negligible. As German courts found themselves unable to award more than notional sums of a few Deutschmark, they began to look towards the European Court of Justice for guidance. There, awarding damages in relation to lost pay and faulted opportunities was permissible and German courts have started to take their lead from Europe, and create a judicial practice which could turn equal treatment into a citizens' right (Hoskyns 1986).

Even after the *EG Anpassungsgesetz* came on to the statute books, differences remained between West Germany and Europe on how to interpret the women's directives. Although the European Commission withdrew its original complaint that West Germany had failed to act on the directives, it has opened a number of cases since 1982 to rectify a shortfall from the spirit of the directives in the German legal adaptations. The first of these, that public service employment was not included, was turned down by the ECJ in 1985 since no discriminatory practices could be proven (*Rechtssache* 248/83). Others continue, among them a complaint against the unspecified exceptions to the equal treatment directive and the limitations on compensation. The Commission would also like the recommendation about gender-neutral advertising strengthened into a requirement. The furthest reaching act of censure concerns equal pay. While West Germany had regarded pay in a narrow sense as remuneration for work done, the commission aims to include the whole area of public and company-specific social security payments and provisions. As a first step, the 1982 Law to Promote Employment and Economic Activity abolished differential contributions by men and women to pension schemes, and introduced a single standard rate (applicable from 1 January 1983). The emphasis on the training and retraining of women mentioned earlier has to be seen also in connection with the European determination to monitor whether or not legislation and labour market practices have responded to the directives on women's equality. Although the European Commission cannot apply sanctions, and the European Court of Justice can only recommend, not enforce, its views, the European initiatives have acted as catalysts of change towards women's equality. In West Germany, they conspired to shift the legislative balance further towards equal rights than might otherwise have happened, or indeed been deemed necessary by West German governments and legislatures (Vallance and Davies 1986: 112ff.).

Between Motherhood and Employment

The women's directives of the European Community focus on equality in the working environment: access to employment, conditions, pay, chances of advancement, training and retirement provisions for women should not differ from those available to men. Underlying this emphasis is a general notion of democracy as based on equality, and of employment as the major route towards the emancipation of women. While West German legislation in the Fifties had concerned itself with the rights of women in the private spheres of marriage, family and parenthood, the following decades regarded working conditions as the real test case for equality. The European Community directives underpinned this orientation to such an extent that emancipation appeared only in reach for those women who were in employment. The conundrum remained unsolved as to whether the dual role of combining family and employment was too much of a burden or, on the other hand, the decisive step towards liberation, and whether women should perhaps discard the traditional roles of wife and mother and remain unattached to fulfil their potential. Should they concentrate on their careers within a male-dominated society and working environment, or should they opt out and find some novel, female avenues of activity?

The Seventies were buzzing with questions and views on how the 'constitutional command' of equality could or should be translated into social realities. The official answers at the time reflected the commitment of the governing SPD to the traditional goals of the socialist women's movement, in particular the belief that women's equality rested on equality of opportunities in employment. While policy intent focused on an integration into the working world as the gateway to women's equality and emancipation, the women's movement took a different view. They were inspired by a search for self-realisation which led to protests against abortion legislation and which made society appear as permeated by patriarchal conventions in the formal and informal norms of everyday life. The women's movements' notion of equality did not look, in the first instance, at opportunities through employment but involved a search for specifically female lifestyles of activity, expression and exercising authority. Despite the differences of emphasis between the SPD-led government and the women's movement, they shared a general concern for the equality of women in society. In the policy intent of the Seventies, the scale had tipped sharply towards regarding employment as the measure of equality. The role of the state would be to create the infrastructure of care facilities, schools, training or retraining programmes which could make equality of opportunity accessible to women. The personalised dimension of female styles and women-specific activities which was favoured in the new women's movement may have encouraged the government to develop more advice centres at local and regional level, but policy articulation remained indebted to more traditional concepts of equal opportunities and the role of women in society.

The change of government from an SPD/FDP coalition with a left-of-centre slant to a CDU/CSU and FDP coalition with a centre–right orientation in October 1982 continued the focus on traditional notions of women's role in society. If the Social Democrats followed a contemporary derivative of the doctrine that work means equality, which had inspired the socialist women's movement in its time, the Christian Democrats adapted the general beliefs of the bourgeois women's movement of the past that women occupy a special place in society, and develop their potential through specifically female pursuits such as homemaking or performing other caring tasks. In the contemporary Conservative perspective on women, motherhood continues to hold prime place, but it has been tied in with the focus on equality as being equality at work to suit contemporary conditions, and in particular to meet the expectations of young-generation women. The Conservative focus on the role of women attempts to tackle the vexed problem of the dual burden of home and work, and produced a legislative compromise which has introduced a new flexibility into the juxtaposition of home and work and a new flexibility of role for women and men.

The first legislative step under the auspices of the Conservative-led coalition government seemed to entail a reaffirmation of motherhood at the expense of employment. In July 1984, the Bundestag passed a law to set up a 'Mother and Child' foundation. It was to receive an annual endowment of DM50 million in order to extend financial and institutional support to pregnant women in need. In October 1985, funding was increased to DM60 million annually. Other legislation (1 January 1985) improved tax concessions for single parents, raised child allowances, and reintroduced child benefit for unemployed adolescents up to the age of 21. In our context, more interesting are the attempts to combine the apparently juxtaposed concepts of motherhood and employment. The legislative package which came on to the statute books on 1 January 1986 contained a reaffirmation of motherhood and its contribution to the well-being of the country, and also a novel step towards separating male/female role prescriptions from the function of mothering.

Two aspects deserve special mention. The first concerns the recognition of child-rearing as in some way equivalent to paid employment. The 1986 legislation took the unparalleled step of allocating pension rights to housewives. For each child, women acquired pension rights equivalent to one year in employment. The small print stipulated, however, that only those women were entitled to a 'baby-year' who had been employed and paid National Insurance contributions before their life as homemakers.[3] Since many women have tended to work as helping family members or employers had treated them as casual labour in order to save the National Insurance contributions, the law might not benefit all women who should be entitled to the new payments. But the step in the direction of pension entitlement for child-rearing has been an interesting and important innovation towards equal treatment in society.

Public responses to the baby-year pensions have on the whole been positive. Criticism was levelled not at the spirit of the law,

3. Women are entitled to draw a pension for child-rearing if they have been in paid employment, and paying National Insurance contributions for at least five years before becoming housewives. However, each child is equivalent to one year's employment, i.e. a women with three children would only need two years' National Insurance contributions, a women with one child four and so on. Women who never worked prior to childbirth are not included in the pension entitlement.

but at its restrictive application. In the 1986 version, only women born in 1921 or later were deemed eligible to receive the new pension. Cutting out women over the age of 65 meant, of course, cutting out the very generation who had borne the brunt of wartime and post-war disruptions, and who had brought up their children single-handed in arduous times. The emotive term '*Trümmerfrauen*' ('rubble-women') was used to accuse the government of inhumanity, neglect, or even callousness. To stem the tide of popular dismay, the Bundestag agreed on 25 June 1987 to include older women into the baby-year pension, starting in October 1987 with those born before 1907, and gradually including all age groups by October 1990. The government decision to defer payments for women in their seventies and late sixties drew fresh contempt and, from the SPD opposition, a charge of speculating that the potential beneficiaries would soon die (*Das Parlament* 11 July 1987). Others stressed the abnormality that the two pieces of legislation on baby-year pension rights have allowed women who were born after 1921 to receive payments earlier than their elders – possibly before their own mothers. Despite the apparent scramble to postpone entitlements and pay out as little as possible, the legislation breaks important new ground in the recognition of child-rearing as a contribution society should reward (*Kindererziehungsleistungsgesetz: Bundestagsdrucksachen* 11/197; 11/541; 11/542). In its intent at making motherhood more attractive the baby-year legislation is in line with the Conservative orientation towards traditional social roles and added recognition of motherhood and family.

It is one of the paradoxes of policy making in West Germany today, that essentially Conservative aims to boost the birth rate and make child-rearing more attractive have resulted in legislation which goes further in abolishing prescribed male and female roles, and in facilitating a transition from work to family and back again, than did the legislative measures designed under the auspices of SPD and FDP in their search for increased equality and participation. The new child-rearing and maternity regulations which came into force in January 1986 are the second major step towards the abolition of prescribed social male/female roles. That they originated with a Conservative government has to be seen in relation to that government's concern over falling birth rates, but also as a recognition of the fact that

West Germans – and especially West German women – do not wish to step back into traditional role patterns. A new emphasis on child-rearing, motherhood and family has to incorporate the orientations towards employment, role flexibility and partnership which emerged as expectations, values and attitudes in society (see Chapter 3).

In practical terms, the new flexibility means that men or women can choose to be carers, and receive the remuneration or protection that goes with it. Compared with the legislation on maternity entitlements, two things have changed: the entitlement is no longer sex-specific; a man or a woman can claim, and they can even change roles during the entitlement period, with the carer going back to work, the partner in employment opting to be the carer. The provisions for child-rearing payments pertain to men or women who had looked after the house full-time, or who had been in employment before the birth of their child (see Table 2.2). Part-time employment of less than twenty hours does not affect entitlement to the payments during the first seven months. While the sums themselves have hardly increased since the revised maternity legislation of 1979, the scope of entitlement has been widened to include male or female homemakers. The law also grants a longer additional time out (child-rearing vacation) than its predecessor with protection from dismissal for both partners and a right to return to equivalent employment after a career break.

Suggestions that the job itself should be kept open were turned down in preliminary discussions within the coalition after the employers' associations let it be known that they would find it impossible to fill responsible jobs with temporary staff without risking a decrease in efficiency and productivity. The commitment to equivalent employment was accepted as a compromise. Although the newly flexible legislation is still too young to assess its impact, some effects can be expected. On a personal and family level, child-rearing and household commitments might become more open between partners. With fathers and mothers both eligible to utilise the new child-rearing incentives, sex disadvantages in employment could have been reduced since employers cannot be certain whether male or female employees will want to take leave to bring up their children. In the long run, the legislative flexibility may serve to

Table 2.2 Child-rearing: synopsis of the legal entitlements (from 1 January 1986)

Child-Rearing Payments	Child-Rearing Vacation
To mothers and/or fathers	To mothers and/or fathers
– who look after their child themselves	– who want to look after their child themselves after the maternity leave entitlement has come to an end
– who are not employed, or not employed full-time (incl. housewives)	
	– who are in full-time employment
Amount of Payment	
DM 600 per month for the duration of:	**Duration of Vacation**
	Directly after maternity leave up to:
– 10 months (1986/87)	– 10 months (1986/87)
– 12 months (from 1988)	– 12 months (from 1988) after the birth of the child
After the 7th month, the amount payable is calculated according to family income	During the Child-Rearing Vacation there is normally protection from dismissals.

reduce the sexist sting in the working environment.

The moves in the 1986/87 legislation to bridge the gap between motherhood and employment were inspired by a Conservative desire to make the home and child-rearing more attractive to women, to increase the birth rate, to take positive action in support of a traditional women's role. Regardless of their ideological overtones, the recent laws created a new scope for women to move between motherhood and work and for husbands to opt for a fair share of domesticity and a novel balance of being a father and a breadwinner. By any standards, this is not an anti-discrimination law. The SPD and FDP proposals for anti-discrimination legislation in the early Eighties, with their emphasis on full equality of women and unrestricted access to leadership positions, were more clearly designed to challenge the hidden injustices in society. The same is true for the anti-discrimination law launched by the Greens which demands that women should occupy half the positions at all levels of employment and authority, and should receive preference over men until equality of numbers and functions has been reached in all walks of life.[4] By comparison, the Conservative moves to bridge the gaps between motherhood and employment are pragmatic in outlook and cautious in their interpretations of equality. Their very pragmatism brought the constitutional promise of equal rights and opportunities for women one step nearer.

References

Abendroth, Wolfgang, *Arbeiterklasse, Staat und Verfassung*, Frankfurt: Europäische Verlagsanstalt, 1975

Adamy, Wilhelm and Johannes Steffen, *Handbuch der Arbeitsbeziehungen*, Bonn: Bundeszentrale für politische Bildung, 1985

Brandt, Willy (ed.) *Frauen heute. Eine Bestandsaufnahme*, Reinbek: Rowohlt, 1978

Bulmer, Simon and William E. Paterson, *West Germany and Europe*, Oxford: Oxford University Press, 1987

Commission of the European Community, *Community Law and Women (Women of Europe 12)*, Brussels, 1983

——, *Community Law and Women (Women of Europe 25)*, Brussels, 1986

Derleder, Peter, 'Die neue Zähmung der Widerspenstigen', *Kritische Justiz*, 1982

Die Frau in der Gesellschaft. Arbeitstexte für den Unterricht, Stuttgart: Reclam, 1977

Dorpfel, Hans Peter, 'Die Gleichberechtigung von Mann und Frau im

4. Two publications by the liberal Friedrich Naumann Foundation present a useful overview and documentary appendix of the political positions in the equality debate and the anti-discrimination proposals of the main parties: Friedrich Naumann Stiftung (ed.), *Gleichberechtigung*, Dokumentation, 3 vols, Bonn/Königswinter 1978–1986 (broch.); and Friedrich Naumann Stiftung (ed.), *Antidiskriminierungsgesetz*, Dokumentation, 2 vols, Königswinter, 1984. For the position of the Greens see Die Grünen, *Vorläufiger Entwurf eines Antidiskriminierungsgesetzes*, Bonn, 1986; 'Entwurf eines Gesetzes zur Aufhebung der Benachteiligung von Frauen in allen gesellschaftlichen Bereichen (Antidiskriminierungsgesetz – ADG)', *Bundestagsdrucksache 10/6137*, 9 Oct. 1987.

Familienrecht der Bundesrepublik Deutschland', *Zeitschrift für Rechtsvergleich*, 1978

Dyson, Kenneth, *The State Tradition in Western Europe*, Oxford: Oxford University Press, 1980

Frauen Europas. Informationsdienst, ed. Kommission der Europäischen Gemeinschaft, Brussels, various years

Frauen in der Bundesrepublik, ed. Bundesminister für Jugend, Familie und Gesundheit, Bonn, 1984 (updated and extended 1986)

Friedrich Naumann Stiftung (ed.), *Gleichberechtigung*. Dokumentation, 3 vols, Bonn, 1978–1986

Hellmich, Andrea, *Frauen zwischen Familie und Beruf. Eine Untersuchung über Voraussetzungen und Nutzen einer Berufskontaktpflege von Frauen in der Familienphase* (ed. Bundesminister für Jugend, Familie, Frauen und Gesundheit), Stuttgart: Kohlhammer, 1986

Helwig, Gisela, *Frau und Familie in beiden deutschen Staaten*, Cologne: Wissenschaft und Politik, 1982 (2nd edn 1987)

Hoskyns, Catherine, 'Women, European Law and Transnational Politics', *International Journal of the Sociology of Law* 14, 1986, pp. 299–315

——, '"Give us Equal Pay and We'll Open our Own Doors" – A Study of the Impact in the Federal Republic of Germany and the Republic of Ireland of the European Community's Policy on Women's Rights'. Paper for the Edinburgh University Conference on Women, Equality and Europe, 1985 (mimeo)

Informationsdienst für Frauenfragen, ed. Deutscher Frauenrat, Bonn, 1951ff.

Jochimsen, Luc, '"Erst kommt der Mann, dann sie . . ."' Über die rechtliche und tatsächliche Situation der Frau in Ehe und Familie', in Willy Brandt (ed.), *Frauen heute* (pp. 88–107), Reinbek: Rowohlt, 1978

Lovenduski, Joni, *Women and European Politics. Contemporary Feminism and Public Policy*, Brighton: Harvester, 1986

Merkl, Peter H., *The Origin of the West German Republic*, New York: Oxford University Press, 1963

Münder, Johannes, Vera Slupik and Regula Schmidt-Bott, *Rechtliche und politische Diskriminierung von Mädchen und Frauen*, Opladen: Leske & Budrich, 1984

Parlamentarischer Rat. (Parliamentary Council), Stenographisches Protokoll über die 42. Sitzung des Hauptausschusses am 18.1.1949 (Stenographic transcript of the 42nd session of the Main Committee, 18.1.1949)

Pfarr, Heide and Klaus Bertelsmann, *Gleichbehandlungsgesetz* (ed. Zentralstelle für Frauenfragen beim Hessischen Ministerpräsidenten), Wiesbaden, 1985

Pfarr, Heide and Ludwig Eitel, 'Equal opportunity policies for women in the Federal Republic of Germany', in Günter Schmid and Renate

Weitzel (eds), *Sex Discrimination and Equal Opportunity in the Labour Market and Employment* (pp. 115–90), Aldershot: Gower, 1984

Reich-Hilweg, Irmgard, *Männer und Frauen sind gleichberechtigt. Der Gleichberechtigungsgrundsatz in der parlamentarischen Auseinandersetzung 1949–1957 und in der Rechtssprechung des Bundesverfassungsgerichtes 1953–1975*, Frankfurt: Europäische Verlagsanstalt, 1979

Säcker, Horst, *Bundesverfassungsgericht. Oberster Hüter der Verfassung*, Munich: Landeszentrale für politische Bildung, 1977

Schenk, Herrad, *Die feministische Herausforderung*, Munich: Beck, 1981

Schmid, Günter and Renate Weitzel (eds), *Sex Discrimination and Equal Opportunity in the Labour Market and Employment*, Aldershot: Gower, 1984

Schumann, Ekkehard, 'Bürgerliches Recht', in *Unser Recht*, Munich: Beck, 1982 (pp. 132–41)

Seifert, Jürgen, *Das Grundgesetz und seine Veränderungen*, Neuwied: Luchterhand, 1983

Späth, Antje, 'Vielfältige Forderungen nach Gleichberechtigung', in Anna-Elisabeth Freier and Annette Kuhn (eds), *Frauen in der Geschichte V*, Düsseldorf: Schwann, 1984

Statistisches Jahrbuch für die Bundesrepublik Deutschland, Stuttgart: Kohlhammer, 1988

Unser Recht. Große Sammlung deutscher Gesetze. Compiled by Ekkehard Schumann, Munich: Beck/dtv, 1982

Vallance, Elizabeth and Elizabeth Davies, *Women of Europe. Women MEPs and Equality Policy*, Cambridge: Cambridge University Press, 1986

Vogel, Angela, 'Frauen und Fauenbewegung', in Wolfgang Benz (ed.), *Die Bundesrepublik Deutschland* vol. II: *Gesellschaft*, Frankfurt: Fischer, 1983

3
Family Life and Lifestyles

In the four generations since the end of the Second World War, the lifestyles of women in West Germany have changed considerably. The constitutional promise of equality and the corresponding legislation have removed many barriers to equal opportunities. No less important have been the changes in living conditions, attitudes and social norms during the lifetime of the Federal Republic. We have seen earlier how Gertrud Bäumer linked urban living to a decline in domestic chores as women gained access to commercial products and services. The middle-class women she had in mind could find time for activities outside their family duties; since then the emergence of advanced industrial society has transformed the living conditions of all social classes in the direction of Bäumer's middle-class woman. Production and reproduction tasks no longer dominate the domestic sphere; free time, personal time, leisure and women's interest in roles outside the family have mobilised the lifestyles and social expectations of women. In West Germany, lifestyles and personal environments changed particularly fast. In the survival culture of the Forties and early Fifties women were thrown back to living conditions which resembled those pre-industrial times. As the West German economic recovery took off the supply of goods and services was soon better than at any time of economic prosperity in the past, and improved incomes enabled the average person to enjoy a better standard of living than anyone in Germany could remember. Today, living standards in West Germany are among the highest in Europe and lifestyles are far removed from the experiences and constraints which determined women's social situation and opportunities only decades ago.

In West Germany, the situation of women has rarely been discussed without normative intentions. Most of the literature which has contributed to our knowledge of women's lifestyles in changing social environments also gave implicit advice on

75

how women should be living and how they should balance the different possible roles between home or motherhood and employment in their lives (e.g. Beck-Gernsdorf 1980; Meyer 1980; Mühlfeld 1982). The social opportunities and capabilities attributed to women tended to amount to hidden recommendations about their suitable role in modern society. When Helmut Schelsky, for instance, wrote his evaluation of young people in the Fifties, his 'sceptical generation' consisted essentially of men. Women were only touched upon in passing since the qualities which Schelsky ascribed to them defined them as bystanders of history rather than actors. Women, Schelsky concluded, lacked the confidence to play relevant roles in broader social contexts. Theirs was the private sphere and their special place was to be towers of emotional resourcefulness and stability within the family (Schelsky 1957: 106–7). Writing ten years later, Elisabeth Pfeil recorded some interesting changes. In her survey of 23-year-olds, she found in 1968 that set notions about different abilities and social roles of men and women had decreased. The majority of young men and women regarded equality as a desirable social goal which might eventually govern society. While the young people of the late Sixties had enjoyed better education and employment opportunities than older generations would have had, and seemed to be changing their expectations about the social roles women could be playing, the author of the study purported to know full well what women could and should be concentrating on in their lives:

> The image of the mother as homemaker who devotes her life to her children and to her husband continues to be powerful. It is rooted in the desire for harmony and an atmosphere of warmth and comfort. In public discussions, this image and the fact that it persists are often castigated as antiquated and as evidence that attitudes are always one step behind social realities. It is doubtful that this explanation is thorough enough. Does not the wish to have mother at home full time during the first two decades of a person's life derive from the experience that our contemporary culture is more strenuous than any which preceded it? The fact that there are some women who can manage to combine full-time working with motherhood, who are naturally dynamic and have an excellent capacity to organise things and do not find it difficult to bring up children, the existence of such women does not mean that one can assume that a dual role of

motherhood and full employment can be lived by everyone. (Pfeil 1968: 99)

Less than a decade after Elisabeth Pfeil expressed her doubts that the family-centred roles of housewife and mother could be combined with employment by anybody but a superwoman, Helge Pross was inspired to write a special study ostensibly in defence of the housewife. Although many women continued to be housewives, and although neither the occupation of 'housewife' nor, indeed, the social expectation that women should care for the home and family had disappeared, what had vanished was the social recognition of homemaking as a useful activity. Helge Pross observed that German housewives had become apologetic about their role. The unspoken social assumptions in the Seventies seemed to have been reversed: women who devoted themselves full-time to the care of their husband and children were now disregarded as 'not-working'. Their role, she argues, did not fit into an environment which had taken to judging people by their position in the occupational hierarchy; here the private sphere did not count (Pross 1975). Against a social climate which seemed to pressurise women into employment by denying them recognition for traditional women's roles, Pross argued for choice and pleaded that the traditional role of housewife should be looked upon more positively.

The examples of advice by authors on the desirable role óf women in the contemporary world show how much the social climate has changed since the survival culture of the war and post-war years. Looking at changes of attitudes and preferences and also changes in family life, this chapter will sketch the cultural and personal environment of women today, and outline the framework in which choices in education, employment or politics would be made. Has the traditional women's realm of homemaking declined as a social reality, in its recognised status, or as a goal to which women aspire? What is the relevance today of the proverbial three Ks – *Kinder, Küche, Kirche* – for women themselves? Are West German women no longer housewives – and if not, what has taken the place of homemaking in women's lives? What do girls and women expect from their lives and how do they envisage balancing their social roles between homemaking and employment?

Families and the Role of Women

In the post-war years, families offered shelter and material and emotional support; in their structure families seemed to revert to the extended kinship networks which had been dissolved since urbanisation and the industrial revolution. Similar to the temporary flexibility of women's roles which we discussed earlier, the new emphasis on the extended family was short-lived. Normalisation of the personal environment meant also a reaffirmation of the nuclear family, i.e. a family group which included only parents and their children. The definition of the family which has been adopted for social and economic legislation in West Germany understands family as based on marriage, and on the parent–child relationship. It normally comprises two generations, a couple and their dependent children, but it may also consist of childless couples or include one or more parents of a couple (*Familie und Arbeitswelt* 1984: 26ff.). Families, in their contemporary size as much as in their transient extension after 1945, have been readily accepted by all age groups as the preferred framework for their private lives.

In the Fifties, the family was regarded as the pillar of social order, and the role of mother as the personal and emotional core of family life. The reaffirmation of the family follows from its important function in the post-war years but also from the focus of the West German population on the normalisation of their private lives. Couples would build their lives together to overcome the deprivations of the post-war years and create a comfortable personal environment. The following excerpt is taken from an autobiographical sketch written by a toolmaker who married in 1950 and built a private environment together with his wife. It is a typical life story for its time. To create its own, materially improved lifestyle was a focal point of family activities:

> Today, the young people start a marriage with owning a car, and we had nothing at all when we started. We could not help it, it was impossible to get anything. And we did not earn the big money, we had to save every penny. . . . We had lots of problems to begin with. The flat was very small, a converted attic. We had to saw the beds shorter to get them into the tiny room where we slept. Every time I turned, I hit my knee on the roof and woke up. We lived for six years in that place. . . . In 1957, we moved into this apartment, and bought

everything at once: furniture for the bedroom, the kitchen, the living room. We had saved all our money for seven years. . . . Only after 1957 could we purchase larger items, and we bought our first car in 1962 . . . and since then we have replaced a lot of things, bought a new three piece suite, a wardrobe, a stereo, a fitted bedroom and kitchen . . . (Deppe 1982: 69–70)

From the empirical studies and the autobiographical accounts which allow us insights into everyday lifestyles in the Fifties, there is no evidence to suggest that social roles had moved away from their traditional grids. Wurzbacher's vision of a new family life, based on equal recognition of men and women and paving the way towards an equal distribution of tasks did not correspond with a social reality which reinstated traditional practices and expectations (Wurzbacher, 1952). The only differences were temporary ones: until children were born, women worked to accumulate savings, to pay for furniture, holidays and luxury goods.

The expectations that a woman should marry, raise a family and build her life around the private sphere remained in force; yet it was mellowed by circumstance and by the life situation of the woman who had no husband or family. In German culture, as in many countries, the spinster, the unmarried woman, had been pitied as the maiden aunt who had been bypassed by real life or who was too ugly of appearance or character to land herself a man. Now, the war and its death toll among single and married men had changed all that. Women without husbands ceased to be a rarity, nor could the war widows and those in whose generation the number of men had been decimated by war be discredited as maiden aunts without prospects. In 1950 every second woman between the ages of twenty and thirty was not married. Two decades later, their number had fallen to about one in four but being unmarried remained a significant social reality for women. The generation who lived through the war as adolescents and young adults saw their lives and prospects changed more drastically than those who had already reached qualifications and defined social roles, or those who were children. This 'lost generation' continued to regard marriage and family life as landmarks of normalisation but could not obtain them for themselves. The lifestyles women developed in

79

post-war society opened a new mobility beyond family living. The need for single women to earn a living, and the mere size of the single women's cohort at the time of social stabilisation and economic expansion in West Germany, contributed to altering the working environment and led to a more favourable view of the career woman with professional competence. Although these women had remained single through circumstance rather than preference, the financial and social independence which they could develop as single working women helped to broaden and diversify the prescriptive role patterns for women in general. These women created new social opportunities: they went on holiday alone, they attended the cinema or theatre with friends or by themselves, they dined in restaurants without a male companion, all things which were frowned upon in the past and would not normally be attempted by the family woman in the Fifties. Beyond the private spheres of homemaking and child-rearing, a place for women in society became increasingly visible. The conventional taboos about what women can or cannot do were increasingly out of step with the realities of women's activities. Unwittingly, the non-married women of the 'lost generation' were trailblazers of change.

Forty years on, the changes in social behaviour are more explicitly linked to expectations and women's perceived social roles. In the Eighties 43% of women in the age cohort between twenty and thirty years were again unmarried: only this time, the shortage of men no longer played a part (*Frauen in Familie*, 1983: 14; 15; 21). The educational reforms since the Sixties have allowed an increasing proportion of young women to obtain qualifications in further and higher education. In doing so, they have tended to postpone marriage (see Chapter 4). Marriage and starting a family have remained important landmarks which West German girls and young women hope to achieve in their personal lives (*Jugend '81* 1982). Compared with the Forties or Fifties, family styles reflect personal preferences with a rapidly growing sector of common-law arrangements. In the life-cycles of women, the family phase itself has decreased in importance. Marriage commences later, and is less focused on children than in the past. In 1980, women tended to be married for nearly three years before the birth of their first child; twenty years earlier, the first child was born less than two years after marriage. Well

Figure 3.1 Families with children under the age of fifteen, 1950 and 1982 (in %)

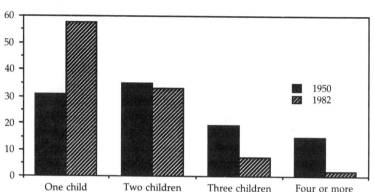

Source: Jugendliche und Erwachsene. Generationen im Vergleich, Opladen: Leske 1985: 290

into the Sixties, one in three first marriages was a *Muß-Ehe,* i.e. entered into to legalise the birth of a child. As contraceptive education became more widely available and as 'the pill' put women in charge of contraceptive practices, the birth rate began to decline, and unwanted or unplanned pregnancies occurred less frequently (Noelle-Neumann and Piel 1983: 232). The so-called *Pillenknick,* the sudden downturn in the birth rate as a result of oral contraceptives, brought the baby boom of the Sixties to a halt, and deaths began to outnumber births in the early Seventies. The post-war baby boom is somewhat of a misnomer, since women did not more children than in the past. The number of live births increased since the size of the generation in their twenties was more numerous than that of their parents had been, and normalisation of lifestyles meant getting married and starting a family.

The following decade witnessed a notable reduction in family size. Traditionally about one in ten marriages has remained childless (*Datenreport* 1983: 54). In the Fifties, one in three families with children had only one child; by the early Eighties, the proportion of one-child families had nearly doubled with a concomitant reduction in the number of families with three or more children (See Figure 3.1).

The One-Child Culture

West Germany seems on her way towards the one-child family. There are many different factors which contributed to the one-child culture. Views have changed about the beneficial influence of a large family on a person's character. A study conducted in 1957, for instance, showed that 88% of the population thought growing up without siblings would harm or ruin a child. Only an environment with siblings, it was felt, could curtail egotistical tendencies and develop social responsibility in children (Noelle-Neumann 1965: 67). As educational philosophy absorbed new ideas of child-centred approaches, not least the writings and teachings of Dr Spock and similar transatlantic advisers on parent/child relations, West Germans began to accept their children more emphatically as individuals, and develop individual relationships with them (Allerbeck and Hoag 1985: 64ff.). The new personalised focus of child-care made the one-child family preferable to a family pattern where several children had to compete for parental attention and material support.

The one-child family can also be seen as a personal and institutional response to some more practical constraints. The rebuilding of West Germany was based on the small three-room apartment in which a half-bedroom was allocated as the so-called children's room. Finding room for more than one child would often have meant moving house or apartment. With the exception of the involuntary dislocations of the post-war era, moving house is not part of the everyday culture (Diewald and Zapf 1984). Even people who live in rented accommodation – and they are in the majority – tend to remain there for a lifetime and the next generation can inherit the right to rent. Home ownership normally ties people and their descendants to a given locality and home. The size of the existing home is, therefore, an important factor in deciding on the number of children a couple may wish to have.

Another pragmatic factor is family income. During the post-war normalisation of personal environments, living standards began to rise alongside wages and salaries. West Germans were able to furnish their homes to contemporary tastes and standards, to eat well, to travel and to enjoy a broader range of activities and services which in the past might have been the privilege of the rich. As living standards improved, a decreasing proportion of family incomes had to be spent on food and clothing, and more was available for leisure pursuits and information. The sense of material well-being has been an important factor in the emergence of democratic attitudes and the acceptance of the West German political system (Conradt 1980). In the private sphere, this sense of material well-being tends to determine the degree of satisfaction or dissatisfaction with personal lifestyles (Berger and Mohr 1986: 35). The emphasis on material well-being and a living standard which matches that of people in one's own environment has militated against large families. The birth of a first child has already been shown to mean a deterioration in the economic situation of a family due to the additional expenditure involved. In those cases where one of the partners – normally the woman – gives up paid employment to look after the child, the family suffers a significant decline in income (*Familie und Arbeitswelt*: 96ff.). Psychological pressures on the couple to adapt to child care, and for the full-time carer the possible isolation from colleagues, friends and neighbours, have also been linked to the tendency towards the one-child family. West German children have to be brought up in style, surrounded by the physical and material comforts befitting an affluent society, and parents expect themselves to conform to these unwritten rules of affluent living. They allow only the better-off to have more than two children without suffering major socio-economic disadvantages through family size. The largest families in West Germany are today found among two groups: the self-employed, who enjoy the highest average family income of all social groups and can afford help in the home; and the foreign workers (*Gastarbeiter*) whose cultural standards still favour large families and who tend to occupy positions near the bottom of the social scale.

For most West Germans, the traditional incentives to rearing a large family are now irrelevant. In the nuclear and urbanised family where the income is earned through paid employment, children have no working role as they do in artisan or farming families. Affiliation to the Catholic Church, which has traditionally rejected birth control, has been on the decline and many active churchgoers follow their own personal preferences as far as family size is concerned. The wish to pass on the family name has also declined as a decisive factor in planning a family. With girls no longer a potential liability for whom the family has to provide a dowry, secure an economically stable marriage and ensure training in such housewifely and social skills as she might need to find a husband, the sex of a child or children is less important to most families than in the past although there is some evidence that boys are often only children while girls have siblings (Seidenspinner and Burger 1982). This would suggest that a certain focus on the *Stammhalter*, the heir to the name, has remained in the everyday culture despite the broad changes in values and lifestyles.

The preference for smaller families has significantly altered the age balance and the balance of sexes in the population. Since 1972, deaths have outnumbered births. As with populations in other advanced industrial societies, West Germans are getting older on average, and the size of the overall population is set to decrease from a peak of 61.6 million in 1980 to 59.6 million in the year 2000 and 46.9 million thirty years later (projections by Ministry of the Interior, 1987). Among the over-fifties, women outnumber men. Although the traditional imbalances in infancy have disappeared since improved medical facilities ensured that male babies enjoy as good a chance of survival as female babies, life expectancy of women has remained higher than that of men.

Family Phases and Lifestyles: A Sketch

The changes in the family structures since the Fifties may be summarised in lifestyle sketches of the average woman. In the early Fifties, she would have married in her mid-twenties. She would normally have had two children, the first born when she was twenty-seven, the second when she was thirty-one years old. Those with three children would have completed their child-bearing phase in their mid-thirties. Since full-time education in West Germany commences when the child is between six and seven years old, the youngest child of the mother-of-two would have started school when the mother was nearly thirty-eight, and depending on the level of qualification attempted the child would have remained in full-time education at school for between ten and thirteen years. By the time the newly wed woman of the early Fifties was fifty years old, her two children would have completed their schooling and started employment, further training or other transitions into adult life. If she had three children, she would normally be in her mid-fifties when her youngest child completed school. After the children entered adulthood or left home, the couple who married in the early Fifties would live together for another ten years or so, with the woman on her own after the death of her husband for a further ten years.

For couples and mothers of the Eighties, the life-cycle would be similar, but with a shortened family phase. The first and often only child is normally born after three years of marriage when the woman is about twenty-eight. She would be in her mid-thirties when it started school and in her mid- or late forties at the time of transition to work or higher education. After that, a woman could expect to live another twenty-five years or so without involvement in child care or educational duties in the family.

The time span in which families care for dependent children has decreased and caring itself has been made easier by the improved equipment of private households with labour-saving devices. Regardless of income group or social class, West German families with children tend to equip themselves with durable consumer goods to assist with everyday chores, mobility and entertainment. In the Sixties, over half the households had a vacuum cleaner and a refrigerator, but cars, telephones or televisions were only for a minority. Just 3% of households were reported to have a freezer. As Table 3.1 shows, the majority of West German households now own all of these items.

As lifestyles have become more affluent consumer durables have lost their status as luxuries beyond reach. Judging by the money spent on them, labour-saving devices, equipment for entertainment, communication and transport are more important today than in the early days of the Federal Republic when core items such as furniture or food had to be bought. In 1960, a family of two adults and two children with an average income tended to spend 5% of their annual budget on household appliances. In 1985, the proportion had risen to 15%. West German families invest in their lifestyles, in the modern technologies to make their personal environment more efficient and

Table 3.1 Consumer durables in private households (in %)

Equipment	1962	1973	1983
Telephone	14	51	88
Car	27	55	65
Vacuum cleaner	65	91	96
Automatic washing machine	34	75	83
Refrigerator	52	93	96
Freezer	3	28	65
Dishwasher	0.5	7	24
Automatic sewing machine	10	37	52
Tape recorder	5	25	35
Camera	42	68	78
Television	36	89	94

Source: Compiled from *Statistische Jahrbücher der Bundesrepublik* for the relevant years.

more attractive to them. The choice between material affluence and family size has been decided: to be able to afford the lifestyle of one's choice, the one-child culture has become firmly entrenched. The changes in family size and lifestyle combined to create more time in which even those women who have opted to be full-time housewives are not involved in child-raising. In the one-child family the number of years dependent children live at home has fallen by comparison with large families and siblings born over a decade or so; the family lives of women have become less child-focused. The protracted periods of widowhood and old age further reduced the place of family and children in a woman's life-cycle. On an everyday level, labour-saving devices have helped to reduce the manual chores of housekeeping which had been such a prominent feature in the immediate post-war years. Family and homemaking need no longer be a full-time and life-long occupation, although women may opt for it.

Attitudes and Expectations

When Helge Pross studied the housewives of the mid-Seventies, she noted that her subjects were not particularly interested in what they were doing – running a home and possibly rearing children – but they had no complaints. Emancipation, as they saw it, the equality of men and women in society, would not follow from housework but from employment and the independent income this would secure (Pross 1975: 13). However, the majority at the time were convinced that they personally could not compete in the world outside, let alone emulate the successes of their husbands and of men in general. While doubting their own ability to change roles between employment and housework they saw no such problems for their husbands and were sure men would cope admirably: 'he is more able, more superior, more intelligent – he is a man' (Pross 1975: 145; similarly, Probst 1981: 86). Ten years earlier Elisabeth Pfeil had noted that young adult women were reluctant to make plans for their future other than thinking they would get married and raise a family (Pfeil 1968: 99).

These women of the Sixties and Seventies lacked the confidence to plan their lives and focus on a preferred lifestyle between the home and the world of work; for their daughters in the Eighties these uncertainties about possible roles and their ability to cope with society's demands are much less daunting – today's generation of young women dares to voice expectations and anticipates a lifestyle of their choice. A study commissioned by the women's magazine *Brigitte* describes especially clearly what young women hope for their lives. The girls in the survey were aged between fifteen and nineteen at the beginning of the Eighties and from a range of educational and vocational backgrounds. One of the main findings of *Mädchen '82* (Seidenspinner and Burger 1982) was that most of the young women in 1982 expected that they would get married and have children (or one child). They had expected the family role as part of their existence as women. However, they also expected to qualify in their chosen career and to be in employment. Motherhood and employment, which have traditionally been seen as mutually exclusive, were now regarded as two complementary activities. To combine motherhood and employment rather than choose between them motivated the young women of 1982. Seidenspinner and Burger point out that most were realists and did not expect to achieve their dual goal without practical adjustments and compromise. Forty-seven per cent planned to obtain a professional or vocational qualification before having children, interrupt their career while the children would be small, and return to work once their children were in full-time education (Seidenspinner and Burger 1982: 13). A further 23% were convinced that they could combine part-time work with having a family and would not have to interrupt their careers; 5% planned to continue full-time working after the birth of their first child and the same proportion stated that they would be happy to give up work and devote themselves full-time to their family.

However, these plans and hopes for future lifestyles do not reflect the practical obstructions they might encounter. *Mädchen '82* shows that the youngest women are the most confident that their expectations can somehow be put into practice. It also shows that girls displayed considerable anxiety as to whether they could obtain sufficiently high qualifications, and that they were willing to compromise and alter their career wishes once they had encountered the obstacle of repeated rejections in their search for work or training. In their access to training and employment women have encountered obstacles and failure despite the more confident general mood. Also, returning to work after several years at home is fraught with difficulties at times of high unemployment (see Chapter 5). Women tend to be out of touch with new developments and risk being employed at a level well below their paper qualifications and potential. The three-phase model of working–homemaking–working again (Myrdal and Klein 1971) has been accused of conditioning women to occupy the lowest rungs of the occupational ladders and the most temporary, dead-end jobs (Schwarzer 1977; Däubler-Gmelin 1977). Although the girls of 1982 may appear naive in their belief that they would somehow manage to find a satisfying lifestyle between family and work, the mobilisation of attitudes which has taken place since their mothers were young adults is important. Looking ahead, the young women today are planning beyond marriage, and they believe that they can succeed in the world outside the private family sphere. The deficit in confidence which was evident in the Sixties and Seventies is no longer as dominant. For mainly as a fall-back position after failing to secure a foothold in the world of employment, the young women in *Mädchen '82* turned their sights to the private world. Thus, marriage and full-time homemaking are within reach as accepted and obtainable social roles for women.

Mothers and Daughters

Girls in the Eighties appear to be more confident, more assertive, and more independent in deciding their own lifestyle than
their mothers or grandmothers had ever been; although they are
prone to cope with disappointment by falling back on traditional
women's roles, the personality make-up of the young generation puts them more on a par with their male contemporaries.
As social expectations and attitudes towards girls have become
less gender-specific, the scope for girls to engage in activities of
their choice has increased. They enjoy similar access to information, entertainment and independent decisions as boys of
their age, and regard their relationship to boys and men in terms
more of partnership than of inferiority or superiority.

Mothers and daughters today have been socialised by different values and have had to conform to different rules of eti-
quette and conduct. In the Fifties, parents kept tight control
over the friends their daughters were allowed to have (sons
were less strictly controlled) and most conflicts erupted over the
time a girl had to return home after an evening out (Preuss-
Lausitz 1983).

Attitudes of young people have received special attention
since the Seventies when the German Shell company began to
sponsor surveys on the lifestyle expectations of the generation
under the age of twenty-five. The 1985 study adopted a somewhat broader approach and offered a cross-generational comparison. On the one hand, it referred back to survey data from
the Fifties to see how young people thought at the time; on the
other hand it repeated those questions which would still be
understood in a similar way and addressed them to the young
people of the Eighties and to adults in the Eighties who had
belonged to the youth cohort of the Fifties. The results show two
processes of change: views clearly differ between youth and
adults of today, and adults of today have adopted more liberal
views than they themselves held when they were young. Table
3.2 focuses on the way people think they have been brought up
and illustrates the value change that has occurred since the
Fifties. In retrospect, adults rate the upbringing as stricter now

Table 3.2 Styles of upbringing in the parental home, 1955 and 1984 (in %)[a]

	Youth 1955 (15–24 years)	Youth 1984 (15–24 years)	Adults 1984 (45–54 years)
Very strict	9	3	19
Strict	36	32	44
Understanding	50	60	36
Too lenient	4	4	1
No answer	1	—	—
	100	100	100

[a] The question read: 'How do you think was your upbringing: very strict, strict, understanding, too lenient?'
Source: Shell study 1985 vol. 3: *Jugendliche und Erwachsene*, Opladen: Leske und Budrich 1985: 151.

than it appeared to them in the Fifties (e.g. very strict: 19% in 1984; 9% in 1955). One of the norms in a strict upbringing stipulated that the young person should obey without questioning orders and without contradicting. The changes outlined in Table 3.2 suggest that young people today are rarely brought up in this way and that adults tend to feel that their own upbringing contained too much obedience and not enough understanding (*Jugendliche und Erwachsene* 1985: 193). Clearly, as parents, they have adopted a different approach towards their own children, the young generation of the Eighties. Well into the Sixties, the majority of children were denied all rights to defend their actions, justify their own conduct or contradict their parents. Although young people felt this to be unfair, most did not challenge it (ibid. p. 104). In 1966, two out of three 10- to 19-year-olds declared that they would not dare to disobey their parents; by 1976, the proportion had fallen to just over four out of ten (ibid p. 229). Girls in the Fifties and Sixties seemed less likely to contradict their parents, and more willing to conform to orders even against their wishes, than did their male contemporaries (Table 3.3). In the Eighties, young people of both sexes listed more issues of conflict and will defend their style, preferences or political views against their parents. The gap between boys and girls still exists as girls report fewer conflicts than boys, but the gap is smaller now than in the Fifties.

Table 3.3 Issues of conflict between young people and their parents: views of adults 1984 on their own youth, and youth 1984 (in %)

Issue	Youth in the 1950s		Youth in the 1980s	
	Boys	Girls	Boys	Girls
School work	69	52	80	69
Going out at night	54	57	68	79
Friendship with boys	—	56	—	56
Untidiness	60	50	86	80
Helping at home	53	50	86	80
Dress	49	48	71	66
Friendship with girls	42	—	33	—
Bad manners	45	31	68	56
Smoking	38	10	42	42
Different political views	18	10	38	30

Source: Shell study, *Jugendliche und Erwachsene*: 118.

For girls, manners, appearance and cleanliness have been regarded as more important than for boys (Noelle-Neumann and Piel 1983: 93). Grooming young ladies to conform with social conventions is still part of today's everyday culture and there is some evidence that girls are still more inclined to conform to these expectations than their male peers (*Jugend '81*: 166).

Studies of gender differences in socialisation patterns have tended to emphasise that improved sex education, contraceptive provision and easier social contacts between the sexes have helped to reduce the taboos which surrounded sexual activity until the mid-Sixties or so, and have enabled girls to engage in sexual relationships without expecting that they would have to lead to marriage. Fears of unwanted pregnancies, which were ever-present until the advent of the contraceptive pill in the early Sixties, receded into history. Girls today are on average younger than their mothers when they have their first sexual experiences, and often have several boyfriends before forming a permanent relationship (Seidenspinner and Burger 1982: 28–9; Sigusch and Schmidt 1973). By the age of nineteen, the majority had sexual experiences and about half had had a steady partner for more than one year. Boys, it seems, have a similar range of sexual contacts to that of girls. Differences between the sexes

Table 3.4 Young people who never contributed to the housework by social background and gender (in %)

Task	Lower class		Middle class		Upper class	
	m	f	m	f	m	f
Cooking: never	74	24	65	16	69	15
Cleaning: never	71	17	57	16	64	18
Laundry: never	94	50	87	49	89	53
Looking after siblings: never	80	75	85	74	77	74
Washing dishes: never	43	11	35	8	42	12

Source: Shell, *Jugend '81*: 333.

which may have existed in the past are no longer prominent. Some traditional attitudes, however, persist and girls are twice as likely as boys to experience conflict with their parents over their involvement with boys (Table 3.3).

The Gender Gap of Everyday Activities

The climate of equality, which is evident in the social experiences and norms which shape the aspirations of young people in the Eighties, have not fully penetrated into the private sphere of family living. The limits of partnership and equality in everyday life are clearly apparent in the uneven distribution of housework. Housework, it has been said, is 'the last reservation of'a gender-specific life experience' (*Jugend '81*: 334). Despite the strides in independence and confidence which have removed many barriers to self-realisation, most girls are expected to help with the housework, the majority of boys are not (Table 3.4). Girls contributed to the household tasks regardless of their social background while boys are least likely to take on 'female' roles in lower-class homes. Of the tasks listed in Table 3.4 only looking after younger siblings does not show a large gender imbalance; as families have become smaller, the task itself is no longer necessary.

Contributing to the day-to-day chores of shopping, cleaning, washing up or cooking is expected of few boys while most girls have, or choose, to make a contribution to the parental household. Girls' own expectations, however, are out of phase with contemporary behaviour. They anticipate a more equal distribution of household tasks than boys have been brought up to offer. Although there is little evidence that girls reject the role of housewife outright, they see their future partner taking an equal share, and they are critical of their own mothers who, they feel, are too devoted to caring for the family and too occupied with housework.

From Conventional to New Women?

Contemporary family life has become *'mütterlastig'* – weighted towards the mother with fathers less involved in everyday matters. When Schelsky studied the 'sceptical generation' of the Fifties, he observed a certain preference for fathers among the young, since father appeared to have time for leisure pursuits and could be approached for confidential advice. 'For these young people, the problems of exaggerated paternal authority no longer exist. A more rational relationship to the parents often creates an especially close link to the father among the young people, which is based on acknowledging his ability to achieve something in life, and less on internally absorbing his authority' (Schelsky 1957: 125). More recent studies have emphasised that fathers tended to remain marginal to the family, wrapped up in their work, detached from the fray of everyday activities and personal crises. In the fatherless society of today, mothers have taken over the roles of confidante and adviser; next to best friends, mothers are the most important persons to help with solving personal problems and providing guidance to their children (*Jugend privat* 1985: 18). At the same time, husbands now look to their wives to talk about problems of work, about politics and other non-private issues, something few would have done in the Fifties. Women, on the other hand, are interested in a broader range of things, and shifts in social conventions have made it easier for women to extend their interests and networks of communication beyond the family.

As gender-specific realms of activity have receded, equality has increasingly been understood to mean partnership, an even-handed distribution of tasks, opportunities and commitments between men and women, husbands and wives (Stamm and Rhyff 1984). The traditional gender gap of expectations has also become a women's generation gap. Among older women, tra-

Table 3.5 Attitudes to marriage and partnership among women aged 15–30

Type	%
The *conventional* woman	39
The *uncertain* woman	31
The *new* woman	30

Source: *Jugend privat*, Sinus Report for the Ministry of Youth, Family and Health, Opladen: Leske & Budrich, 1985: 34.

ditional patterns and lifestyles have remained unquestioned. We saw earlier in this chapter that even the single (or widowed) working women of the Fifties who had changed the scope of socially acceptable behaviour for women continued to view the private world of marriage and homemaking as the role women ought to play, if circumstances permitted. New ideas about women's social roles and the meaning of equality between men and women in everyday life gained ground among younger women and moulded attitudes and social behaviour. The process of change has been uneven, and views among young-generation women are by no means uniform. In fact, conventional role patterns exist side-by-side with a new focus on partnership and equality as some prefer the traditional notion that women are natural mothers and homemakers while others stake their claim to equality in their private lives (Lupri 1983). These two types have been called the 'conventional' and the 'new' woman: the former settled in her endorsement of traditional behaviour, the latter settled in her commitment to the reality of partnership (*Jugend privat* 1985). Table 3.5 suggests that conventional women in the young generation (39%) outnumber the adherents of equality (30%). Together young women who have opted for a definite interpretation of their social role – be it conventional or 'new' – amount to more than two-thirds of the young generation. However, the third group highlights the uneven pace of social change most clearly: these 'uncertain' women accept the principles of equality and partnership and also endorse motherhood and homemaking as women's roles. In their private lives, they appeared to switch between roles and were unable to be as convinced as either of the other two types that they knew what women should do in contemporary society and how they could balance their own expectations with those in their environment.

The simultaneous existence and similar frequency of three types of woman – the conventional, the uncertain and the 'new' woman – suggest that traditional role models for women as mothers and homemakers have not been replaced by clear-cut new ones based on partnership. The notion of types itself may be too static to account for the fluid pace of attitudinal change. Detailed studies of individual lifestyles have shown that the distribution of tasks and the role expectations of women differ at different stages in the family cycles. Glatzer and Herget, for instance, present the findings of a representative survey of everyday life and related attitudes in the early Eighties. They report that the husbands in families without children took on the largest share of the housework, only slightly lower than that of their wives. At this stage in the family cycles the majority of women would be in employment. The similarity of socio-economic roles appears to be mirrored in the private roles. Once children were born, the husbands' commitment decreased and that of their wives increased, although men in the survey claimed to spend up to three hours daily playing with their children. Of five set household tasks, married women regularly performed 4.7, men about one (Glatzer and Herget 1984: 127). The lives of married couples without children with both part-ners in employment seem to come closest to the expectatioris that men and women should play equal roles. The birth of the first child meant a reinstatement of conventional practices. In the family phase, child care and housework have remained the unchallenged domains of women, and the expectations of part-nership have yet to be fulfilled in this part of the private sphere.

Satisfaction and Dissatisfaction with Lifestyles

The pivotal place of women in the home, and in charge of the home, is not altogether popular with women today. They are less satisfied with the distribution of labour in the home than men, and voice frequent complaints about the practicalities of household management in their private spheres (Glatzer and Herget 1984: 132). One in three women (32%) and 7% of the men felt that they had to 'give more than they received'. Women in West Germany have always been more sceptical than men about achieving happiness in marriage (Noelle-Neumann and Piel 1983: 26). In the Eighties, the general doubts about married life can be traced more specifically to social and economic roles, in particular the balance of home and work. The most unhappy segment of women appear to be those in part-time employment (38.7%) whose husbands take few responsibilities in the home but who are carrying the dual burden of homemaking and work. One in three women who are full-time housewives also felt they contributed more than their fair share to the home and family (32.2%). Women in full-time employment were the most satisfied group (Glatzer and Herget 1984: 135). Some of the reasons for the dissatisfaction of women with their personal environments may be emotional, relating to a lack of recognition for their achievements, social isolation, unsuitable hours of employment or the overall lack of choice in determining their own lifestyle and its balance between home and work. Material conditions, however, are at least as important as circumstantial and personal factors. Regardless of who works and for how long, women in families with higher incomes are clearly more satisfied with their personal environment than women who live in less advantaged circumstances (Berger and Mohr 1986: 35).

Discrepancies between role expectations and role opportunities are the most powerful source of personal dissatisfaction. For women, the expectation of finding suitable work outside the home and of combining homemaking and employment could often not be met. The reasons might range from a shortage of suitable openings to a qualification deficit in the woman herself, the objections of the husband or other obstacles such as distance from a possible place of work or personal health. That frustrated expectations of employment have been at least as important in generating discontent as an uneven distribution of household chores between men and women became apparent once mass unemployment began to bite. Looking for paid employment became less feasible for full-time housewives when some 10% of the labour force were out of work and seeking employment. Women adapted their expectations to the new constraints, and showed themselves more content with being full-time housewives than at times of better opportunities (ibid.: 39). This response is parallel to that observed by Seidenspinner and

Burger among young girls who tended to adjust their hopes of combining work and family once they experienced obstacles in the labour market: then a life as a housewife was seen as a possible alternative. The new emphasis in the Eighties by the Conservative-led government on family life and motherhood also contributed to a climate in which being a housewife is publicly presented and could be individually perceived as a positive choice. The views which Helge Pross had encountered in the mid-Seventies, that being a housewife meant a lifestyle of 'solitary confinement' or was a symptom of unemancipated backwardness, have been modified in the light of contracting opportunities in the world of work. The changes in role patterns for women, and the shift towards expectations at least of a partnership between men and women, have enabled women to take a more active part in society, even without socio-economic integration through employment.

The new participatory political culture since the Seventies has made it easier for women to become involved in political parties and other types of political activity. In women's personal opportunities the family sphere of homemaking or child care continues to hold a central place, but other avenues of involvement have emerged in which women can articulate preferences and choose a style of commitment which suits them. Although the transition to partnership values has only just begun, changing family sizes, a reduction in time spent on domestic chores, a loosening of social conventions and a range of participatory opportunities in social, economic and political life have mobilised women's lifestyles and created some of the preconditions for transforming the constitutional promise of equality into a social and personal reality.

References

Allerbeck, Klaus and Wendy Hoag, *Jugend ohne Zukunft?* Munich: Piper, 1985

Beck-Gernsdorf, Elisabeth, *Das halbierte Leben. Männerwelt Beruf –*

Frauenwelt Familie, Frankfurt: Fischer, 1980

Berger, Regina and Hans Michael Mohr, 'Lebensqualität in der Bundesrepublik', *Soziale Welt*, 1986

Conradt, David, 'Changing German Political Culture', in Gabriel Almond and Sidney Verba (eds), *The Civic Culture Revisited*, Boston: Little Brown, 1980

Datenreport, ed. Presse- und Informationsamt der Bundesregierung, Bonn, 1983, 1987

Däubler-Gmelin, Herta, *Frauenarbeitslosigkeit oder Reserve zurück an den Herd*, Reinbek: Rowohlt, 1977

Deppe, Wilfried, *Drei Generationen Arbeiterleben*, Frankfurt: Campus, 1982

Diewald, Martin and Wolfgang Zapf, 'Wohnbedingungen und Wohnzufriedenheit', in Wolfgang Glatzer and Wolfgang Zapf (eds), *Lebensqualität in der Bundesrepublik*, Frankfurt: Campus, 1984 (pp. 73–96)

Familie und Arbeitswelt, book series by the Ministry of Youth, Family and Health, vol. 143, Stuttgart: Kohlhammer, 1984

Frauen in Familie, Beruf und Gesellschaft, Statistisches Bundesamt, Stuttgart: Kohlhammer, 1983, 1987

Glatzer, Wolfgang and Hermann Herget, 'Ehe, Familie, Haushalt', in Wolfgang Glatzer and Wolfgang Zapf (eds), *Lebensqualität in der Bundesrepublik*, Frankfurt: Campus, 1984 (pp. 124–40)

Jugend '81. Lebensentwürfe, Alltagskultur, Zukunftsbilder (Deutsche Shell), Opladen: Leske & Budrich, 1982

Jugend privat, Sinus Report for the Ministry of Youth, Family and Health, Opladen: Leske & Budrich, 1985

Jugendliche und Erwachsene '85. Generationen im Vergleich. Jugend der fünfziger Heute-Jahre. Jugendwerk der Deutschen Shell vol. 3, Opladen: Leske & Budrich, 1985

Lupri, Eugen (ed.) *The Changing Position of Women in Family and Society – A Cross-National Comparison*, Brill (International Studies in Sociology and Social Anthropology 3), 1983

Meyer, Heinz, *Das Frau-Sein*, Opladen: Westdeutscher Verlag, 1980

Mühlfeld, Claus, *Ehe und Familie*, Opladen: Westdeutscher Verlag, 1982

Myrdal, Gunnar and Viola Klein, *Die Doppelrolle der Frau in Familie und Beruf*, Cologne: Politik und Wissenschaft, 1971

Noelle-Neumann, Elisabeth, *Jahrbuch der öffentlichen Meinung*, Allensbach, 1965

—— and Robert Piel, *Eine Generation später*, Allensbach, 1983

Pfeil, Elisabeth et al., *Die 23 jährigen. Eine Generationenuntersuchung des Geburtsjahrganges 1941*, Tübingen: Mohr, 1968

Preuss-Lausitz, Ulf et al., *Kriegskinder, Konsumkinder, Krisenkinder. Zur Sozialisationsgeschichte seit dem zweiten Weltkrieg*, Weinheim/Basel: Beltz, 1983

Probst, Ulrich, *Männer und Frauen sind gleichberechtigt. Zur politischen Emanzipation der Frau in der Bundesrepublik Deutschland*, Munich: Bayr. Landeszentrale, 1981

Pross, Helge, *Die Wirklichkeit der deutschen Hausfrau*, Munich: Beck, 1975

Schelsky, Helmut, *Die skeptische Generation*, Düsseldorf: Diederichs, 1957

Schwarzer, Alice, *Der kleine Unterschied und seine großen Folgen*, Frankfurt: Fischer, 1977

Seidenspinner, Gerlinde and Angelika Burger, *Mädchen '82*, Munich: Deutsches Jugendinstitut, 1982

Sigusch, Volkmar and Gunter Schmidt, *Jugendsexualität*, Stuttgart: Enke, 1973

Stamm, L. and C.D. Rhyff (eds), *Social Power and Influence of Women*, New York: Westview Press, 1984

Wurzbacher, Gerhard, *Leitbilder gegenwärtigen deutschen Familienlebens*, Stuttgart: Enke, 1952

4
Women in Education: Schools, Vocational Training and Universities

'Traditional prejudices are a major reason why the importance of general and in particular of vocational education for women continues to be underestimated' (*Bericht* 1972: 1). In 1972 a note of regret set the tone of a government report on the situation of women. It was published nearly a decade after educational reform had moved to the top of the political agenda in West Germany amidst fears that an 'educational catastrophe' (Picht 1964) was imminent. Had not the Soviet Union taken the lead at the cutting edge of scientific and technological innovation when it launched the first ever spacecraft, Sputnik, in 1957 (Becker 1983)? Could Western democracies survive without exhausting all their educational reserves and bringing able young people from all walks of life into advanced and higher education (Dahrendorf 1965)? Working-class children and women seemed most disadvantaged and strongly under-represented at advanced secondary and tertiary levels. Table 4.1 contains the data which Ralf Dahrendorf used in 1965 to draw attention to the poor participation rate of women at higher levels of education. The higher the level of educational qualification, the greater was the shortfall of women: in the lower forms of the selective grammar schools, 41% of the pupils were girls; their share had declined to 36% at A-level (*Abitur*), and to 17% on graduation from university.

Explanations why girls underperformed in the education system pointed to traditional views of female roles in society and also in core components of the curriculum (Borris 1972). Post-war reconstruction of the educational system had largely consisted of ridding textbooks and teaching practices of the most blatant facets of National Socialist ideology. The new emphasis on wider access and the participation of previously disadvantaged groups now implied changes in the quantity and in the

Table 4.1 Women in advanced education (1965)

Share of women	%	Women's 'deficit' (in %)	
Population	49		
Grammar school (3rd year)	41	−8	(compared to share of age cohort)
Abitur	36	−5	(leaving before completion)
University entry	26	−10	(compared to women with *Abitur*)
Graduation from university	17	−9	(leaving without graduating)

Source: Ralf Dahrendorf, *Bildung ist Bürgerrecht*, Hamburg: Nannen, 1965.

quality of educational provision, in particular at advanced level. This, in essence, was the purpose of educational reforms which originated in the Sixties and laid the foundations for broader access to post-elementary education at secondary and at tertiary level in the ensuing decades (Max-Planck Institute 1980).

Women emerged as the main beneficiaries. Since the Seventies, West Germany experienced something of a revolution in the educational participation of women, a *Fräuleinwunder* of enhanced opportunities and improved access. Women under the age of forty appeared to have entered the era of educational equality (Hradil 1987: 41). The scope and the limitations of women's equal chances in education are the theme of this chapter. Women, it is argued, have eagerly embraced the German educational culture of formal qualifications. In schools, their bid for equality may be called a success story: they not only caught up with their male peers in secondary education, they overtook them with higher participation rates and with better grades (Hurrelmann et al. 1982). Beyond general schooling in vocational or tertiary education, young women have encountered more substantive obstacles; the *Fräuleinwunder* in school-based education has not been matched by a similar miracle in employment-related education (Sixth Youth Report 1984). At both poles of the spectrum, vocational training and university qualifications, the transition from school to work continues to be fraught with gender-based differences of access, opportunities and intent. When the educational *Fräuleinwunder* got under way in the Seventies, chances of a smooth transition from school to work had already deteriorated. By the time girls were educated in larger numbers and to higher levels, the oil shock and the world economic recession brought endemic mass unemployment in West Germany for the first time since the Fifties. The entry of West Germany's young, educated and vocationally motivated women occurred in an age of economic uncertainties. Its benchmarks have been widespread concern about employment prospects, about matching educational achievements to career avenues and the related fears that individual expectations and life-plans will not be met by experiences and realities.

Educating Gretchen – Girls in the School System

Since its inception in the nineteenth century the German educational system has been based on two core principles which have determined its overall organisational structure to this day: the first purpose of education has been to provide sufficient training in numeracy, literacy and technical skills in order to equip the country with a competent and adaptable workforce and, in the days of the Prussian monarchy at least, with obedient and respectful subjects. The second purpose of education has been to train a small elite to advanced level, and for leadership positions.

The basic need for general education was to be served by a network of *Volksschulen* with compulsory attendance for a specified number of years. The educational reforms in the Sixties redefined the sector of compulsory schooling into an elementary part, *Grundschulen*, for children of all abilities between the ages of six and ten or twelve, depending on regional arrangements, and a secondary part which came to be known as *Hauptschule*, 'main school', and is designed to educate young people up to the ages of fifteen with a normally optional tenth year in some of the *Länder*. The pupils would be those young people who did not pass selective tests for more advanced schools or who failed to achieve the standards required in the next higher level and were demoted. Table 4.2 shows how the balance in the West German school system has shifted from basic education only to intermediate or advanced schooling. In the Fifties, the majority

Table 4.2 Educational participation of 13-year-olds by types of school

Year	Types of school			
	Main school (*Hauptschule*) %	Intermediate school (*Realschule*) %	Grammar school (*Gymnasium*) %	Comprehensive (*Gesamtschule*) %
1955	72	8	15	—
1960	70	11	15	—
1965	66	13	16	—
1970	55	19	20	—
1975	46	21	24	3
1980	39	25	27	4
1985	37	26	28	4

Sources: Datenreport (ed. Statistisches Bundesamt, Bonn) 1983: 63; 1987: 57.

of 13-year-olds would attend the lowest level school; by the mid-Eighties, only 37% did so. In the same period, the grammar school doubled its share of an age cohort, and the intermediate *Realschule* trebled it. Comprehensive schools have been created during the educational reforms but have not emerged as a major school type.

Basic compulsory schooling in West Germany (see Figure 4.1) is followed by compulsory vocational schooling until the age of eighteen. This schooling is part-time if young people are employed as apprentices in authorised enterprises and firms; it is full-time for students who opted for special vocational schools (*Berufsfachschule/Fachschule*) or for those who could not obtain a training place. The dual system of vocational training, which combines an enterprise-based apprenticeship with part-time *Berufsschule*, has been the backbone of the industrial, artisan and administrative labour force in West Germany, and the recognised entry-route to skilled employment (*Berufsausbildung* 1983; *Lernen für die Arbeitswelt* 1986; *Competence and Competition* 1984).

A similar function of preparing young people for the skilled segment of the labour market falls to the network of intermediate schools, the *Realschulen*. Their focus is more clearly vocational than that of the *Hauptschulen*, with special interest in clerical and administrative tasks, and public services. Pupils from these schools gain the O-level equivalent *Mittlere Reife* and may opt for vocational training in the dual system, but they also qualify for attendance at full-time schools and colleges with a vocational specialisation. The *Realschulen* occupy a place between higher education and skills for the masses (*Schulwesen* 1984).

If the *Hauptschulen* and possibly the *Realschulen* are the institutional equivalent of the commitment to education for all, grammar schools were designed to prepare a small, intellectually able elite to university entrance standard. They served the second principal aim of German education: that of training a few for leadership. In the original design, no more than 5% of an age cohort would be deemed suitable to join this elite. Selectivity at entry, and 'weeding out' of weaker students in the process of education conspired to retain the role of elite recruitment for West German grammar schools and universities well into the Sixties. It is here that Dahrendorf pressed for change, and that educational reforms adjusted modes of selectivity and the number of places offered in the various types of school in order to broaden access and encourage participation in advanced secondary and in higher education. A number of specific provisions and adjustments underpinned these aims: for instance, school transport was made available to assist young people in rural areas. In the Fifties, Catholic girls from farming communities had been the educationally most disadvantaged group. Between 1969 and 1982 grants were paid to all secondary pupils, a measure intended to enable young people from poorer homes to delay full-time entry into the labour market in favour of prolonged and more advanced education. At the stage of selection for advanced schooling, formal written examinations were replaced in most West German regions by a period of assessment, or a special two-year orientation phase. The three-tier structure of selective schools itself has survived the shift towards extended participation at the higher levels, although some comprehensive schools have been created, and transfer between tiers has been facilitated throughout the system. Moving between tiers now allows pupils to accumulate qualifications by concluding one type of school with an examination success before entering the next higher type at the appropriate level. In general terms, each type of school leads to a specific qualifying examination or leaving certificate which in turn entitles the

Figure 4.1 The basic structure of the education system in the Federal Republic of Germany

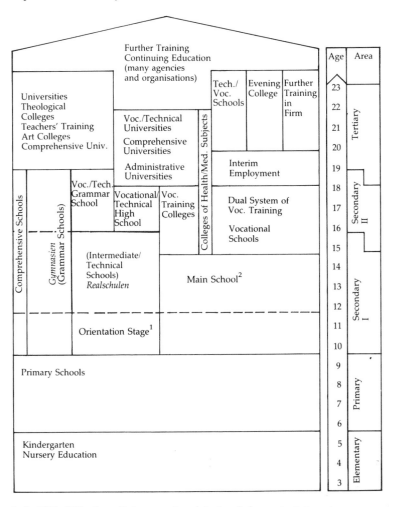

1. In 1981, 64% of pupils in years 5 and 6 attended an orientation stage.
2. Some 20% of pupils in *Hauptschüler* have attended a 10th year of schooling in 1981.
Note: The age range always refers to the minimum age at entry and an uninterrupted rise through the education system.
The size of rectangles in the diagram is not matched to attendance numbers.

holder to further schooling or to vocational/professional training. The hierarchy of schools is reflected in the hierarchy of school-leaving qualifications from *Hauptschulabschluß* at the lower end to the *Abitur* at the higher.

For women and their participation in the educational system, two aspects of West German educational practice have been of particular significance: schools continue to be ranked hierarchically in the three-tier structure but pupils who succeed in examinations can rise to the next higher tier. Moving up step by step to higher levels of formal qualifications provides a second chance for those who had earlier fallen through the selectivity grid.

Of similar importance is the close linkage between general and vocational education. That educational qualifications should feed into vocational training or schooling and that education should be a gateway to future employment is never out of sight in the German educational system. At the basic level, the progression leads from non-selective schools to apprenticeships; at the advanced level, it leads from grammar schools to university education, although the vocational purpose of academic training is implicit rather than explicit in West Germany. Formal qualifications and recognised levels of training and expertise carry considerable weight in West German society. In the working environment, learning 'on the job' only opens the most lowly positions while public examinations, certificates and degrees are not only recognised as proof of an individual's ability but are prerequisites for holding any type of skilled job. The stress on formal qualifications is underpinned by a tradition of pride in one's expertise, be it as a locksmith, as a chemical engineer or as a qualified florist (Friebel 1985).

This socio-economic culture of graded achievements and formal qualifications of schooling and vocational expertise has determined the participation of women at the different levels of education. As women began to set their sights beyond the traditional role of housewife and mother, and look towards a place in the working environment, they did so within the traditions of formal educational and vocational qualifications. Integration into the world of work did not mean finding employment merely to earn some money, to meet people, to lead a fuller life. From the outset, the process of socio-economic mobilisation involved for women, as it had always done for men, obtaining status and expertise in and through the system of examinations, certificates and defined hurdles of expertise. For women in West Germany, the culture of graded achievement and certified expertise had the advantage of clearly defining the steps which had to be taken in the bid for a recognised place in the labour market. It had the disadvantage of obscuring the factors which might militate against female certificate holders on any level of expertise (Seidenspinner et al. 1984). Ranging from prejudice about women's intellectual calibre or desirable social roles to seemingly practical obstacles such as the lack of lavatory facilities to explain why a factory or office cannot accommodate female trainees or employees, a cluster of attitudes influence women's chances for equality in everyday life. In this context, the hidden messages in the socialisation of girls have also been stressed as important: role patterns for women in the family, stereotypes of women in the media or in school textbooks (*Alltag und Biographie* from 1984). Studies of gender-specific behaviour and personal conduct have highlighted the bonus of assertiveness and self-presentation in boys, and the corresponding tendency in girls to look for compromise, to be modest, unassuming and adaptable.

Hidden reservations about the place of women have shaped the participation of women in educational and vocational/ professional training. These have been highlighted by champions of women's rights and torchbearers of equal opportunities, who tended to advocate non-compliance with the male rules in an achievement-orientated world (Lovenduski 1986). The majority of West German women, by contrast, responded to the system and to the hidden reservations about equality with a *Bildungsmotivation*, a drive to build success on formalised qualifications.

Top-of-the-Form Girls

Once improved living standards and a new perception of the uses of educational qualifications mellowed traditional reservations about advanced education, women became ardent contenders for the opportunities afforded to them. Girls took full part in a general shift towards higher and tertiary education. In

Table 4.3 Participation in full-time education by age and gender
1970–1980 (%)

Age	1970/71		1980/81	
	Men	Women	Men	Women
15	59	59	86	90
16	35	32	60	67
17	24	23	38	45
18	19	17	40	42
19	16	14	9	15
20	15	11	12	17
21	13	8	18	17
22	15	6	16	18
23	14	4	18	11
24	12	3	17	10

Source: Eurostat, Bildung und Ausbildung, *Statistisches Bulletin* 2, 1982; *Frauen in Zahlen*, Nachtrag zu Nr. 14: 26.

the early Seventies, young women would leave the educational system earlier than men, i.e. aim for less advanced educational qualifications (Table 4.3). By the early Eighties the situation had been reversed at secondary and vocational level and a higher proportion of women than men remained in full-time education up to the age of twenty. After that – at university and tertiary level – men were more likely to remain in education than women.

For girls, the advances into secondary schooling beyond the minimum leaving age have been spectacular. They have outclassed their parents, and also their male peers. Girls, it seems, perform better at school than boys; they are less frequently required to repeat a year, they obtain better marks, and are more successful in passing their qualifying examinations (Köhler 1980). They are good as well as eager students, aiming for post-elementary levels of secondary schooling. If girls were represented in accordance with their share of the relevant age cohort, they would account for just under 50% of pupils. This is true for the primary level; at the secondary level they have reversed the deficit of holding a majority at the lowest level, to holding a majority at intermediate and advanced level. Boys now outnumber girls in the *Hauptschule*. In the intermediate *Realschule* girls have consolidated their traditional position of strength from 52 to 54%. The top branch of the three-tier selective system, the grammar school, experienced the furthest reaching transformation. In the Fifties, one in three pupils here were girls; in the Eighties, girls accounted for half the pupil population in grammar schools. The attrition rate among girls who often left grammar school with *Mittlere Reife* at the age of sixteen has nearly vanished. In 1984, West German grammar schools had 51% girls in their lower forms and 50% girls in their sixth forms or graduation classes (*Frauen in der Bundesrepublik 1986: 9*).

Looking at the participation rate of girls in secondary education today, it seems that young women have entered the era of equality. The age-old pattern of minimum education for girls appears to have been reversed: girls are more strongly represented in the two higher tiers of secondary education, and those aged between fifteen and twenty remain longer in full-time schooling than young men of the same age group. Since the mid-Seventies, women have also played an increasingly prominent role in evening colleges. These are part-time colleges which provide courses for adults who want to complete GCSE or A-level equivalent examinations. The students would normally have missed out on formal educational qualifications or would be looking for advancement in their careers. Using this 'second educational track' (*Zweiter Bildungsweg*) signifies ambition and perceived personal disadvantage. Both converge in the *Bildungsmotivation* of young women in contemporary West Germany.

The expansion of educational facilities coincided with the entry of West Germany's largest generation into the school system. The number of births had risen since the late Fifties and culminated in 1964. By 1970, the age cohort of six-year-olds entering the school system had doubled from 600,000 to well over one million; nearly half of them were girls, and members of that generation of women whose educational zeal gave rise to the *Fräuleinwunder*. From the mid-Seventies to the mid-Eighties, when numbers began to tail off, between 400,000 and 600,000 women annually have completed secondary education and sought further qualifications at vocational schools, in the dual training system or at tertiary level in universities and similar institutions.

Generational Perspectives – From School to Work

While the *Fräuleinwunder* of equal access has reshaped secondary education, access to the vocational sectors has proved more difficult to achieve for women. Before examining the varied experiences of transition from general to vocational or professional education, some broad changes in the participation of women are worth noting. Compared with men, women continue to lag behind in vocational qualifications at all levels. The equal representation which we observed for secondary schools cannot be found in the more immediate transition to a working environment. However, some important shifts and improvements in the position of women have taken place. In the younger age groups, who reaped some of the benefits of educational mobilisation and opportunities mentioned earlier, women are more qualified than their older sisters. At the basic level of vocational qualifications, that of completed apprenticeships, younger women have nearly caught up with men; the changes in qualification are particularly striking if we look at women over the age of fifty. Table 4.4 compares men and women within two age cohorts: those aged 30–35 and those aged 50–55. Given that the data were compiled in 1978, they include the war experience and its impact on the lives of the older of the two groups; the younger ones were born in the post-war era and their opportunities are those of the children of democracy. Of the older women, the majority (59%) held no vocational qualifications compared with only one in four men of that generation. Among the younger women, just over one in three reported to have no vocational qualification; the remainder had qualified, some even at a managerial or advanced tertiary level (10%).

Among the younger generations, the process towards equality of qualifications has been set in motion. Older women faced traditional role expectations which were not geared towards vocational qualifications, or they lived through National Socialism with its confused women's policy of advocating motherhood, restricting the admission of girls to universities, and then again recruiting girls into industrial training and, in the war years, into universities with few restrictions. Table 4.5 presents a profile of qualification in the West German labour force in the mid-Eighties. As far as schooling is concerned, women and men

110

Table 4.4 Vocational education by age cohorts and gender (1978; in %)

Age	(a) No completed voc. education	(b) Voc. qualifications apprenticeship	(c) Foreman technical	(d) University tertiary/higher	(c)+(d)
30–35					
Men	20	57	9	14	23
Women	36	54	3	7	10
50–55					
Men	25	57	10	8	18
Women	59	37	2	3	5

Source: Infratest survey 1981, quoted in Hradil 1987: 42.

Table 4.5 Secondary schooling and vocational education of West Germans in employment, by gender and age (in %)

Age groups	Secondary schooling[a]					
	Basic level		Intermediate level		Advanced level	
	m	f	m	f	m	f
All ages	74	70	15	22	11	8
25 – under 35	65	61	19	25	16	14
35 – under 45	75	74	15	19	11	7
45 – under 55	80	81	12	14	8	5
55 and over	77	77	13	17	10	6

Age groups	Vocational education[b]							
	None		College based		Dual system		University/tertiary	
	m	f	m	f	m	f	m	f
All ages	21	40	14	11	56	43	9	6
25 – under 35	13	25	13	12	59	51	15	12
35 – under 45	18	41	16	11	54	42	12	6
45 – under 55	28	60	14	9	51	28	7	3
55 and over	29	61	13	8	50	26	8	5

[a] The three levels are in German: (1) Volks-, Hauptschule; (2) Mittlere Reife; (3) Hochschul-, Fachschulreife.
[b] The four modes of vocational education are in German: None: Keine abgeschlossene Berufsausbildung; Fach- und Berufsfachschule; Betriebliche Berufsausbildung: Hochschul-, Fachhochschulausbildung.
Source: Quintessenzen aus der Arbeitsmarkt- und Berufsforschung 4, 1984: 12.

achieved fairly similar standards within an age cohort; the women's 'deficit' at the top end of advanced education seems all but compensated for by their higher participation at the inter-mediate level. In the field of vocational qualifications, the changes have been transformations: young women are much better qualified than their older female colleagues; for women, the qualification gap between generations is considerable, e.g. 25% of the youngest but 61% of the oldest were without qualifi-cations, or 51% of the youngest and only 26% of the oldest women fully qualified in the dual system. Men have improved their levels of qualifications, but not as sharply as women across the generations.

Today's working women under forty have nearly closed the gap in college- and university-based vocational/professional qualifications, and have come close to it in apprenticeships. In the past, unskilled women constituted the largest segment of the female labour force; today, skilled women do. Although a gender gap does remain, the structures of women's and men's vocational qualifications have come to resemble one another. Since improvements in the transition from school to vocational or professional qualifications are dependent on the *Fräulein-wunder* of educational participation and qualifications, it seems likely that the gap will close further as more young women with the dual motivation towards education and work make their mark in contemporary society.

Judging from the preferences of young women of all ability ranges, leading a full life now means as much education as possible and as much training as possible. While education and vocational qualifications may have carried little weight at a time when parents expected their daughters to find financial security through marriage – a notion which was often shared by the daughters themselves – today's young women have discovered the promise of qualifications. The life of their choice combines everything: equal chances to qualify, and also equal chances as their mothers and grandmothers had to marry and raise a family. Only nowadays, young women tend to regard these diverse activities as part of the same life, not as mutually exclus-ive ventures. They look to education, engage in training, attend vocational schools and appear determined to spend a number of years improving on their qualifications with a view to using all of them in their working environment. This is a generation of motivated women. They are eager to utilise opportunities in education and training, and they tend to expect that such opportunities exist and would be equal. Younger women and adolescents in particular are brimming with optimism about the multi-dimensional lives they wish to lead and the qualifications they wish to obtain (Seidenspinner and Burger, 1982/3). Those who have already faced failure and rejected applications for training or employment are, on the whole, more doubtful about their chances to succeed. Even for those young women of today who struggle at the lowest end of the educational hierarchy, remaining unqualified is experienced as failure not as choice.

Threshold or Barrier? Vocational Training for Women

If educational qualifications were to be the passport by which young people could secure vocational training places and prepare themselves for skilled and secure employment in the future, the educational *Fräuleinwunder* would amount to a women's bonus. The real experiences of young women in the transition from school to work suggest that on the contrary, entry to the dual system of training operates a gender barrier and young women find it difficult to realise their vocational intentions. The educational accomplishments and the vocational motivations of the present-day generation of young women have not removed the barriers to equal opportunities to training and future employment.

The most favoured avenue to skilled employment in West Germany has been the apprenticeship or dual system. As mentioned earlier, an apprentice works under contract for an employer and also attends vocational school part-time, to study a curriculum of general and work-related subjects. Training has been completed successfully once public examinations in practical skills and in theory have been passed, normally after three years. In the wake of the 1969 *Berufsbildungsförderungsgesetz* (Employment Promotion Act), legislation designed to broaden access to vocational training, shorter programmes were introduced in retailing and a number of service sectors (Heinz and Krüger 1981: 665).

In addition to the dual system, West Germany has a number of taught courses in the broad field of vocational training. With the exception of advanced training in *Fachoberschulen* or *Fachschulen*, taught courses tend to cater for those who failed to find a place in the dual training system. For the lower end of the ability spectrum a school-based preparatory vocational year is intended to ease the transition from school to work. Pupils can obtain a qualified school-leaving certificate if they failed to do so before, or learn various work-related skills. Although overall numbers on these one-year taught programmes have fallen somewhat, nearly 150,000 young people were registered on one of them in 1984 (*Berufsbildungsbericht* 1985: 129). The majority of pupils on these one-year courses (between 65 and 80%) are girls. For them, it is a waiting area until opportunities in the dual system come along. Virtually all pupils in the Vocational Foundation Year or the Preparatory Year are determined to move up into full-scale vocational training.[1] The dual system of apprenticeship training, then, is the principal type of training young people aim for, and the principal point in the transition from school to work where the gender gap of unequal chances first becomes evident.

For young people with basic education only (*Hauptschule*) vocational training in the dual system has been the preferred mode of transition from school to working life (Friebel 1983). Despite their educational motivations and high standards young women have found it difficult to realise their expectations about training and vocational qualifications. A recent survey showed that at the age of fifteen, 56% of female school leavers intended to qualify via an apprenticeship; 39% had been taken on (Seiden-

---

1. The situation governing the Vocational Foundation Year is complicated for a number of reasons: (a) vocational schooling in West Germany, like all schooling, is the responsibility of the regions (*Länder*) and provisions between regions can vary. Therefore, the *Berufsgrundbildungsjahr* has not been introduced throughout the Federal Republic. (b) Where it has been introduced, its status is unclear. For some training programmes, it constitutes the compulsory first year, i.e. trainees then enter the dual system in the second year of training. For other programmes, it is not recognised by the relevant Chambers of Commerce or the Craft Chambers as an integral part of vocational training. However, young people who completed this year have to be admitted to the second year of training – a provision which reduces the in-firm training component in the first year of training, and has made it difficult for young people who passed the Foundation Year to transfer into the dual system of training.

Table 4.6 Vocational training three years after leaving school

Type of training	Success rate (in %)	
	m	f
Apprenticeship in the dual system (first destination)	71	54
Apprenticeship in the dual system after full-time vocational schooling (second destination)	6	9
Vocational schooling only	11	22
No vocational training	12	15

Source: Mitteilungen aus der Arbeitsmarkt- und Berufsforschung 1, 1982.

spinner and Burger 1982: 29). Data collected by the research institute affiliated to the Federal Employment Office show that there is little difference in the proportion of young men and young women who are not in vocational training three years after leaving school. Differences, however, do exist in the access to this training. Table 4.6 shows that in 1982 more young men than young women had secured a training place in the dual system. College-based vocational courses were more important as avenues of qualification for women than for men. Some qualifications, of course, can only be obtained at college; laboratory assistants, for example, are only trained in colleges, not in the dual system. For many women, however, as for West Germans in general, college-based training does not enjoy the high status of training in the dual system, and is regarded as second best.

As Table 4.6 shows, in 1982 one in five women trained in a full-time vocational school; the very accessibility of school-based vocational training explains its importance for women. Young men have tended to find it easier to move directly into apprenticeships and had to rely less frequently on full-time vocational courses. A number of studies have underlined the determination of young women to obtain a place in the dual system of training. They attempt to optimise their chances by gathering more information about training places in their area and by writing at least twice as many letters of application than their male peers. Family connections and direct contacts with a potential employer are the major avenues of recruitment for boys, but work less well for girls who instead have to rely on chance and intensify their search. Many utilise advertisements or take the penultimate step before unemployment and register with the Employment Exchange Office (56%). In most of these cases, finding a training place would often mean that personal preferences of craft or profession have to be sacrificed to the expediency of gaining access to a skill at all (*Frauen und Arbeitsmarkt* 1984: 16).

Channels and Choices in Vocational Training

There are a number of factors which contribute to the gender-based disadvantage in the transition from school to work. In the dual system of vocational training, half the places are earmarked by the employers for male applicants and one quarter for female applicants, while the remaining one quarter are open to both sexes (*Berufsbildungsbericht* 1987; 1988). Throughout the Seventies and Eighties, the gender distribution in the dual system has remained nearly constant, with 62–63% male and 37–38% female apprentices. This is to say, young women do not appear to have benefited from their increased educational motivation and qualifications. A special analysis of women in the labour market even found that young men who failed to obtain any qualifications at school and do not hold a school leaver's certificate normally enjoy the same chances of being taken on as an apprentice in the dual system as a young woman who gained such a certificate. For a young woman who left school without qualifications, the prospects of training in the dual system are poor. In order to enjoy equal opportunities at the threshold of vocational training, girls need a higher level of education than their male competitors (*Frauen und Arbeitsmarkt* 1984: 16). The higher the formal educational qualifications the lower the failure rate among women and the smaller the gender differences in finding a training place. In this perspective, the drive for educational qualifications is not so much a bid by women for advanced positions but an insurance policy against remaining at the unskilled margins of the labour market.

As mentioned earlier, the socio-economic climate of the Seventies militated against women. When the generation of educational mobility encountered the transition from school to work, access to training in the dual system had become especially difficult (*Berufsausbildung und Arbeitsmarkt* 1977: 15). In

117

the Fifties and early Sixties, West German employers were unable to find enough apprentices, and for a time one in every two places remained unfilled. With the entry of the baby-boom generation into the labour market, the demand for places in the dual system rocketed while the number of places on offer decreased. In addition to the discrepancies in the distribution between male and female training places, the cohort of young and motivated women has never known a situation that more places were on offer than were required. On the contrary, theirs has been an experience of shortage, thwarted intentions and intense competition. Although successive governments since the mid-Seventies have tried to create additional places through appeals and financial incentives to potential employers, the situation has not been eased in the long run. In 1985, for instance, 756,000 potential applicants chased 719,000 places (*Berufsbildungsbericht* 1986: 25). Throughout the Federal Republic, the number of training places on offer declined by 1.1% between 1984 and 1985; the rate of decline varied between regions from 4.5% in the Saar region to 0.2% in North Rhine-Westphalia. Of the young people who had not found an apprenticeship within a year of application, 70% were women (*Berufsbildungsbericht* 1985; 1986).

The provision of training places in the dual system has to be seen in the context of changes in the labour market. Since the early Seventies, the overall number of people in employment has declined and the relative importance between economic sectors has changed (see Chapter 5). Between 1970 and 1985, 2.2 million jobs disappeared in manufacturing and a further one million in agriculture. Some of these losses seemed offset by an increase of employment opportunities in the tertiary sector. In the Seventies, about one million new jobs were created here, but the increase has slowed down to about 200,000 between 1980 and 1984 (*Berufsbildungsbericht* 1986: 57). Certain branches of industry were particularly hard hit: in textiles and leather, both traditional areas of women's employment, the number of jobs declined by 60%; mining lost 66%. Other sectors registered a boost: demand has shifted towards technicians, electricians, maintenance staff, organisational and administrative staff notably with expertise in information technology. In all of these, the proportion of women trainees or employees is small.

The reorientations in the labour market have not been directly reflected in the dual training system. Since nearly half the trainees are employed in small craft workshops which between them employ only 19% of the labour force, a mismatch between skills produced and skills required is inevitable (*Berufswege und Arbeitsmarkt* 1977: 22–3). Skill shortages and discrepancies have been especially marked in the technical fields and in manufacturing. The West German car industry, for instance, employs large numbers of qualified bakers or butchers who have received on-the-job training to cope with their new tasks. In order to train a potential skilled labour force of the future, successive West German governments have funded training initiatives which cover part or all of the cost of training incurred by the employer, or which offer college-based qualifications.

Men's Jobs or Women's Jobs?

The shortfall in qualified technical and manufacturing staff paired with a general interest in broadening equal opportunities prompted the government in the mid-Seventies to offer special programmes for girls. The so-called initiative 'Girls in Men's Jobs' (*Mädchen in Männerberufe*) was launched in 1976 and is continuing despite a change of government from an SPD/FDP coalition to a CDU/CSU/FDP coalition in 1982. The programme has been focused on vocational training in those fields where traditionally 80% or more of the trainees had been male. As an incentive to take on girls, the government has covered the cost to companies of female trainees in a 'male' field. Given these incentives, the programme did have some successes. In 1976, 2% of female apprentices in the dual system were training in a 'male' field; ten years later, 80% did so. Table 4.7 lists the increases of women trainees in the main technical and engineering-related fields.

However, in most of the fields to which girls have now been admitted, the recruitment of apprentices has declined as traditional technologies and manufacturing processes give way to new developments (*Materialien für Arbeitsmarkt- und Berufsforschung (MatAB)* 3, 1986: 6). The initiative *Mädchen in Männerberufe* has placed a spotlight on unequal chances for girls but with its orientation towards declining trades it can make only a

Table 4.7 Girls in 'men's jobs', 1976–1986 (in % per trade)

Trade	1976	1986
Turner	0.1	3.5
Locksmith (industrial)	0.0	1.4
Precision toolmaker	0.6	9.8
Toolmaker	0.1	2.3
Communications engineer	2.1	7.5
Carpenter	1.0	8.2
Painter and decorator	0.7	8.4

Source: Statistisches Bundesamt (ed.), *Berufliche Bildung*, Wiesbaden, 1981; *Berufsbildungsbericht*, Bonn, 1987.

small contribution towards redressing the gender imbalance in vocational training in West Germany.

At the time of writing, the range of vocational opportunities for girls, and their preferences, have changed little since the Fifties. Then, nine in every ten girls in vocational training were concentrated in just twenty approved programmes, while over 600 were on offer. In 1984, three out of four girls were bunched in just twenty of a possible 412 programmes, nearly 60% trained in ten occupations and close to 40% in the top five (see Appendix I). Not only has diversification in the vocational field remained modest; with one or two exceptions, girls today tend to choose the same areas of vocational training as their mothers had done thirty years ago. Moreover, most of the diversification has been a result of vocational reform as traditional trades or sales functions were redefined to suit modern needs. A similar pattern of female preferences is apparent in the specialisations chosen by West German young women who attend vocational training schools (*Berufsfachschulen* or *Fachschulen*). Here, 86% opt for training in the service sector; the caring professions in the health service are virtually exclusively female and only a few young women become technicians (4%) or enter manufacturing industry (3%) (*Bildung im Zahlenspiegel* 1982).

Despite a decade of educational mobility and vocational orientation, the scope of female training has hardly changed. Young women choose from a narrow range, and also from a range which in itself is unlikely to lead to advanced qualification and leadership positions. These choices are often dictated by circumstance. As mentioned earlier, girls tend to try very hard to find training, and tend to be less successful than boys in finding training places. 'Women's' jobs appear to have been more accessible and have therefore retained their strong positions among women's contemporary choices. Even the expansion of training provisions since 1977, which was to facilitate the transition from school to work for the baby-boom generation, occurred in the conventional fields and left gender imbalances intact. Traditional female training areas such as hairdressing and retailing have been among the fastest growing areas as far as the provision of training places is concerned, and between them absorbed one in six girls looking for vocational training in the last ten years.

From Training to Work – Views and Experiences

The uneven provision of training places had other important effects on the situation of girls. The shortage and the narrow range forced over half the female applicants to accept a substitute career. By contrast, the majority of the boys trained in the area of their prime choice. Girls have been more dissatisfied with the training they receive, and are more inclined to abandon it before qualifying. One in four girls learning to be hairdressers give up prematurely, so do one in five sales assistants in the food trade, or one in six dentist's assistants. A 1982 survey óf young people in vocational training found that less than half (49%) the women but the majority of men (61%) would undertake the same training again (*MatAB* 9, 1986).

The additional provision of vocational training places did not normally dovetail with the needs for skilled personnel in the enterprise which undertook the training, or in the occupational field as a whole. After training, a certain degree of occupational mobility is inevitable: newly qualified people either want to work elsewhere, or cannot be taken on by their former employer. The increase in training opportunities allowed more young people, including more women, to qualify but the labour market was unable to absorb all of them at their level of expertise. On the other hand, employment opportunities in service sector occupations, for instance, have increased throughout the post-war period, while training places failed to catch up. One in

Table 4.8 Unemployment among men and women under the age of 25 with completed vocational training, 1982–1985

	1982	1983	1984	1985
Total (in 1,000s)	551	623	582	564
	%	%	%	%
Men	51	49	48	47
Women	49	51	52	53

Source: *Berufsbildungsbericht* 1986: 65.

four apprentices are trained in the service sector which employs 64% of all working women. Unemployment is one possible result of the mismatch between training and manpower needs. In the Eighties, unemployment of women under the age of twenty-five who completed their vocational training has been on the increase.[2] In 1982, more young men than young women were unemployed; in 1985, tables had turned and young women accounted for 53% of the young unemployed with vocational training (Table 4.8).

In the context of discussing women's vocational training, unemployment highlights the problems of transition from apprenticeships to secure employment. As mentioned earlier, many of the training programmes do not correspond to labour market trends and employment would either mean that women with certified skills work in semi-skilled or unskilled areas, or that finding skilled work would necessitate retraining and updating. The fields with the highest rates of unemployment both directly after training and among experienced and qualified staff are also among the most popular vocational goals for girls: hairdressing, doctor's receptionists, pharmaceutical assistants, retailing (*MatAB* 3, 1986: 13). Women have been reluctant learners in an environment in which skills are often out of phase with opportunities, and in which updating and retraining have be-

---

2. The argument here focuses on unemployment among young people with completed vocational training. Looking at unemployment overall, women are further disadvantaged since they are more strongly represented among the unskilled or semi-skilled. In 1987, nearly 50% of the unemployed were women compared with just under 40% in the labour force. The rate of unemployment among women lay at 11%, that of men at 8% on average (*Statistisches Jahrbuch* 1988: 110; *Datenreport* 1987: 72).

come an essential dimension of skilled employment. The lower the educational level, the more uncertain women tend to be about coping with the demands, and about their ability to achieve further qualifications (Andressen et al. 1981). In particular, women with *Mittlere Reife* have been more difficult to recruit into updating and retraining programmes than their male colleagues. The confidence which these women had in their school days that educational qualifications were within their reach appears to have dissipated during vocational training, and in the experience of unemployment afterwards. Those who do learn new skills tend to opt for general courses (84%) with just 16% embarking on full-scale vocational training. Again, four-fifths (80%) tend to choose traditional women's occupations for their second attempt at making the transition into employment (*Frauen in der Bundesrepublik* 1986: 15–16).

The experience of vocational training itself has weakened the vocational motivation of women. Even after training, women appear to develop a weaker sense of pride in their expertise, and are less determined than men to develop this expertise. A 1986 study of the transition from training to work showed that on average 63% of women with completed vocational training, and 54% of men were prepared to work in a field that was different from their specific area of expertise. Young people who had trained in the field of their first choice were more determined to match their employment to their training than those who had trained in a substitute skill. We have seen earlier that women are less likely than men to find the training they had originally intended. The discrepancies between training places and employment opportunities in the typical women's occupations leave their mark on attitudes to work: confidence in the quality of the training and the employment prospects attached breed confidence in the ability of the individual to be successful. Ambivalent or negative experiences in training and in the transition to employment generated the view that success depends, in the last analysis, on chance and luck (*MatAB* 5, 1986: 8). Even after training, and after achieving better pass rates and marks at qualifying examinations than their male colleagues, women are less certain about the usefulness of their specialist skill and more willing to make do with employment in which their specialism plays no part. The 1986 study on the transition from training to employment listed thirteen fields in which over 60% of the newly qualified young people declared that they would accept work in other areas. Of the thirteen vocational specialisms, eleven were among the top fifteen choices for women apprentices (*MatAB* 5, 1986: 3). For women, moving into other areas often means demotion to semi-skilled activities, loss of earning capacity, and under-utilisation of their educational and vocational qualifications (*Frauen und Arbeitsmarkt*, 28; 32).

The catch-22 situation of cumulative disadvantage does not stop here. Confidence in one's expertise and abilities has also been singled out as an important prerequisite for occupational success such as advancement to managerial or leadership positions (*MatAB* 7, 1986: 5). Women, who on the whole score less well in terms of confidence, clearly lag behind in terms of advancement. At the post-vocational stage the next higher step in West Germany, and one which entitles the holder to open a business or to train apprentices, is the *Meisterprüfung*. Women, who occupy nearly 40% of the training places, accounted for only 8% of the candidates at the examinations for *Meister* in 1985. It is small consolation that as with their performance in the education system today, women tend to achieve a higher pass rate and better marks in these examinations than men. Favoured subjects for advanced vocational qualifications are again 'women's' subjects such as hairdressing or ladies' tailoring.

High-Flyers and the Vocational Perspective

Recently, one group entered vocational training who seem to defy the web of discouragement and lack of opportunities which renders job qualifications such an uncertain investment for many women apprentices. Since the mid-Seventies, vocational training in the dual system has been perceived by A-level students as an attractive alternative to university studies. Young women in particular began to see training in the dual system or in specialist vocational schools as a more reliable and speedier preparation for secure employment than a university degree would afford. Today, one in four women with *Abitur* enlist in vocational training. In 1985, they constituted 62% of A-level entrants to the dual system; some 70% of examination successes by apprentices with *Abitur* are accomplished by women (Tessaring and Werner 1981: 46ff.; *MatAB* 1, 1986; *Bildung und Wissenschaft* 11 Dec. 1983: 188). One in five applicants who had applied for a place in vocational training with the Federal Employment Office had passed their *Abitur*; over half had been educated to the level of *Mittlere Reife*. The shift in girls' schooling towards higher educational qualifications has changed the face of vocational training: as the educational standards on entry to vocational training are rising, those at the lower end of the educational spectrum are in danger of being squeezed out of training altogether. This is particularly true for girls since the chances for boys without school qualifications to find a training place are nearly four times as good as those of girls in a similar position (*Berufsbildungsbericht* 1986: 30).

With highly qualified young women entering the vocational training system, one might have expected a diversification of women's jobs, and a reduction of the gender gap. In one or two instances, the gender gap has in fact narrowed: young women with *Abitur* who remained unemployed after completing vocational training were as motivated as men in the same position to enrol on additional courses or undertake training. The chances of women with *Abitur* and successful training in the dual system of rising to intermediate managerial levels do not match those of men with equivalent qualifications, but are clearly better than for women without *Abitur* (Bernadoni and Werner 1987). At the entry point into vocational training, however, women with *Abitur* appear to be as narrow in their choice of trades or careers as their less educated sisters. Instead of hairdressing and retailing, they opt for careers in banking, in various office and administrative skills and as assistants to professionals such as accountants or doctors. With the exception of retailing and dentist's assistant, all vocational training programmes in the service sector which are top choices for women are also among the top choices for women with *Abitur*. In banking, for instance, every second apprentice now holds *Abitur* qualifications (*MatAB* 1, 1986: 4). Vocational training programmes in the airline business have become a reserve for applicants with *Abitur*. In the service industry and in administrative areas candidates for vocational training are increasingly expected to hold school qualifications beyond *Hauptschule*.

The influx of highly educated people into vocational training

has been dubbed a *Verdrängungswettbewerb*, a displacement competition. Candidates who would by all criteria of curriculum
design and selection principles be eminently suitable for vocational training do not stand a chance against their educated
rivals. Even vocational schools have bowed to the trend and
often run special classes where apprentices with *Abitur* can
acquire more advanced knowledge in theory and material science related to their trade or craft than the rank-and-file apprentice would be able to do. For women the possible ill-effects of the
Verdrängungswettbewerb are especially harsh, since applicants of
all educational backgrounds tend to bunch in so small a number
of occupational fields, and the direct competition between
high-flyers and other applicants could make it more difficult for
girls to find training places of their choice and in line with their
abilities.

Why is it that young women with *Abitur* prefer to become
Azubis – *Auszubildende* – rather than proceed to higher education? It seems that *Abiturienten* in West Germany today fall
into two groups in their orientations towards future employment. The first group is concerned about employment prospects
and expects that the acquisition of specialist skills and vocational
expertise will optimise their personal employment prospects.
This search for security is more widespread among women than
among men, and appears to persuade them to enter the dual
training system. The second group consists of *Abiturienten* who
have firmly decided to proceed to university and who tend to
attach less importance to considerations of job security and
employment prospects after graduation. Women here hold the
same views as men. In the absence of detailed research into this
discrepancy of vocational perceptions, explanations have to be
tentative. It has been suggested that the numerical increase of
pupils in grammar schools brought a sizeable proportion of
young people from non-academic backgrounds into advanced
education. Here, the relatively undefined vocational purpose of
academic training may be regarded as undesirable risk-taking.
For young women, traditional reservations about combining
higher education with a woman's life may also play a part.
Despite the apparently neutral quality of school-based qualifications where an *Abitur* or any other qualification holds equal
value regardless of the subjects or options on which it is based,

the educational experience of women themselves is not strictly equal. The majority continue to opt for 'female' subjects such as arts, languages and social studies to the detriment of sciences, technology and mathematics and some have even ascribed the higher marks achieved by girls to the spread of subjects studied (Krinner 1986). Notwithstanding the educational equality of girls as far as formal qualifications are concerned, a gender gap of preferences has persisted, and continues to influence school leavers at all levels. Whether curricula are discriminatory, whether girls are guided towards a narrow band of subjects or candidly discouraged from branching out, differences exist and the causes will vary from case to case. A major factor, however, is the gender-specific preferences of the girls themselves for suitable and presumably secure 'women's' jobs through vocational training.

The steady shift of young women with *Abitur* from higher education to vocational training confirms the high regard for the dual system in German everyday culture. For the individual woman, vocational training may also provide a half-way house between the educational background and social values of her parents, family and personal environment on the one hand, and on the other hand her surge towards the educational elite through grammar school. Parents of grammar school pupils are more involved in advising their daughters than their sons which career they should follow (Becher et al. 1983: 179). Vocational training tends to blend in with family traditions, and promise subsequent employment in line with this training. Did not the mothers of today's generation of educated young women largely miss out on skilled employment, and the security or status it entails, since many did not or could not obtain vocational qualifications? To that extent, the daughters are moving one notch up on the ladder of social mobility – not towards emancipation, but towards the modern-day equivalent of their mothers' way of life. Measured against the age-old aims of grammar schools to prepare their graduates for university, these women set their aims low. Measured against the modest accomplishments of people in their own environment, these daughters have caught up with their fathers and often overtaken them in education and in vocational skills. In this perspective, the women's option from *Abitur* to *Azubi* contains a flicker of emancipative spirit. Yet it also reflects the lack of confidence among girls that they would be good enough to compete at the top, gain a university place and obtain a degree. That a shortage of university places in certain areas has generated an intense competition for first-class marks in schools may have contributed to the transition from grammar school to training. By opting for a seemingly less competitive environment these women also opt for an environment in which they can expect to hold a place at the upper end.

Higher Education for Women – Elite Training or Finishing School?

In the political culture of West Germany, higher education has always enjoyed an elevated status: those who graduated from university would be addressed by their academic title, whether they were popping into the corner shop for a loaf of bread or taking their seat at a board meeting. Higher education has been regarded as a benchmark of excellence and as evidence of a privileged socio-economic position even for those who left without completing their examinations.

On a more tangible level, university education has, of course, been career training. Not only can access to professional areas such as law, medicine or engineering be gained only through success at a higher level of education, this has also been the normal prerequisite for a significant segment of civil service positions, of top managerial functions in industry and business, and leading roles in the media, in publishing and the arts. It would not be far wrong to call German universities training schools for the civil service since it has been customary for up to 80% of graduates to take up public employment of some kind at the national or regional (*Land*) level.

The tradition of professional recruitment on the basis of recognised entry qualifications has given universities their strong positions as training schools for elites in all branches of economic and administrative life. The German emphasis on formalised qualifications and on job specifications which detail the type of expertise an applicant is required to possess, have militated against a practice of assessment on the grounds of

Table 4.9 Women at university, 1950–1988

Year	Total (in 1,000s)	% of student population
1950/51	25	19
1955/56	35	23
1960/61	65	26
1965/66	84	30
1970/71	130	31
1975/76	176	32
1980/81	278	38
1985/86	371	41
1987/88	392	42

Sources: *Frauen in Familie, Beruf und Gesellschaft*, Mainz: Kohlhammer, 1987: 123; *Statistisches Jahrbuch* 1988, Stuttgart: Kohlhammer, 1988: 359.

personality, communicative qualities or similarly flexible criteria. A university education rounded off by success in the final examination can be regarded as a visible and defined vocational path. In addition, students who intend to become civil servants have to pass a special set of examinations, administered by the institutions of tertiary education but designed and monitored by the state. For those who can secure the state positions they had hoped to obtain, this *Staatsexamen* constitutes an entry ticket to lifelong employment.

The increased participation of young West Germans and of women in higher education could be building on the perception of universities as training schools for secure employment in higher income groups, with examinations as all-important entry tickets. In the Fifties, 3% of an age cohort would complete a university education; today close to 20% do so. Student numbers have rocketed from 130,000 in 1950 to over one million as the baby-boom generation grew into tertiary education, and as the participation rate increased (*Der Spiegel* 20, 1985). In universities, the participation rate of women has risen from 19% in 1950 to over 40% today (Table 4.9).

Counting the tertiary sector as a whole – universities, polytechnics (*Fachhochschulen*) and Art Colleges – half a million women (537,000) were students in higher education in the winter term 1987/88. Contrary to expectations, student numbers have continued to rise. Given the age structure of the West German population and the generational effect of the drop in the birth rate, it had been widely predicted that fewer students would enter higher education. Instead, students tend to enter university after having completed vocational or other training first. This practice of dual qualifications applies to male and female students although not in equal proportions. In 1988, 58% of freshers had been in work or training before their studies, 28% had qualified in the dual system of vocational training, the remainder had served in the armed forces, in social work in lieu of military service, or had been in employment of some kind (*Kulturchronik* 6, 1988: 36).

Before examining women's participation in tertiary education in more detail, some comments about the significance of academic training in the modern environment may be useful for evaluating education with reference to social and economic opportunities. The high regard for academic qualifications has already been mentioned. Similar to vocational training but on a more ambitious level, university studies and especially success in university examinations are generally recognised as evidence of personal and intellectual calibre. Thus, university studies have been viewed positively by prospective graduates; in turn, once larger numbers of graduates became available they have been readily absorbed into the working environments. Specific jobs which in the past did not need academic qualifications as a prerequisite became increasingly 'academic' and reserved for graduates. According to calculations by the Federal Institute for Employment Research, the quota of academics in the economy, i.e. the proportion of academics among new appointments, rose from 2% in 1960 to 9% in 1982 with projections of an increase to 15% in the year 2000 (Table 4.10). In the West German working environment of the future, qualifications in the tertiary sector and completed vocational training will be in demand: the very areas in which women have consolidated their position and increased their stake.

Until the turn of the century, the number of positions for which applicants are expected to hold university or equivalent qualifications is expected to rise by 60% to 3.7 million. Higher education as training for the labour market has a strong future. In the short term, employment opportunities will expand faster for academically trained personnel than for any other sector of the labour force. In the Sixties, demand for university graduates

Table 4.10 Education and training today and tomorrow

Education/Training	1982 %	2000 %	Difference in 1,000s
Higher education	8.5	14.8	+1,552
Special vocational/*Fachschule*	6.6	6.7	+23
Vocational training	52.9	58.7	+1,315
Unskilled/semi-skilled	32.0	19.8	−3,172

Source: 'Die Zukunft der Arbeitslandschaft. IAB Prognos Projektion zur Entwicklung des Arbeitskräftebedarfs bis 2000', *MatAB* 6, 1986: 8.

in the social sciences, mathematics and related sciences, and in the humanities expanded particularly fast with excellent employment opportunities in all fields of education (Naumann 1980: 86–7). In years to come, demand is most likely to rise in occupational fields relating to planning, information technology, development and research as well as at all levels of management.

This note of optimism has, however, not been reflected in popular concerns about the uses of university education. Commentators and prospective applicants for university places have been concerned about the recent trend towards graduate unemployment as the real or likely scenario of the future (*Spiegel* series 20, 1985ff). For the first two decades or so of post-war German development, people with advanced education and university degrees had been in short supply. Unemployment among graduates might amount to 1% or so, but tended to be temporary and negligible. Changes in technology, in administrative practices, in policy styles, and in the size of the generation needing education and institutional backup seemed to produce an apparently limitless need for university graduates. In the Seventies, employment opportunities became more sluggish and by 1986, 5% of graduates in higher education were registered as unemployed. Although unemployment hit nongraduates much harder (9%), its very existence among graduates seemed an anomaly which went against the grain of received wisdom about the employability of graduates and against the accumulated expectations and aspirations of the young generation. Their increased participation in grammar school and university education had been based on the view that advanced education would open advanced vocational opportunities. However, soon after larger numbers of highly qualified young people began to enter the labour market, that market had contracted and was unable to absorb all of them at the level of expertise for which they had trained, or at the level of remuneration or status which they and their parents had expected would crown advanced education. As mentioned earlier, women – who had been the most recent arrivals in advanced and higher education – were hit by contracting opportunities before they could establish broader career paths for their growing numbers.

The difficulties of labour market integration were exacerbated by discrepancies between career and subject choices of individuals and labour market needs. Since the West German constitution guarantees the freedom of occupation and profession to every individual, admission to any field of higher education has normally not been restricted. As we shall see later, medical studies are an exception to this rule and have operated a so-called *numerus clausus* of limiting admissions. In general, however, bottlenecks of an over-supply of graduates in certain fields followed the expansion in student numbers and the simultaneous reduction of employment opportunities since the mid-Seventies. Unemployment among graduates has been bunched in fields such as librarianship, social work, teaching, sociology and humanities. At tertiary level, most of these are fields with a high proportion of women students; they are also the fields which are not expected to benefit from the projected increase in the demand for graduates. A government report on graduate unemployment noted in 1986 that demand for employment had fallen somewhat in those areas where unemployment was high; here, fewer new graduates entered the labour market looking for jobs (*Bildung und Wissenschaft* 1–2, 1987: 29). This could mean that career choices, and the corresponding subject choices at tertiary level, have been modified in the light of vocational considerations and that prospective students opt for 'safe' subjects. It could also point to changed transition patterns from tertiary education into employment. Of particular importance here are the bridging or retraining programmes which have been introduced by the government in order to fund graduates for one year after graduation in a work placement which could lead to future employment. In 1986, some 15,000 new graduates who had been unsuccessful in their search for employment attended such a programme. In numerical terms even more effective has been the trend towards a second degree. Today, an estimated 180,000 graduates who had been unable to find employment have decided to remain in tertiary education and continue with their studies (*Grund- und Strukturdaten*, 1987; *Bildung und Wissenschaft* 9/10, 1987: 10).

The mismatch between graduate specialisation and current labour market demand is greater than unemployment statistics can reveal. The long-term prospects seem bright for certain fields, but reorientations and a shift in preferences between subjects take time to work their way through. Women, whose good credentials at school carried them in greater numbers into higher education, soon experienced the bitter taste of dwindling opportunities. Today, the place of West German women in higher education, and their bid for advanced vocational qualifications and positions through higher education in the Eighties and Nineties, have been overshadowed by the mismatch between preferences and career opportunities in the current economic environment.

Not a Woman's World?

The *Fräuleinwunder* of equal representation of women at grammar school, and equal success in *Abitur* passes, has not continued into higher education. With just under 40% of the whole student population in higher education, women fall somewhat short of equal representation with men, but they are no longer a minority group whose place and role at university might be in doubt. When the discrepancy between the performance of girls at school and their access to institutions of higher education elicited a public and academic debate in the mid-Sixties, the universities themselves were blamed for deterring women and preventing them from fulfilling their personal and intellectual potential. Women, it seemed, had much more to overcome than merely a reluctance of their parents to fund prolonged education or socio-economic expectations about their future social roles. Some suggested that the structure of university life blocked access and opportunities for women: 'The university originated as a training place by men for men, and has, in essence, remained so' (Pross 1969: 45). Others argued that women in higher education were a challenge to the inherited system of higher education and a catalyst of reform:

> Despite all pronouncements of equality of treatment, the German university continues to regard itself as the kind of institution it has been in law until the early part of the 20th century, not just a prerogative of men, but their very own institution, which advocates the male cause against the opposite sex. Where the influx of women as students or as teaching staff is concerned, the university is therefore by no means a neutral medium or an open area where the conflict of interests between the two sexes could be sorted out. . . . The fight of women for equal treatment with men at the university thus turns from a fight between men and women to a conflict of woman herself with the whole university system. (Nitsch et al. 1967: 438)

Two decades after these early explanations were voiced as to why women were under-represented in higher education, the buoyant participation rates of girls in grammar schools and their good performance in qualifying examinations left their mark, and women have narrowed the gender gap in the student population. The university reforms of the Seventies also dismantled some of the traditions and styles which struck the commentators of the Sixties as enclaves of male exclusivity. Hierarchical structures have been modified, communication patterns mellowed to exclude the subservience and formality which seemed to be the hallmark of a traditional German university. The student as the bag-carrying servant may continue to exist, but at least nominally decision making structures, curricula and modes of assessment have been rendered more rational and thus more likely to encourage equal treatment.

University reform also included a certain degree of curricular reform which accommodated women's preferences of duration and style of study. Traditionally, German universities did not have structured programmes. In most subjects, students have always had to pass certain courses or subjects before being allowed to proceed to the next higher level; but the decisions when to take these tests, how to combine courses and pace the programme over a number of years, and when enough had been learned to attempt the final examination have been left to the student. For the last three points, this is still the case, and continues to be perceived as an added difficulty of coping with higher education. In order to make sure of success in examinations, West German students tend to study further courses, and add on additional years of revision, preparation and accumulation of knowledge. Compared with students of similar age in other European countries, West German undergraduates are more insecure and likely to suffer from anxiety. The fear of failing examinations and the need for the individual to determine when he or she knows enough to pass are the main causes of unease. Among women the uncertainties about performance and attainment tend to be particularly strong.

Of the possible targets for university reform, only the structure of the initial syllabus received lasting attention. In a number of fields, in particular those where the large number of students bred impersonality and encouraged disorientation, a programme of basic or introductory courses was introduced. Often they may be taken at any time, and in any order, but passing them is a prerequisite for admission to intermediate or advanced work. A more open-ended format of university studies has, however, been defended by those who argue that intellectual development and research capacity cannot be taught quickly or through a set menu, but need time to unfold. Originality and individuality should be fostered through university studies, and conditions should allow for them to emerge and consolidate (Habermas 1969). On the other hand, the contemporary function of universities as mass institutions for advanced vocational training depends on course organisation and structure to monitor course contents and student progress, and also curtail the time taken by the average student from first enrolment to final examination. This approach has been dominant in the vocationally defined *Fachhochschule* which normally offers defined courses of study with compulsory syllabi. In the university environment the conflicting concepts about the purpose and the pace of higher education continue to coexist.

The different paces of tertiary studies are reflected in the different completion times between types of institution. In 1983, the average university student would need 6.7 years or 13.4 semesters (*Bildung und Wissenschaft* 9/10, 1987: 12) to complete the course with a final examination. Many would study for eight

135

or more years, with a few finishing in the minimum time of four. Completing a degree at a *Fachhochschule* has been quicker. In 1983, it took just over four years or 8.2 semesters on average. The assumption that studying takes time, and that the number of years spent in higher education can be neither foreseen nor easily controlled is entrenched in the German political culture. Students in general tend to react angrily when expectations are voiced that study times should be reduced. Women, as mentioned earlier, have always voiced majority support for a shorter duration of tertiary studies and have tended to opt for an apparently vocational mould with a well-defined course sequence, and specified aims and examination requirements.

Subject Choices and Vocational Orientations

Given the changes in the socio-economic environment and in the educational climate, subject preferences and vocational orientations of women in tertiary education have remained surprisingly constant. Top of the list has been the academic preparation for the teaching profession. Until the reform of higher education, teachers' training was conducted in two institutional settings depending on the level of schooling for which the prospective teacher intended to train. Teachers up to intermediate level would attend a three-year course at an educational college (*Pädagogische Hochschule*). After a compulsory state examination, full qualifications would be achieved through a period of teaching practice in the relevant type of school (Sommer 1986). Over 80% of students at educational college were women. Since the university reforms educational colleges and universities have frequently merged, but teachers' training for primary and intermediate levels has remained a predominantly female affair. Teaching staff at grammar schools attend universities and complete state examinations in the subjects in which they wish to specialise. The pattern of state examination is the same as for primary teaching – an academic examination followed by examinations based on teaching practice. Although the gender imbalance in this tier of teachers' training is less severe than in primary teaching, women still constitute a majority. In the mid-Eighties, 65% of women who enrolled to study at a university stated their intention to qualify for teaching.

In their subject choices, women have remained indebted to the focus on languages, humanities and arts. Of the fifteen most popular subjects at universities, eleven fell into these categories; in German, English and French, women tend to outnumber men by about two to one. This pattern can, of course, be traced back to the schools. Attempts to explain it have ranged from social conditioning which prevents women from venturing into 'male' options, to accusations that certain types of institution or teaching style make it impossible for girls and women to develop inquisitiveness and realise their full intellectual potential (good summary in Hoecker 1987). There are some signs of diversification, however. Women today are more enterprising in their subject choices. In the early Sixties, over 70% of women students were registered for one of the ten most popular subjects; in the mid-Eighties, the bunching of choices had been reduced to 54%, i.e. women were more prepared than in the past to leave the beaten track and choose from a wider range, and they have spread their preferences more widely than men (see Appendix II).

To sum up: during the process of diversification, management studies emerged as the most popular subject among women students. The majority of subjects which women prefer at the tertiary level lead to a recognisable professional qualification and modes of employment after completing the relevant degree. Medicine, law, management studies and fields which figure in the school curriculum and prepare for a career in teaching have this vocational slant, although employment prospects do not always match the vocational design of the course of study. In their adjustments to university and their utilisation of advanced educational opportunities, the majority of women have been reluctant to embrace the German academic ethos of open-ended studies with no apparent link to employment. Women students responded to contracting employment opportunities by broadening their range of choices and by consolidating their perception of tertiary education as primarily vocational training which should and will lead to a professional qualification and to related employment.

The Broken Mould

The view of tertiary education as vocational training for a specific profession guides the majority of present-day course choices of women, their preferences for shorter programmes of study and also for intermediate levels of examinations. Women appear to be pragmatic in their approach to university and reluctant to aim for the top. To understand the intermediate pitch of women's tertiary education, we must briefly sketch the examination and qualification structure which dominates it.

German institutions of higher education offer four types of degree qualification, each with its specified assessments and minimum duration of study. As mentioned earlier, universities and polytechnics (*Fachhochschulen*) do not operate a maximum time of study, although the more structured courses tend to facilitate early completion. In West Germany, a course of study at a *Fachhochschule* is more clearly structured and geared towards early completion than a course at university where students themselves normally have to define when and how they are to pass the required courses and qualifying examinations. *Fachhochschulen* award their own degrees; they are called graduations and normally take four years to complete. Universities allow a broader range of examinations: the doctorate is considered the most advanced and is also the least well defined, being based on original research work under supervision. It is a prerequisite for teaching positions in the higher education sector. Depending on the subject, universities now also offer slightly less advanced examinations which provide candidates with a diploma or a master's degree qualification. In order to ensure that students complete their courses, these examinations have been emphasised in recent years and can be a prerequisite for doctoral studies. The fourth examination offered by universities is the state examination for teacher training; here universities cooperate with the relevant *Land* in setting and administering the examinations. The main purpose of the state examination, as mentioned earlier, has been to control the quality of candidates entering the public service, notably the teaching professions.

As Table 4.11 shows, women are more motivated towards examinations today than they were ten years ago. Their share among all types of examination has increased, particularly at the

138

Table 4.11 Examination successes of women in higher education, 1973–1984

Year	All examinations		Diplomas and MAs %	Doctorates %	State exams (teaching) %	Graduations (Fachhochsch) %
	Total	%				
1973	27,133	28	18	17	55	13
1980	40,992	35	28	20	57	27
1984	51,188	38	33	24	62	34

Source: Frauen in Familie, Beruf und Gesellschaft 1987: 133.

pragmatic/intermediate levels of diplomas or graduations. In the same spirit of vocational orientation, women constitute close to two-thirds of the prospective teachers. At the doctoral level, they have strengthened their position but with a proportion of only one in four doctorates, women's share remains lower here than among the student population or the successful candidates in an examination cohort. If we count all but the doctorate as vocationally focused or intermediate academic examinations, nearly nine out of ten women who qualify in higher education do so below the most advanced level. Teaching qualifications continue to attract a high proportion of women (62%) but fewer women today than in the early Seventies take the state examination; since the peak of teachers' training in 1977, the number of those who passed the state examination has declined by one-third (*Frauen in Familie, Beruf und Gesellschaft* 1987: 125).

The profile of women's academic performance in the Seventies highlights two important changes in the approach to higher education: the participation rate of women in examinations has increased, and teaching as a career choice has lost some of its appeal. To explain these changes, we have to consider the broader social and economic context of academic study in West Germany. In the Fifties and Sixties, women who attended university fell into two categories: those who came from academic backgrounds where university education was regarded as a normal phase of general personal development and those in whose families nobody had yet attended university. For the first group, university appeared to provide a valued cultural and intellectual experience. Some even claimed that it functioned as a marriage bureau. Examinations were of secondary importance and many left university without attempting any qualifying examination (Kath et al. 1966: 27). For the second group, university education provided access to professional qualifications. These students were often girls from non-academic working-class or lower middle-class families with a high vocational motivation, and the determination to obtain a final qualification. Teaching constituted their main professional option.

Compared with the Fifties and Sixties, women today are more clearly motivated to obtain recognised qualifications. The class differences in the vocational focus continue to be relevant; but since the expansion in educational qualifications has brought few additional working-class children into secondary or tertiary education, the real change of attitudes relates to the approaches of young women from middle-class and academic backgrounds. They now share the determination which had traditionally inspired working-class or lower middle-class girls in higher education, to utilise their studies in a suitable career.

The Collapse of Teaching as a Career and its Impact on Women

Putting these vocational expectations into practice after graduation, however, became increasingly difficult as graduate unemployment in West Germany began to rise. As we have gleaned from the pattern of final examinations, the vocational aspirations of women have been strongly focused on teaching. Teaching provided a clear vocational goal for the new generation of women who have entered university since the mid-Sixties and who have been motivated to achieve academic success and qualify through examinations for their chosen career. Less than a decade after the educational *Fräuleinwunder*, and a boom in the recruitment of teachers, teaching has virtually collapsed as a viable profession for newcomers. The very focus of their vocational determination has set women once again adrift as the linkage between employment and academic studies has become uncertain.

Employment opportunities for teachers at all levels of primary and secondary schooling rose rapidly after the Sixties, and have dropped sharply since the early Eighties. At the height of teachers' recruitment in the Seventies most candidates who passed the first state examination at the end of their university studies would proceed to the second stage and complete their state examination with the compulsory teaching practice and assessment. There was very little wastage along this career path. Although the first state examination entitles the holder to an in-service training place in a school, success in the practical examination does not guarantee appointment as a teacher. Since the late Seventies, the proportion of fully qualified teachers who were appointed to full-time posts has dropped sharply. In the mid-Eighties, only half the qualified teachers could remain in the profession. Thus more than 12,000 candidates of the 22,000 who had passed their second state examination and had qualified for a full appointment were not in fact appointed to a post (Sommer 1986: 81–2). In 1988, most West German *Länder* did not appoint new teachers, with the exception of some specialist fields in vocational schools. Unemployment has become a sizeable problem among newly qualified teachers, although some of the government programmes for unemployed academics which were mentioned earlier have cushioned the overall effect. By 1984, some 28,000 teachers were registered as unemployed; trade union estimates speak of at least twice that number of unemployed teachers.

Although the drift into teacher training has begun to decline, and numbers of examination passes have fallen since the early Eighties, the influx into the profession has been slowed down but by no means halted. It is rumoured that the universities have contributed to stemming the tide in their own fashion by increasing the failure rate in state examinations from near zero at the time of peak demand for teachers to over 11% in the Eighties (*Bildung und Wissenschaft* 9/10, 1987). However, the demand for teachers is, of course, closely linked to population sizes. Despite the declining birth rate, a rise in demand for teachers has already been predicted to cope with the children of the baby-boom generation of the early Sixties. Among students entering university, teaching as a career is again viewed with more optimism; applications for courses of study which conclude with the state examination and lead towards a teaching qualification have risen by 35% in 1987/8, the first rise for over ten years. As before, most of the aspiring teachers are women (*Bildung und Wissenschaft* 1/2, 1988).

The precarious employment opportunities for graduates in general and for teachers in particular elicited two kinds of response among educated young women – one vocational, the other personal in orientation. Vocationally motivated young women have broadened their focus and moved into new fields of study in order to prepare themselves for employment success. Women motivated by personal inclinations have remained undeterred by the spectre of unemployment and chosen their field even if it did not appear to hold the promise of employment after graduation. Young women who undertake apprenticeship training after their *Abitur* fall into the first category. They frequently come from homes where education is regarded as a lever of upward social mobility. In the past, teaching would have provided that mobility. As opportunities in teaching became rare, this group looked for similarly defined, vocationally focused qualifications, notably in business administration (where applications have risen by 40%), in the polytechnic sector (*Fachhochschulen*) which offers sandwich courses with a practical component, or outside the tertiary sector. The second group is larger and resembles the women in the Fifties with their tentative commitment to competitive university qualifications. Their situation is characterised by the paradox that they subscribe to a vocational focus – to become a teacher, a social worker, a sociologist or to choose another profession where unemployment has been rampant – in the full knowledge of their uncertain vocational prospects. Theirs is an ambivalent vocational focus which seems to aim for employment and for marginality at the same time.

Training to be Oneself?

A number of recent studies have cast some light on the question why young people opt for academic careers which appear to lack vocational prospects, to what extent teachers in particular are prepared to consider other fields of activity, and how unemployment after graduation might affect personal and vocational behaviour.

Choosing a subject of study appears to be closely linked to personality and value orientations. Regardless of gender, a sense of achievement or of satisfaction may be derived, for instance, from social contacts, personal communications, factual knowledge, independence of action or size of income. It has been suggested that the choices of subjects at school and the choices of career paths in adult life correspond to clusters of value orientations. Thus, men and women who opt for teaching or for one of the caring professions appear to have a social approach to their career. They tend to be less interested in independence, in their level of income or their socio-economic status but they value personal contacts, in particular with young people. The potential teacher expects a different type of satisfaction from work than the potential lawyer, manager or engineer. Interests are, above all, focused on persons, not on objects or

143

facts (Havers 1986: 68–9). A successful choice of vocation would be one where value orientations and work tally. For teachers, the value orientations would be of the social and communicative kind, with an emphasis on personal contacts. Among women, this type of value preference appears to be more prevalent than among men but where it occurs in men it is assumed to have the same effect: to gear the individual towards a career in teaching or related fields. For women, of course, teaching has always carried the added attraction that child-rearing and employment can be more readily combined if working-times and holidays coincide.

Unemployed prospective teachers who believe that teaching builds on special personality strengths have not been willingly persuaded to look for other types of work. Apparently, teachers of this type define their identity through their personal perform- ance in the teaching situation. They find it difficult to imagine themselves in an occupational role which would not be based on this linkage between personality and activity. The academic expertise which they accumulated during their studies tends to be viewed as secondary, not as an asset to give increased flexibility. Even unemployed teachers regard themselves, above all, as teachers rather than as qualified experts in foreign languages, historians, masters of the German language, or knowledgeable in geography (Havers 1986: 77; Stooß 1983). This personal dimension in the vocational motivation has apparently prevented students from exploring other employment possi- bilities which would utilise the skills they acquired during their education rather than the personality traits they value in them- selves (Havers et al. 1983).

How would graduate entrants to the labour market react if they were faced with unemployment? This was the subject matter of a survey among students who had completed their *Abitur* in 1976 and were still at university in 1980. The study assumed that most would be at an advanced stage of their course and ready to anticipate a transition to the labour market. The questions were designed to test the vocational motivation, the willingness to retrain, the determination to avoid unemploy- ment, or the tolerance towards it. It also intended to gauge the extent to which young people were inclined to turn their backs on vocational practices and social norms by opting for an alternative lifestyle to suit themselves. Did unemployment breed radicalisation, and a defiance of socio-economic conventions and practices? And if so, which type of student, of which gender and from which subject group would choose to 'opt out'?

Some of the findings of the study are presented in Table 4.12. It shows male and female orientations and also links subject choices and institutions to vocational motivation. The way chosen in this study to assess vocational motivation was to ask students what they would do if they found themselves unemployed after completing their course of study. Across the institutions and subject areas, women were not as vocationally determined as men; they were more willing to forgo income (column I) or to accept unemployment (column III) but less interested in additional qualifications (column II) which might cushion the effects of unemployment. In all categories, women were more emphatically interested in pleasing themselves in the way they make a living rather than conforming to the inhospitable world of work. With some variation between subjects, the vocational motivation of women seems to be less well defined than that of men, with a tendency to withdraw to a marginal position of alternative living in the face of employment barriers (column IV). These adherents of a so-called 'alternative' lifestyle are not interested in finding a way of fitting into conventional employment patterns or existing slots in the labour market. In German, this group has been called the *Aussteiger*, those who turn their backs on society and established behaviour patterns. Arts and social sciences subjects in universities and *Fachhochschulen* attract a larger cohort of potential *Aussteiger* than the classical male fields of engineering or technology. *Aussteigen* could mean finding a closed circle of like-minded friends to develop a lifestyle which has freed itself from the conventions that inform the everyday culture and the working lives of the people at large; in this sense, it is a tool of protest and potential opposition. For women, opting for an alternative lifestyle and 'looking for an alternative way of making a living for myself' could, of course, also refer to a withdrawal into the private sphere of stay-at-home wife or mother who would use her personality resources to create her own environment. In both cases, the vocational focus of women's higher education seems tentative. The tendency among women to look for *Bildung* – self-development –

145

Table 4.12 Students' reactions in case of unemployment (in %)[a]

| | | | STUDENTS PREPARED TO ACCEPT: | | |
| | I. Less money | II. Additional qualifications | III. Unemployment | | IV. Alternative lifestyle |
			6 months	1 year	
All students	87	80	51	20	16
Male students	86	82	47	16	14
Female students	90	79	60	28	20
Prospective teachers	87	78	64	31	17
Male	89	83	60	31	15
Female	87	75	66	33	18
University students	88	82	49	19	15
Male	87	82	46	16	14
Female	91	82	56	25	20
for selected subjects:					
Engineering	82	83	38	9	7
Medicine/pharmacy	95	83	41	15	10
Sociology/psychology	88	87	64	33	26
Languages/arts	92	82	49	25	29
Students at advanced colleges	81	81	42	11	13
Male	78	81	39	9	11
Female	92	78	53	19	25

for selected subjects:

Technical/science	79	80	39	8	10
Economics/management	80	84	37	9	9
Social work	85	87	56	27	33

[a] The study included students who completed *Abitur* in 1976, and were in tertiary education in 1978, and also in 1980/81. Students were asked to rank their preferences on a four-point scale from 1: most likely, to 4: unlikely. Percentages summarise rankings 1+2. The statements in full:

    I: I shall accept less money for a limited time if I can realise my vocational expectations.
   II: I shall try to improve my employment prospects by obtaining additional qualifications.
  III: I shall accept unemployment up to 6 months; I shall accept unemployment up to one year.
  IV: I shall turn my back on the whole traditional range of employment and look for an alternative way of making a living
     for myself.

rather than qualifications through higher education and to sidestep training for employment resembles women's uncertain educational motivations in the early Sixties. Now the concern with self-development is based on new reasons and carries a new critical sting against the mismatch of expectations and opportunities in their contemporary social environment.

References

Alltag und Biographie von Mädchen (ed. Sachverständigenkommission Sechster Jugendbericht, 17 vols), Opladen: Leske & Budrich, 1984f.

Andressen, Marion et al., *Berufliche Wiedereingliederung arbeitsloser/ berufsloser Frauen*, Schriftenreihe des Bundesministerium für Jugend, Familie und Gesundheit, Bd. 87, Stuttgart: Kohlhammer, 1981

Becher, Ursula et al., Evaluation der Berufsberatung der Bundesanstalt für Arbeit. *Die Orientierungsmaßnahmen in der gymnasialen Oberstufe*, Beiträge aus der Arbeitsmarkt- und Berufsforschung 79, Nuremberg, 1983

Becker, Hellmut, 'Bildungspolitik', in Wolfgang Benz (ed.), *Die Bundesrepublik Deutschland*, vol. 2: *Gesellschaft*, Frankfurt: Fischer, 1983 (pp. 324–50)

'Bericht der Bundesregierung über die Maßnahmen zur Verbesserung der Situation der Frau, 1972', in Deutscher Bundestag Wissenschaftlicher Dienst (ed.), *Frau und Gesellschaft*, Materialien no. 86, Bonn, 1984

Bernadoni, Claudia and Vera Werner, *Ohne Seil und Haken. Frauen auf dem Weg nach oben*, Munich: Saur, 1987

Berufsausbildung, Special Issue of *Bildung und Wissenschaft* 2/3, 1983

Berufsausbildung und Arbeitsmarkt. Quintessenzen aus der Arbeitsmarkt- und Berufsforschung 8, Nuremberg, 1977

Berufsbildungsbericht, ed. Bundesminister für Bildung und Wissenschaft, Bad Honnef: Bock (various years; annual reports)

Bildung im Zahlenspiegel, ed. Bundesminister für Bildung und Wissenschaft, Bonn, 1982

Borris, Maria, *Die Benachteiligung der Mädchen in Schulen der Bundesrepublik und Westberlin*, Frankfurt: Europäische Verlagsanstalt, 1972

Competence and Competition. Training and education in the Federal Republic of Germany, the United States and Japan. Report prepared by the MSC and NEDO, London, 1984

Dahrendorf, Ralf, *Bildung ist Bürgerrecht. Plädoyer für eine expansive Bildungspolitik*, Hamburg: Nannen, 1965

Datenreport, ed. Statistisches Bundesamt, Bonn: Bundeszentrale für politische Bildung, 1987

Frauen in der Bundesrepublik Deutschland, ed. Bundesministerium für Jugend, Familie, Frauen und Gesundheit, Bonn, 1986

Frauen in Familie, Beruf und Gesellschaft, ed. Statistisches Bundesamt, Mainz: Kohlhammer, 1987

Frauen und Arbeitsmarkt. Quintessenzen aus der Arbeitsmarkt- und Berufsforschung 4, Nuremberg, 1984 (2nd edn)

Friebel, Harry, *Von der Schule in den Beruf*, Opladen: Westdeutscher Verlag, 1983

——, *Berufliche Qualifikation und Persönlichkeitsentwicklung*, Opladen: Westdeutscher Verlag, 1985

Grund- und Strukturdaten, ed. Bundesminister für Bildung und Wissenschaft, Bonn, 1987

Habermas, Jürgen, *Protestbewegung und Hochschulreform*, Frankfurt: Suhrkamp, 1969

Havers, Norbert, 'Berufswahlmotive und berufliche Mobilitätsbarrieren von Lehramtsstudenten', in Manfred Sommer (ed.), *Lehrerarbeitslosigkeit und Lehrerausbildung*, Opladen: Westdeutscher Verlag, 1986 (pp. 67–77)

—— et al., *Alternative Einsatzfelder für Lehrer?* Beiträge aus der Arbeitsmarkt- und Berufsforschung, Nuremberg, 1983

Heinz, Walter R. and Helga Krüger, 'Berufsfindung unter dem Diktat des Arbeitsmarktes', *Zeitschrift für Pädagogik* vol. 27, 1981, no. 5

Hoecker, Beate, *Frauen in der Politik*, Opladen: Leske & Budrich, 1987

Hradil, Stefan, *Sozialstrukturanalyse in einer fortgeschrittenen Gesellschaft*, Opladen: Leske & Budrich, 1987

Hurrelmann, Klaus et al., *Bildungsbeteiligung von Mädchen im Allgemeinbildenden Schulbereich*, Unpublished report, University of Bielefeld, 1982 (in preparation of the Sixth Youth Report, 1984)

Kath, Gerhart et al., *Studienweg und Studienerfolg*, Berlin: Institut für Bildungsforschung, Studien und Berichte 6, 1966

Köhler, Helmut, 'Amtliche Bildungsstatistik im Wandel', in Max Planck Institut für Bildungsforschung (ed.), *Bildung in der Bundesrepublik*, vol. 2, Reinbek: Rowohlt, 1980

Krinner, Alfred, 'Mädchen in schulischer, betrieblicher und Hochschulausbildung', in *Bayern in Zahlen* 3, 1986, pp. 53–7

Lernen für die Arbeitswelt. Special Issue 'Berufsbildung in der Bundesrepublik', Bildung und Wissenschaft 3/4, 1986

Lovenduski, Joni, *Women and European Politics. Contemporary Feminism and Public Policy*, Brighton: Harvester, 1986

Max Planck Institut für Bildungsforschung (ed.), *Bildung in der Bundesrepublik Deutschland. Daten und Analysen*, 2 vols, Reinbek: Rowohlt, 1980

Naumann, Jens, 'Entwicklungstendenzen des Bildungswesens der Bundesrepublik Deutschland im Rahmen wirtschaftlicher und demographischer Veränderungen' in *Bildung in der Bundesrepublik*, ed. Max Planck Institut für Bildungsforschung, Reinbek: Rowohlt, 1980, pp. 21–103

Nitsch, Wolfgang et al., *Die Hochschule in der Demokratie*, Neuwied: Luchterhand, 1967

Picht, Georg, *Die deutsche Bildungskatastrophe. Analysen und Dokumente*, Freiburg: Olten, 1964

Pross, Helge, *Über die Bildungschancen von Mädchen in der Bundesrepublik*, Frankfurt: Suhrkamp, 1969

Schulwesen in der Bundesrepublik Deutschland, Das, Special Issue of *Bildung und Wissenschaft* 10/1, 1984

Seidenspinner, Gerlinde and Angelika Burger, *Mädchen '82*, Munich: Deutsches Jugendinstitut, 1982

——, *Mädchen im Übergang von der Schule in die Arbeitswelt*, Expert Report 15a for the Sixth Youth Report, Munich, 1982/3 (unpublished)

—— et al., *Vom Nutzen weiblicher Lohnarbeit. Alltag und Biographie von Mädchen 3*, Opladen: Leske & Budrich, 1984

Sixth Youth Report: *Verbesserung der Chancengleichheit von Mädchen in der Bundesrepublik Deutschland*. Bundestagsdrucksache 10/1007, 15 Feb. 1984

Sommer, Manfred (ed.), *Lehrerarbeitslosigkeit und Lehrerausbildung*, Opladen: Westdeutscher Verlag, 1986

Statistisches Jahrbuch der Bundesrepublik Deutschland, ed. Statistisches Bundesamt, Mainz: Kohlhammer, 1988

Stooß, Friedemann 'Zur Frage der Beschäftigung oder Umschulung arbeitloser Lehrer', in Norbert Havers et al., *Alternative Einsatzfelder für Lehrer?*, Beiträge aus der Arbeitsmarkt- und Berufsforschung, Nuremberg, 1983

Tessaring, Manfred and Heinz Werner, *Beschäftigung und Arbeitsmarkt für Hochschulabsolventen in den Ländern der Europäischen Gemeinschaft*, Beiträge aus der Arbeitsmarkt- und Berufsforschung 46, Nuremberg, 1981

5
Women in Employment: Structural Changes and Personal Opportunities

At a time when socio-economic forecasters are predicting an end of the 'working society' with employment receding in importance for the individual, women appear to be living against the grain of change. For men, the participation in the labour market has indeed fallen. In the early Seventies, 88% of men between the ages of fifteen and sixty-five were in employment or registered as unemployed, i.e. potentially active in the labour market. A decade later, the proportion of working men had fallen to 83%. For women, the changes took the opposite direction, and the participation of women of working age increased from 48 to 52% over the same period. Among women, employment has gained in prominence and plays a bigger part in their personal lives.

The shift towards the non-working mode of advanced industrial society can be traced to two major factors: young people today tend to remain longer in full-time education or training and are older than previous generations when they enter the labour market, and people retire at an earlier age from their working lives than had been customary in the past. The postponed transition of young people into the world of work has affected both men and women and so cannot explain why the participation of women in the labour market has increased. It has even been suggested that women under twenty-five will further delay the transition from education or training to work as they seek higher qualifications and engage in extended periods of training (*Mitteilungen aus der Arbeitsmarkt- und Berufsforschung (MittAB)* 3, 1970: 296). At the opposite end of the employment cycle, women tend to retire earlier than men. Again, the duration of working lives can do little to explain why women's share in the world of work has increased at a time when non-working is gaining ground.

What has changed is the motivation among West German women towards employment. This motivation to work can build on the educational motivation and the orientation among women to obtain vocational qualifications, which were discussed in the previous chapter. Without at this stage examining career opportunities and the access of women to positions of leadership, the motivation to work is evident in two distinctive ways: more women remain in the labour market today even after marriage and childbirth than in the founding years of the Federal Republic, and those who take one or more career breaks tend to return to employment sooner than women had done in the past. In the early Fifties, 25% of married women went out to work; today, 43% do (*Datenreport* 1987: 82).

When Myrdal and Klein developed their famous model of how women could combine their dual roles of being home-makers and going out to work, they thought in terms of a prolonged break of fifteen years or so after training and a brief taste of full-time employment (Myrdal and Klein 1956). Women, it was argued, could and possibly should return to work once their children were independent enough to dispense with full-time care. Working outside the home was seen as a useful way of gaining social contacts, some financial benefit and added self-esteem. It was also seen as desirable social engineering which would open new pastures for mothers who might otherwise stifle their offsprings' lives by being over-protective.

In the light of the Eighties, the Myrdal and Klein model seems all too indebted to the notion that women should do whatever was best for others – even go out to work. When it was formulated, it was received in a different mood as a package of practical, apparently workable suggestions on how to resolve the dichotomy of women's two roles. Since then, the expectation that homemaking and employment can be bridged in some way has gained ground among West German women (Boss 1981). The younger generations in particular have embraced the spirit of the dual-role model and set out in life with the dual aim of family and work. Compared with the original model, women are more employment-orientated and less inclined to live their lives in separate phases. Longitudinal studies of labour market participation have shown that the balance between family and work has been more complex: at no point or

Table 5.1 Women in employment (1965–1985) by age (in % of age cohort)

Year	15–20	20–25	25–30	30–35	35–40	40–45	45–50	50–55	55–60	60+
1965	57	52	40	37	37	38	38	33	28	19
1975	58	62	51	47	46	47	46	40	32	14
1985	41	71	66	60	60	60	56	50	40	10

Source: *Frauen in Familie und Beruf*, Bundesministerium für Jugend, Familie, Frauen und Gesundheit, 1986: 12; Gisela Helwig, *Frau und Familie*, Cologne: Wissenschaft und Politik, 1987: 40.

age has there been a surge back into the labour market after, say, a decade of homemaking for one generation. In the Fifties and Sixties, employment of women decreased sharply when they were in their late twenties, and then continued to fall gradually until retirement. In the Eighties, a similar pattern has prevailed, but more women have remained at work, and employment tends to remain at about the same level between the ages of thirty and fifty-five. The age cohort which should, according to Myrdal and Klein, have taken the family break – the 30- to 45-year-olds – have increased their labour market participation by 59% in the last twenty years. Table 5.1 shows that with the exception of the youngest who tend to remain in education, women today are more active in the labour market than in the past, with the highest increases in the women who, judging by their age, are or could be in the family phase. Working, it seems, has become a widely accepted and practised part of women's lives in contemporary society.

A Working Life of Career Breaks

Despite the apparent employment motivation, the involvement of women in the labour market has remained uneven and punctuated by family commitments, notably child-rearing. A study of employment patterns and career breaks analysed the reasons given by men and women for leaving their employment. The picture presented in Figure 5.1 details the reasons since 1970, and includes projections until 1990. Retirement has been the most important reason for both men and women,

Figure 5.1 Reasons for leaving employment:[a] men and women

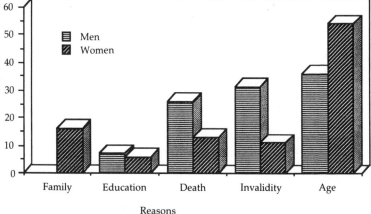

Reasons

[a] The data combine a trend analysis since 1970 with projections until 1990.
Source: 'Wachstum und Arbeitsmarkt. Perspektiven 1980–2000', in *Quintessenzen aus der Arbeitsmarkt- und Berufsforschung* 1, 1975: 12.

followed – for men – by invalidity or death. In our context, however, the column marked 'family' is of particular interest since it includes the people who leave their employment to bring up children or attend to other family-centred affairs. For women, this is the second most important reason for leaving their employment; for men it is so infrequent a reason that it does not show up in the statistics.

For a woman one or more career breaks are a major experience of her working life. Although more women today than in the Fifties work after marriage and also after having children, few do so without interrupting their employment. In the early Eighties, only 16% of West German women with children had remained in employment without a career break. Labour market participation has been lowest among married women with children under three years of age, or with several children to look after. Single mothers, widows or divorcees are more inclined to seek employment while their children are of pre-school age (45%) than women who live in complete families (34%). Financial constraints are the single most important reason for working; the higher the family income, the less likely are

154

mothers of young children to enter into employment. The poor provisions in West Germany of full-time day care facilities for children under the age of three make it difficult for women to rely on established child-care networks. That kindergartens and schools normally finish at midday also militates against women seeking employment (*Familie und Arbeitswelt*: 56–7). The half-day pattern means in practical terms that someone has to be at home to prepare the midday meal and to supervise younger children in the afternoon.

West German women have opted for the temporary career break in order to combine their own employment motivation with the requirements of their families and children. In the founding decades of the Federal Republic, those women who wanted to return to work after bringing up their children would do so after a break averaging fifteen years. Today, women tend to return after half that time; the average length of a career break has dropped to eight years (although individual patterns vary from a few years to decades; Hellmich 1986).

The most detailed study to date on the duration of career breaks and the different family situations which influence the decision to leave employment was conducted in the late Seventies under the auspices of the research institute affiliated to the Federal Employment Office, the Bundesanstalt für Arbeit. The survey focused on women who were not in employment at the time and aimed at determining the factors which might influence their decision to return. Some of the findings are presented in Table 5.2. It highlights the career intentions and personal situations of those women who were planning a return to the labour market, 44% of all respondents in the study; the remaining 56% did not intend to return to paid employment in the future. Younger women who had not been outside the labour market for long were more motivated to return ('definitely') than those who had not been employed for ten or more years, and were heading towards retirement age ('perhaps'). Table 5.2 suggests that the age of the children is less important for the wish to work – although it is a major consideration in the actual decision to return to work – than the time which has elapsed since the last employment, or the age of the mother. Women whose children were teenagers or older were in fact the least inclined to head for employment. This suggests that the major

Table 5.2 Planned return of women to the labour market after career break

	Definitely %	Perhaps %	Total %
All respondents who wished to return	16	28	44
Age of the women			
Under 20	38	18	56
20 – under 25	42	30	72
25 – under 30	32	42	74
30 – under 35	25	44	69
35 – under 40	21	37	58
40 – under 45	13	30	43
45 – under 50	6	26	32
50 – under 55	3	15	18
55 – under 60	1	7	8
60 and over	0	3	3
Age of the youngest child			
Under 6 years	28	43	71
6 – under 15	18	34	52
15 and over	4	14	18
Time elapsed since last being in employment			
Less than 1 year	36	28	64
1 – under 3 years	24	35	59
3 – under 5 years	20	36	56
5 – under 10 years	19	35	54
10 years and more	8	22	30

Source: H. Hofbauer, 'Zum Erwerbsverhalten verheirateter Frauen', in *Mitteilungen aus der Arbeitsmarkt- und Berufsforschung* 2, 1979.

factor in the shifting balance between homemaking and the motivation to work is a generational effect.

The profile of career breaks and intentions to return to work matches our earlier findings that young women since the Sixties have enjoyed and used educational and vocational opportunities and shown themselves to be motivated to obtain qualifications and to participate in the labour market. We can now develop this point and state that the motivation among younger generation women to qualify and to work has shaped their lives after marriage and the onset of the family role, and that these women aim to return to work as soon as feasible, often taking several family-induced career breaks. Older women are less concerned with combining family and employment, and are less exposed to the unsettling effects of career breaks. Education, however, has been a major role in motivating women towards employment and regardless of age, women with higher qualifications are the least likely to interrupt their work and are keenest to resume it if they did take a career break. The lower skilled or unskilled tend to be less motivated to return to work, except for financial reasons.

For women in contemporary society, working plays a larger part in life than it had done for women in past decades. Again, we can gain more specific insights into the factors which influence women's decisions to leave their employment, and comparisons over time show the changes in the social situation and in the attitudes of women in post-war Germany. The data in Table 5.3 are taken from a survey on women's integration into the labour market and focus on those women who were not working at the time. In the Fifties, just 15% of women who were housewives had been working for ten years or more before leaving their employment; in the Seventies, 40% of the housewives had worked this long (Table 5.3). In the past, women took their career breaks earlier – 66% at the age of twenty-five or under; today, women remain in employment longer and are older when they interrupt or leave it. In the Fifties, most became homemakers on marriage and two out of three of the nonworking women had no children on leaving work. In the Seventies, one in four did not have children when they left their employment; the remainder, however, only left when children were born. One in four worked until after the second or subsequent children were born.

The participation of West German women in the labour market is punctuated by career breaks and phases of nonemployment as they struggle to match their motivation to work with their motivation to live a family life, and have children. If a change of values has taken place and men should have started to opt for homemaking instead of their wives, this is as yet too novel and too feeble to be reflected in the statistical profile of employment patterns. What is evident here is that women continue to shoulder the burden of child care. If they are

Table 5.3 Women's employment and social situation before the
career break: a comparison of the Fifties and Seventies

Career break was taken in	1957 and before	1973–1977
Duration of employment before		
career break	%	%
Less than 5 years	43	31
5 to under 10 years	42	29
10 years and longer	15	40
Overall	100	100
Age of respondents when taking		
career break		
Less than 25 years	66	36
25 to under 30 years	25	24
30 years and over	9	40
Overall	100	100
Number of children when taking		
career break		
No children	67	26
One child	28	50
Two or more children	5	24
Overall	100	100

*Source: Frauen und Arbeitsmarkt. Quintessenzen aus der Arbeitsmarkt- und Berufsfor-
schung (QuintAB) 4, 1984: 26.*

employment-motivated, and wish to return to the labour
market, they adjust their careers and move in and out of the
labour market during the years of child-rearing. The motivation
to work has intensified since the Fifties. Rather than opting for
consecutive phases, those women today who wish to work opt,
as much as possible, for living both lives at the same time, that
of the working woman and that of the mother. For women who
are the head of the household, there is often little choice if they
want to ensure a reasonable standard of living, and 61% on
average are in employment (*Familie und Arbeitswelt* 41).
Although married women with children may be more protected
from economic pressures than non-married women, 41% of
women whose husbands are in employment also go out to work
(ibid. p. 40). It has been calculated that four out of ten children
under the age of eighteen have mothers who are in paid employment. For the majority of these women their present-day

employment follows at least one career break for the sake of homemaking.

The intensified motivation to work among the well-qualified younger generation of women has not been easily accommodated in contemporary German society. The reality of career breaks for most working women or a return to the role of full-time housewife seems to place the generation of motivated and educated women of today at a similar disadvantage in the world of work as their less competitive and qualified elders encountered decades before.

The Employment of Women and the Future of the Working Environment

In 1988, the total labour force in West Germany numbered close to 26 million; just under 10 million were women. On the surface, little seems to have changed since the early days of the Federal Republic when 36% of the labour force were female. The changes which did occur concern the structure rather than the size of the West German labour force. In the post-war era the balance between sectors of the economy shifted with primary industries such as agriculture or mining declining in importance as producers of national wealth, and in particular as employers, while the tertiary sector expanded. West Germany has maintained a relatively strong secondary sector and nearly 40% of the labour force today are working in production, in manufacturing or similar occupations. Employment in the secondary sector has, however, fallen since the early Seventies and West Germany is moving closer to becoming what Dahrendorf has called a 'service class society' (Dahrendorf 1967).

The employment of women seems to have reached that stage already. The shift in women's employment from the primary to the tertiary sector of the economy since the early Fifties amounts to a transformation (Hofbauer 1979; Baethge et al. 1984). In 1950, agriculture was the most important area, employing one in three women; one in four worked in industry; the remaining 40% in the tertiary sector (Table 5.4). By 1985, agriculture employed 7% of working women; manufacturing industry again employed one in four women, after a peak of 35% in 1970 and a sharp

Table 5.4 Women at work by branches of the economy, 1950–1985

Branch of the economy	1950 %	1960 %	1970 %	1985 %
Agriculture/mining	34	20	11	7
Manufacturing industry	25	31	35	25
Trade	11	17	18	15
Transport/communications	2	2	3	3
Banking/insurance	1	2	3	4
Services (industry/professions)	12	18	22	32
Private households	9	4	3	3
Public administration	4	4	5	8
No answer/no data	3	—	—	—

Note: Percentage figures were rounded to the nearest number, and may not add up to one hundred.

Sources: Data based on Census and Occupational Statistics, published in *QuintAB* 2, 1973, and *Statistisches Jahrbuch*, ed. Statistisches Bundesamt, 1986.

decline during the Seventies as the economic recession and rationalisation took their toll. Close to 70% of working women in the Eighties are employed in the tertiary sector of the economy (Müller 1980; 1983).

The changes in the nature of employment can also be understood in terms of the emergence of information processing. Modern economic activity is inconceivable without an extensive network of communication, administration and distribution. From the typing pool to the telephone service, communication and information processing have become the backbone of economic activity, with whole industries specialising in it. In the last decade or so, the advent of the office computer has made information processing more effective, and further expanded its role in the world of employment. The decline of employment in the primary and secondary sectors of industry, and the expansion of tertiary employment can also be seen as an expansion – even an explosion – of employment in information processing. In 1950 18% of the West German labour force were exclusively concerned with information processing; in 1982, their share had risen to 35% with the trend still rising. Taking information processing and services together they comprise over half the contemporary labour force (Table 5.5).

Since the early Sixties, increases in employment in the sec-

Table 5.5 Employment since 1882 and the emergence of information processing (in % of labour force)

Year	Employment in economic sectors:[a]					
	I	II	III	IV	II+IV	III+IV
1882	45	30	11	12	42	23
1907	35	35	13	13	48	26
1925	30	36	19	13	49	32
1939	26	37	22	14	51	36
1950	21	39	22	18	57	40
1961	13	40	25	22	62	47
1970	8	39	25	28	67	53
1982	6	34	26	34	68	60

[a] I. Agriculture; II. Manufacturing industry; III. Service; IV. Information.
Source: Mitteilungen aus der Arbeitsmarkt- und Berufsforschung 4, 1984.

ondary and tertiary sectors have been increase in information processing. In concrete terms, the information boom brought an expansion in office work, and accelerated the increase of female employment in white-collar occupations. Today, seven out of ten West German women are employed in offices, and therefore in information processing of some kind.

Women's Work and New Technologies

On the face of it, the strong position of women in the white-collar sector and in the fast growing segment of information-related employment seems to place them in a competitive position for the working environment of the future (Stutenbäumer-Hübner 1987; Lane 1988). The parameters of employment change have, however, moved since the advent of the typewriter and the adding machine assisted the entry of women into the previously male-dominated office environment at the turn of the century. Today, technological innovation, new technologies and rationalisation of employment processes combine to redraw the map of paid employment (see Appendix III). A closer look at the balance of skills women can offer and those which will be in greater demand suggests that in the transition to the labour landscape of the year 2000, women may be losing out (Volkholz 1987; Bolte and Büttner 1986). The employment of women in information processing services is less flexible than might at first appear. The concentration of expertise in a narrow band which we have already observed for training programmes is carried over into a narrow band of jobs: 90% of the female labour force are employed in only twelve occupational areas (Appendix IV). One in four women are employed in unskilled or semi-skilled office work, a further 20% in skilled office work. Only this type of office work could be included with management and planning tasks and belong to the top end of the occupational range. The majority of the occupational groups fit into the lower or intermediate range in an employment hierarchy which is based on the scope for decision making and leadership. The occupations themselves which are dominated by women do not lack a scope for responsibility and devotion, or even job satisfaction, but they do seem to be lodged as services or labour support in the intermediate or lower ranges of employment.

The question of what women do at work and how this differs from the work done by men has been examined recently to evaluate the usage of new technologies. The detailed evaluation of existing labour processes has rendered some interesting contrasts between men and women which extend our knowledge about gender differences between occupational fields. A comparison of the main activity involved at work – regardless of the specific name or classification of a job – shows that men are more frequently engaged in production, repairs and maintenance and women in trading or office work (Table 5.6). This is only to be expected given the activities which constitute male- or female-dominated areas of employment. The data in Table 5.6, however, also compare less obvious activities such as planning, management and controlling. These are the hidden activities which are not necessarily evident from occupational classifications, but they are the skills which characterise the workforce of the future. For the workforce of today, they can be interpreted as the potential to be competitive in the future and in a position to play a leading role. It is here that women are losing out. Grouped by the main activity in their present employment, women are not altogether excluded from the top end but dominate the bottom end of the scale. In the tasks of the future such as controlling, planning, research and development, maintenance and management, men outnumber women by at least three to one.

Table 5.6 Men and women in employment by their main activity, 1980

Main activity	Women	Men
Production	√	√√√√√√√√√
Repairs	√	√√√√√√√v
Machine maintenance	√	√√√√
Planning and construction	√	√√√
Management	√	√√√
Transport	√	√√
Controlling	√	√v
Other services	√v	√
Trading	√√v	√
Office work	√√√√v	√

Note: The symbols depict equal numbers in the workforce: v = half of √.

Source: Bundesminister für Forschung und Technologie, *Frauenbeschäftigung und neue Technologien*, Vorstudie von Batelle Institut, Frankfurt and Infratest, Munich, Bonn, 1983.

As new technologies and new labour processes change the working environment, the skilled person of the future will combine technical and managerial tasks, and assume responsibility usually as a member of a team for decisions relating to his or her work (Aleman and von Schatz 1987; Scharfenberg 1986). In the contemporary world of work, the majority of women have no experience in decision making of this nature, since their work supports rather than initiates decisions (Willms-Herget 1987). In key sectors of white-collar activity such as banking or insurance, 70% of women are employed with tasks which are routine and repetitive, and thus easily carried out by a new technology device (Krebsbach-Gnath 1985: 52). Women in manufacturing industries have frequently been employed as unskilled or semi-skilled workers on assembly lines where nimble fingers were required, or in textiles and clothing production. Many of these tasks have been simplified through new technology or given over to production robots altogether (Kern and Schumann 1984).

New Technologies Applied: Some Examples

A case study of the electronics industry describes how the day-to-day work of women at an assembly line changed after their product was improved through new technology. The original task consisted of soldering 500 tiny colour-coded parts to build a conductor. The parts had to be handled by tweezers, and the skill of the workers consisted in correct recognition of the parts, correct mounting and, of course, speed. To assemble one conductor took thirty minutes on average. Technological advances in this field involved using micro-chips. Now a conductor needed only 50 component parts, soldering had become unnecessary and the electrical connections could be installed by machine. The new type of conductor needed only a third of the time to assemble, and was one hundred times more powerful than its predecessor. For the workforce, these changes reduced the quality of the labour process, since the expert knowledge about the sequence of assembly was now redundant and precision soldering skills had become obsolete. The rapid increase in productivity also increased the risk of unemployment (Bednarz-Braun 1984).

In its most drastic form, the introduction of new technology can lead to the disappearance of the place of work altogether. Since there are no statistics which clearly link unemployment with the introduction of new technologies, their impact on the working situation can only be assessed on the basis of specialist studies and the estimates advanced in them (*Frauenbeschäftigung und neue Technologien* 1987). Job losses in the wake of new technology are expected in a number of areas with above average employment of women, such as in office work (between 20% and 40%), in general trade and retailing (10%), in printing (30%), in banking (25%) and in industrial production (a decline of about 500,000). An expert report by the West German trade union federation has suggested that well over one million jobs which are now predominantly held by women will have disappeared by the end of the decade (Deutscher Gewerkschaftsbund 1985: 223). A survey of office work concluded that by 1990 one in four clerical jobs will have disappeared in the wake of computerisation; a government report on new technology anticipated that up to 2.5 million places of work in administration and office work – most of them held by women – will no longer exist at the end of the decade (Steppke 1980: 171f.).

One concrete example for which the impact of technological innovation on the employment of women has been shown in detail is the West German post office (Schwuchow, 1985: 243ff.). In 1985, the post office was West Germany's largest civilian employer with a workforce of 540,000, just over one-third of them women (187,000). Of these, 71% were so-called *Tarifkräfte*, mostly blue-collar workers; 12% were civil servants, and the remainder apprentices or trainee civil servants. Just over half the women worked full-time (55%), the others part-time (45%). Although on paper the post office is an equal opportunities employer, the majority of women worked at intermediate and non-technical levels, especially in the telegraph service, in the West German national savings bank equivalent or in part-time postal deliveries. Between 1986 and 1990 the introduction of computers into these areas will reduce the number of allocated full-time work places by nearly 18,000. Since many women here are working part-time, about twice that number are expected to lose their jobs. Taking all areas of post office employment together, 40,000 work places are to be disestablished through rationalisations by 1990, in addition to the 28,000 already dispensed with during the last ten years (Schwuchow 1985: 247).

The reductions in the post office labour force have changed the gender balance within occupational areas, and also highlight the structural disadvantage of women in traditional fields with a low technical skill content. In the West German post office, formerly 'female' domains such as the telephone and telegraph service now employ 58% women and 42% men. To some extent, the new gender balance reflects organisational restructuring after rationalisation measures and the larger job losses among women. It also points to a higher occupational flexibility among men who find it easier to move into new areas and, as we shall see later, receive more support to qualify for new tasks. In the post office, the main set of qualifications needed in the new working environment is technical. Here women have been slow to create or utilise opportunities. In 1980, just 3% of the technical trainees were women. The proportion had doubled to 6% in 1983 but still fell far short of future demand, and remained marginal in comparison with the main orientations of the female labour force. With demand for skilled labour already strong in the technical field and set to increase in the future (Rothkirch and von Weidig 1986), women in the post office and also elsewhere have yet to step out into this future in greater numbers.

The Tasks of the Future and the Realities of Office Work

The impact of new technologies on clerical or office work has been similarly far reaching and points to a new polarisation in the female labour force: at one end, highly skilled women occupy positions of leadership; on the other end, the segment of semi-skilled and unskilled women in the labour force is artificially extended as women from intermediate positions are demoted through new technologies into general support and service functions (Stooß 1987). This process has become apparent in one of the mainstays of female employment, office work. Compared with the early Sixties, office-based employment has increased by 2 million overall. The league table of skills also shows that women have improved their share in the administrative sector, which includes managerial functions, and in skilled clerical (*kaufmännische*) tasks (Table 5.7). The general dogsbody work in support of the office infrastructure constitutes the least skilled of the occupational categories in office work, and in the early Sixties most of the infrastructure workforce were women. Table 5.7 shows that this kind of work is no longer the stronghold of female employment it has been in the past, although women have remained over-represented (Baethge and Oberbeck 1986). Within the general area of office work, infrastructure work is most likely to be affected by unemployment since many tasks can be automated or may disappear in reorganisations of the labour process (Stooß et al. 1988). For women in skilled clerical work the utilisation of new technologies can open avenues of responsibility, as the tasks become increasingly weighted towards planning and mapping out key decisions of a managerial type. For the majority of women, however, the effects of new technologies appear to point in the opposite direction. Administrative and planning-related responsibilities tend to be allocated to a number of computer workstations and the tasks involved in office work resemble general support work. As new technologies change the working environments, women in particular are in danger of being demoted from clerical to infrastructure work, once their special skills are no longer needed (Dobberthien et al. 1986). In the traditional fields of women's employment, new technologies and related changes in the working environment seem to have

Table 5.7 Women in office work, 1961–1982

	1961 %	1970 %	1980 %	1982 %
Women in office work	40	39	48	46
By occupational area:				
Administrative	28	34	41	44
Skilled clerical	40	39	52	48
Technical	7	9	10	10
Services	43	54	59	63
Infrastructure	98	81	76	61
Total in workforce (in millions)	5.3	6.1	7.3	7.6

Source: L. Troll, 'Büroberufe im Wandel', *MatAB* 1, 1984.

lowered the status and qualifications of women and retained or even widened the gap between those who frame the decisions and set the pace, and those who assist, serve and support.

Change and Innovation: Prospects for Women

At times of rapid technological change due to new machinery, new products or new work organisation, additional qualifications are frequently the major safeguard against losing ground in the world of work. Updating and expanding qualifications in line with new developments can cushion against unemployment and against a process by which skills and qualifications which have been acquired in the past no longer suffice for the future. In West Germany, *Weiterbildung*, the permanent development of individual expertise through special training programmes or courses, has become a core component of the contemporary working environment. The workforce of the present will only suffice for the future and produce the quality goods and services needed in a country which, like West Germany, depends heavily on exports, if the workforce is both highly skilled and highly flexible to adapt to new developments in production processes and communication technology, and to retain an innovative edge. Against the backcloth of such a general focus on *Weiterbildung* and the enhancement of skills and qualifications in the contemporary West German business

environment, we need to evaluate how women have participated and benefited from these developments, and what effect
Weiterbildung had on the gender gap in employment.

We saw earlier that women in general appear to be reluctant
to engage in further training, although the motivation to acquire
new skills and undertake further training has grown in line with
formal educational and vocational qualifications. Women who
have completed their *Abitur* have been just as eager as men to
make use of programmes or courses to develop their skills. The
participation of women in updating and retraining programmes
cannot be linked to motivation alone, although the correlation
between level of expertise and motivation is important. No less
important is whether courses are, in fact, on offer, and whether
women enjoy equal access to them (Krebsbach-Gnath and
Schmid-Jörg 1985). A study of in-service courses designed to
familiarise staff with new developments including technologies
and to enhance the effectiveness of staff in the business organisation revealed an uneven pattern of gender-related obstacles
(Hegelheimer 1981). In three of the four sectors studied – banking, the computer industry and retailing – single women under
the age of thirty had better chances of further training than other
women employees. Since successful participation in in-firm
training measures tends to be regarded as a precondition of
internal promotion to managerial tasks, women are selected for
these courses as potential managers. In fact, less than 1% of
top-level managers in the companies in the survey were
women, and the in-firm training for women was aimed above all
at the lowest and intermediate managerial levels such as fore-
man, group leader, project organiser, deputy manager. Here, 10
to 15% were female. Despite the apparent differences in opportunities, women employees in industry and business felt they
had equal access to training measures, and could benefit from
them as much as men. In public service, the fourth sector of the
economy covered in the survey, married women with children
had better access to further training and also to managerial posts
(10%) than in the other three. Yet, women were generally more
critical of their opportunities for in-service training and did not
believe that their chances of advancement matched those of men
(Hegelheimer 1981: 39).

For the average woman white-collar or blue-collar worker

without managerial ambitions and the educational qualifications to underpin them, provisions for training have been worse. In the main field of female employment, office work, few training programmes in new technology or other aspects of innovation and updating appear to be on offer. One in five women who regularly use new technology in office work did not receive any training, i.e. they could not be expected to perform administrative or planning tasks (Krebsbach-Gnath 1985). A government-commissioned survey on qualification measures in West German industry and business found in 1983 that the majority of programmes related to production processes and were designed to benefit skilled workers who were threatened by redundancy through new technologies or new product development (Mendius 1983: 229ff.). Even in industries where one in three production workers were women – in printing or the electrical industry for instance – women were not included in the measures: these were aimed at skilled workers only, while women in production tended to be semi-skilled or unskilled. In printing, the introduction of computer typesetting might have provided an excellent opportunity for office staff with keyboard and word-processing skills to qualify for the new positions in production. No women were, however, included in retraining or updating programmes, since a transition towards the new technology was only envisaged for skilled typesetters and printers – all of them men.

In areas of employment with a high proportion of women very few qualifying measures were on offer. Where additional qualifications could be obtained, they tended to be so-called 'other qualifications', i.e. preparing participants to cope with a specific production process or a new piece of machinery and training them to be semi-skilled in this area. Here, the proportion of women in women-dominated industries such as textiles and leather (67%) or electrical goods (50%) was in line with their place in the workforce. Core sectors of women's employment such as banking, insurance, retailing, and the broad field of office work offered next to no special qualification programmes for non-managerial employees, and certainly none which would have enhanced the chances for women to make optimal use of the new technological developments in their fields of employment. Overall, 13% of the participants in additional qualification measures were women, and the proportion would have been lower still had not the government appealed to companies to give preferential consideration to the further training of women.

The gender gap in training and retraining reflects motivation, provision, and the place of women in the employment structure. On the whole, positions occupied by women are rarely earmarked as priority areas for training in new technologies or production processes. If the worker and employee of the future is to be flexible, to possess more than one skill and be adaptable, and be trained to innovate and initiate, women have so far been written out of this job specification, and have remained on the sidelines of modernisation (Kern and Schumann 1984). Even in a company such as Karstadt, whose training and retraining programmes are among the best in West Germany, women enjoy only limited opportunities to utilise retraining chances and turn them into managerial advancement. The company insists that staff do not rise within the same store or in the same locality from intermediate to top positions. The mobility which is a prerequisite for rising into the top management through *Weiterbildung* and further training does not appear to be a deterrent for men, but it is a deterrent for women, and few are able to move. The only area where women have a firm foothold on the managerial path is the area of training and retraining itself – here the majority of top personnel are women.[1] It has been amply demonstrated that men continue to dominate leadership and management positions (Bernadoni and Werner 1987). In West Germany, the majority of women managing directors are, in fact, controlling firms owned by their families (Kehrmann Institute 1985; Deutsche Bank, *Bulletin*, December 1986).

New Technologies and Reduced Opportunities

In the contemporary working environment, women are doubly disadvantaged. The first disadvantage is one of qualification. Women have frequently trained in areas which are declining,

1. This information was obtained from the Personnel Manager and Manager of the Training/Retraining Department of Karstadt (Hanover) during a working visit in December 1988, within the framework of the European Community Programme for Experts in Vocational Training.

and their working skills are under threat from new technologies or are becoming less central to the economic activities of the future. The second disadvantage is one of opportunity to keep pace with change and to enhance qualifications during a working life through *Weiterbildung*. Gaining access to retraining and additional qualification measures has been difficult for women partly because measures were not on offer or they could not be combined with family and other calls on women's time. There is also the problem that the linkage between taking part in *Weiterbildung* and promotion chances is uncertain for women – those in part-time employment are unlikely to gain promotion, and those in full-time employment may not be able to meet the conditions of promotion, such as geographical mobility. The uneven effect of updating and enhancement of qualifications on the opportunities for women in employment continues a pattern which is already apparent in the implementation of new technologies themselves. A study of new technologies in administrative processes found that half the men engaged in administration had a computer on their desk or a terminal accessible in their own personal office; women who on paper held equivalent positions enjoyed less convenient access to computers, and only 25% used computers to conduct their administrative tasks (Krebsbach-Gnath 1983; 1985). A similar result emerged from a review of employment in data processing: in 1986, four times as many men as women were employed in data processing; more men than women held university degrees or vocational qualifications; conversely, more women than men held no formal qualifications at all. Although all these women were actually employed in data processing and seemed to have made the step from a pre-technological to a new-technology working environment, the majority were employed in the least skilled segments of the occupational field (Drostal 1987: 7).

In short, women have fallen behind in the scramble to utilise new technology. For the majority, the new processes of production or work organisation have not enhanced the working environment or fostered career chances; in fact, many women experience new technologies negatively as a deterioration in their working environments or relative qualifications. In the early Eighties, the Batelle Institute survey on new technologies compared how men and women perceived the changes in their

171

working environment. As could be expected from the previous discussion, twice as many men as women in the companies which were evaluated in the study had used new technologies, and for men, the experiences with these technologies seemed to be more encouraging than for women (Table 5.8). One out of three men, but only one out of twenty women who were working with new technologies rated their effects positively. The majority of men also remained sceptical and stressed negative effect but among women an overwhelming 95% rated the changes as mostly negative. Since 1970, women's views had mellowed a little but had in essence remained the same.

As we have seen, the changes brought about by technological innovation have not benefited the majority of working women; women's employment with its slant towards giving assistance/ services and away from planning or control lends itself to being bypassed by new technologies, or indeed challenged in its very existence; and women themselves have been reluctant converts to the new processes and procedures they would have to acquire. Together, these factors have conspired to place women at a disadvantage in the contemporary working environment with its new technologies and skill requirements; they also appear to conspire to make women less adaptable in developing the leadership skills, planning qualities or technical competence which will dominate the working environment of the future. The full force of these changes has only come into the open in the Seventies. Their detrimental effects on the employment status of women were partly hidden as long as women could move easily from the production sector to the tertiary sector, which offered additional openings until recently. The strong position of women in white-collar employment seemed to put women in line for the tasks and functions which would be needed in the year 2000. However, with office-based work, information processing and the various service tasks undergoing a technological reorientation, women are again losing their foothold. This time, employment in established sectors of the economy is no longer on offer. Employment prospects for women, therefore, have taken two distinct directions: the first can be called a retrogressive step in modern disguise. The computer, it has been argued, makes an excellent home-based work station and the woman of the future will work from home, processing information and

Table 5.8 New technologies: views of their impact among men and women. Question to men and women working with new technologies: how has your work been affected by new technologies?

Type of impact	Women (1970) %	Women (1980) %	Men (1980) %
More positive than negative	4	3	29
Both negative and positive	1	1	6
More negative than positive	49	54	37
Only negative	46	42	28
Respondents overall (N)	6,228	6,570	13,451

Source: Camilla Krebsbach-Gnath et al., *Frauenbeschäftigung und neue Technologien*. Munich: Batelle Institute, 1983: 216.

conducting operations in her own time and environment for her distant employer or company (Klug et al. 1987). The three Ks of the twenty-first century, *Kinder, Küche, Komputer*, could resurrect the isolation, comparatively low pay and marginal status of the traditional outworker. Such developments do not appear to match the educational and vocational motivation of contemporary women, nor their qualifications or abilities. Being a hi-tech outworker is, however, a real possibility women will have to face and cope with in the future.

The second development in the wake of new technology concerns the rise in part-time working in tertiary occupations, with women employed to fill 'gaps in the technology' in jobs which are likely to disappear as soon as the bit of missing technology has been installed, or changes in production or labour processes remove the need for a gap-filler (Stooß and Troll 1982: 180; Büchtemann et al. 1986). The West German labour market response to new technologies and the accelerated entry of women into that market have tended to push women into the cul-de-sac of low skills, of support functions and of jobs without prospects of advancement. In the past, the qualification deficit of West German working women may have made women a ready target for such a *de facto* demotion; the entry of young, well qualified women with a strong vocational motivation should constitute a better safeguard of women's opportunities at work in the future. The best safeguard, however, appears to be the projected skill shortage in the 1990s and beyond. It has been suggested that the entry of the *Pillenknick* generations into the labour market will bring a reduction of the potential work-force by over 500,000. Assuming that the demand for labour and expertise has not been decimated by new technologies, ample opportunities should exist for experts of either gender, provided their expertise is geared to the tasks of the future.

Part-Time Working – Exploitation or Emancipation?

In the Seventies, part-time employment was the fastest growing sector of the labour market with an expansion rate of over 40%. In the Eighties, growth of the part-time positions on offer has slowed down to about 13%. Compared with the early Sixties, part-time employment has more than trebled from around one million to well over 3 million. In 1987, some 15% of the labour force were in part-time employment. Essentially, part-time working is a woman's domain; today, one in three women in paid employment are working part-time and nearly nine out of every ten part-timers are women. Despite such a sizeable segment of part-timers in the female labour force, demand is considerably larger than the number of part-time positions on offer. In February 1987, for instance, over 200,000 people were registered as unemployed and seeking part-time employment while the Federal Employment Office had only 17,000 part-time positions on its books. The so-called silent reserve – *Stille Reserve* – is even larger. These are women who are not registered as unemployed, and do not appear in the statistics but are looking for part-time work. Three in four women who wish to return after a career break would prefer to work part-time. In addition, over half the women who were in full-time work in the mid-Eighties would rather have worked part-time (Jenkins 1984: 208). This *Stille Reserve* of part-timers has been estimated at 700,000 people, most of them women. Surveys on work satisfaction also indicate that women working part-time tend to be more contented with their work than women in full-time employment. In short, part-time employment seems to be popular with West German women, demand for this type of employment has remained high, and women have such a dominant stake in this area that it can be regarded as a major sector of their world of work.

Part-time working has, of course, always had a place in the employment of women. Home helps, cleaners, seasonal or hourly shop workers were well established before the expansion of the sector in the Seventies. The traditional part-time position has been at the unskilled end of the labour market with corresponding low pay and status. The influx of part-timers into employment since the Seventies has not altered this situation fundamentally, but has wrought some interesting shifts in the qualification and status structure of the part-time labour force. The tertiary sector has consolidated its position as the major area for part-time staff, and the employment structure for part-timers is similar to that of all working women: just over 70% in services and trade, just over 20% in industry, and the remainder in agriculture and related fields.

Table 5.9 presents an overview of the complex pattern of part-time and full-time working in the various sectors of the economy. Part-time working is a women's realm in two ways: the shorter the weekly hours, the higher the proportion of women at work in that category. Nine out of ten people who work less than twenty-one hours per week are women. These types of part-time job are most commonly found in agriculture or in the services sector and are less numerous in manufacturing. The majority of women here work a regular full-time week; women who work full-time work on average longer hours than in the other two sectors. Table 5.9 also shows that the services sector is by far the largest with 2.3 million women working part-time and 4.6 million full-time out of a total workforce of just over 10 million.

If we look at the occupational fields for the part-time employment of women, some have been familiar for generations: barmaids, seamstresses, shop assistants. However, important new opportunities have also arisen outside traditional part-time areas, in fields which require higher qualifications or are within the professional range (see Appendix V). Today, nearly four in ten female teachers in primary schools are working part-time; so are half the women employed as accountants. These openings would not have existed in the Fifties and Sixties, when part-time professional posts were not on offer.

The growth of part-time work has, on the whole, accom-

Table 5.9 Women at work by sectors of the economy and working hours, 1984

Weekly hours	Workforce %	Women (in 1000s)	Women in pt/ft workforce %	Women employed in: Agriculture %	Manufacturing %	Others[a] %
Part-time employment						
Under 21	7	18	91	19	13	19
21–30	5	11	88	13	10	12
31–35	1	2	74	4	2	2
All part-time	14	31	88	36	25	33
Total part-time (in 1,000s)	3,600	3,200	—	240	660	2,300
Full-time employment						
36–41	72	59	31	15	71	58
Over 41	15	11	26	49	4	9
All full-time	86	69	30	64	75	67
Total full-time (in 1,000s)	23,000	7,000	—	430	1,950	4,620

[a] Including distributive trades, transport and telecommunications.
Source: Adapted from *Wirtschaft und Statistik* 7, 1986: 490.

Table 5.10 Part-time employment of women by size of enterprise

Size of enterprise	% of women in part-time employment
Large companies (labour force of 100 +)	26
among these, very large companies with labour force of 1,000 or more	(17)
Small and medium-sized companies (labour force up to 99)	74
among these, small firms in the tertiary sector	(41)
Part-time employment (all companies)	100

Source: From Bundesinstitut für Berufsbildung/Institut für Arbeitsmarkt- und Berufsforschung Study of Part-time Working, in *Quintessenzen aus der Arbeitsmarkt- und Berufsforschung* (*QuintAB*) 4, 1984: 30.

panied rather than changed the structure of female employment. It is concentrated in the same few occupations, the majority in the services sector. One other aspect, however, should be highlighted. Part-time employment has been concentrated in small or medium-sized firms with a labour force of less than one hundred people. Three in four part-timers work in such small enterprises; the remainder in larger companies (Table 5.10). While smaller firms provide opportunities for women to take on part-time work and thus play a positive role in the contemporary business environment, working conditions in such companies are frequently less favourable than in larger ones. These conditions can include the usage of up-to-date equipment, machinery and technologies and also cover working hours and general working conditions or benefits. The woman who works at peak times in a supermarket may learn to operate an electronic cash register, and gain some familiarity with advanced technology in retailing. The woman who works part-time in a corner shop will normally use out-of-date equipment and experience a working environment which does not equip her to adapt to new labour processes and skill requirements in her field. Part-timers in small companies and businesses are in danger of falling behind in their potential qualifications, since their working environment is itself outdated. The advantage that small businesses provide opportunities for part-time work (which is, as we have seen, very much sought after) has to be balanced against the disadvantage that part-timers do not enjoy job security, and those in small companies even lack access to the social benefits which are commonplace in larger firms and range from the works canteen to discounts, preferential share holdings or access to leisure facilities, to name just a few of the different possibilities for enhancing the working environment. None of those can be provided in the small company to cushion the risk which all part-timers run: of being rapidly dismissed when markets fluctuate or business policy reduces the demand for labour.

Despite its popularity with women, part-time working has not enhanced anything but the quick-and-ready opportunity to earn some money. On the ambitious level of employing women in line with their qualifications and potential, and rewarding them with job security, promotion chances and substantive opportunities of equal employment, part-time working has been a hindrance rather than an asset in the search for equality. It has consolidated the gender gap in the labour market, and the position of women at the less favoured end as far as status, prospects, and pay are concerned. Compared with their part-time sisters, women in full-time employment are on average better educated and qualified, more likely to use their specialist training in their work and less likely to change their work-place or lose their jobs.

Part-Time Working and Job Security

To understand fully the element of insecurity connected with part-time working, we have to look more closely at the working hours themselves. Table 5.9 listed the distribution of part-time and full-time working in the Eighties. Within the part-time bracket, i.e. a working week of less than thirty-six hours, the significant divide is at twenty-one hours. Anybody who works more than this number of hours enjoys similar benefits to those of a full-time person: health insurance, unemployment insurance, pension scheme; anybody who works less than twenty-one hours does not. With more than half the part-time women working less than twenty-one weekly hours, the implications of the two modes of part-time working are worth exploring (see Table 5.11).

For part-timers who work more than twenty hours per week, the only major difference is that most of them are employed in the tertiary sector, in particular in distributive trades and basic office work. According to West German labour legislation, part-timers of this category are liable to full National Insurance payments, and are in turn eligible to receive benefits in the case of unemployment. The second type of part-time work is called *geringfügige Beschäftigung*, 'minor employment' in the bureaucratic language of the West German labour administration. It comprises all work of less than twenty weekly hours. People in this category are exempt from National Insurance payments and are, in turn, not eligible to receive unemployment benefit. How many women are employed in this manner is impossible to estimate. The figures which we do have – 18% of the female labour force, and over half of all women in part-time employment – are too low, since this kind of work does not have to be registered with the Federal Employment Office and working agreements are often too informal to be listed in statistics. Minor employment, then, is an important mode of female employment (Brinkmann and Köhler 1981).

A comparison of full-time employment with different types of part-time working shows the generally negative social effects of minor employment (synopsis: Table 5.11). The majority òf women in this kind of employment belong to socially weak groups. They are either very young (with small children) or over sixty years old; in both cases they appear to work to make ends meet and alleviate financial hardship. For older women, it is often a case of supplementing an inadequately low pension; for the young woman with small children it is an attempt to combat the drop in living standards which hits young families, or else these women are single parents who are living on the poverty line. Women in minor employment tend to live in larger than average households, and their educational and vocational standards are lower than in the other two employment groups. They frequently work outside their vocational/professional expertise in unskilled or semi-skilled positions, normally at the lowest end of the spectrum, and tend to move in and out of unemployment and jobs (Landenberger 1987: 19). Minor employment

Table 5.11 Structural differences between women working full-time, part-time and in minor employment

Personal and occupational characteristics	Women working full-time (A)	Women working part-time (B)	Women in minor or temporary work
Age	Concentration between 20 and 30	Concentration between 30 and 50	As for B, but also under 30/over 60s
Marital status	About half married; often single/divorced	Mostly married	Predominantly married; some single or widowed
Size of family	Often 1–2 person family; frequently no children under 16	Often 3 and more persons in family; and children under 16	Mostly 3 or more person families; highest proportion of children under 16
Education/training (qualified)	50% *Mittlere Reife* and above; only 20% no vocational qualifications	Only 35% *Mittlere Reife* and above; 30% no vocational qualifications	Only 30% *Mittlere Reife* or higher; 70% basic schooling; 50% unqualified
Work in the area of qualified training	About 50% work in occupation for which they are qualified	Less than 50% work in occupation for which they are qualified	Only 25% in work for which they are qualified; 75% in work for which not trained
Task performed	Often qualified manual admin. or service functions	Basic sales and services	Mostly unskilled sales, services

Economic area	Often in production/ industry	Mostly in trade, manufacturing	Frequently in catering, laundries, cleaning, and service organisations
Duration of employment with present employer	Long duration of employment	As for A	Mostly short duration
Change of employer	Rarely	As for A	More frequently
Unemployment in previous year (1983)	Rarely	As for A	About 10%
Change of working time in previous year	Hardly	Frequent change between full-time and part-time working	Frequent change between minor employment, non-working and unemployment
Gross pay (blue-collar and basic white-collar)	About DM 10.50	About DM 10.50	About DM 9.50
National Insurance contributions	Full National Insurance	In most cases National Insurance	60% no National Insurance

Source: M. Landenberger in *Aus Politik und Zeitgeschichte* B 21, 1987: 18.

reinforces the low status of women in the occupational hierarchy; it also appears to reinforce the bunching in a narrow band of clerical or retailing jobs. Regardless of the role such employment may play for the individual, in a broader perspective it hampers the mobilisation in the labour market which one might expect as a result of the improved standards of education and training among the younger generation women.

Part-time working rarely creates opportunities; rather it appears to decrease them and reduce the competitive edge of women's qualifications and employment potential. A 1979 survey on part-time working found that the majority of women had to accept downward occupational mobility (58%). Of those who had completed vocational training, 30% could use it, 40% could not (Beitr.AB 70, 1979). More than half who had trained for administrative or clerical occupations performed unskilled or semi-skilled manual work; a similar proportion of women who had learned a trade were employed as part-time labourers. In some cases, mobility had been upward, from blue-collar to white-collar work, from clerical white-collar to managerial work. On the whole, however, the adjustment process has been downhill; the part-time work which women were able to find was in most cases below their qualifications and expertise.

Exploitation or Opportunity?

Given the doubtful benefits and certain disadvantages of part-time working, it may seem surprising that demand for it is so high and also that women who work part-time are, on the whole, satisfied with their work. One reason for this satisfaction may be circumstantial: at a time of high unemployment and an acute shortage of part-time work the fact that a woman has secured a part-time position at all seems more important than the occupational status or equality of opportunities it promises in the long run. Many women who take on part-time work have already accepted that their vocational expertise and their employment may not match, let alone be enhanced through working. Part-time employment tends to be taken on by women with families and children, whose private duties militate against full-time employment and for whom some employment seems better than nothing; the other group of women to opt for part-time working are those who return into the labour market after a career break. Having already interrupted their vocational qualifications they lost skills by default and have adjusted their expectations downwards. Without special retraining and pre-paratory measures they are normally unable to return to their original job and a part-time job is experienced not as a de-motion, but as a welcome entry point into the labour market.

A further reason for women to take on part-time work, even if it involves a vocational or professional demotion, relates to the social legislation on National Insurance payments and pension rights. Employment has been the major means of accumulating an entitlement to a state pension. Although the Conservative/ Liberal government introduced some pension rights for mothers who gave up their previous employment to look full-time after their children (see Chapter 3), up to 1986 the only avenue to a pension was employment. In order to qualify for full retirement pay, men or women have to contribute National Insurance payments, i.e. be in employment, for at least twenty-six years. Part-timers would have to work for the same number of years, although they will only be entitled to a proportion of a full pension in accordance with their weekly working hours. Women who attempt to accumulate their own pension rights in addition to those of their husbands, or because they are not insured via a husband, have to look to the labour market to do so (Landenberger 1985). The well-off can make voluntary contri-butions to National Insurance and build up pension entitle-ments provided that the woman or man, as the case may be, has been in paid employment in the past. The majority of West German women, however, rely on employment to gain their own pension entitlements. Part-time work of twenty or more hours per week can play a major role here since it involves National Insurance payments and can thus prepare the ground for future pension rights. As an additional avenue to securing reasonable provision in old age for women, part-time working is all the more important since pension entitlements at present are quite inadequate. In 1986, many widows received such low pensions that they had to depend on social security payments to reach the stipulated minimum income; pensions paid to women have been on average one-third lower than those paid to men (Landenberger 1987: 24). In this perspective, part-time working is a device used by women to plan for the twenty years or so after retirement which they can now expect to live. The immediate job status or career prospects of their employment appear to be less decisive in their choice of work and the satisfaction with it than the longer-term view towards a reasonable standard of living in the closing years of life.

Women in part-time work have not perceived their socio-economic position as disadvantaged. The main source of discontent concerns the distribution of working hours rather than the more fundamental issues of women's equality, opportunities and expertise. In evaluating the socio-economic function of part-time working, personal perceptions can only provide guidance, not analysis or answers. If we broaden the frame of reference and assess the role of part-time work in the contemporary economic environment, its impact on the position of women is less clear-cut. With its proliferation of low-skilled and unskilled clerical tasks, personal services or domestic support work, part-time employment underpins the negative tendencies already observed in the impact of new technologies. Women are channelled into the auxiliary positions in the labour market, and the promise of their vocational motivation and potential remains largely untapped. Can we, therefore, conclude with the critics of part-time working that the motivation of women to keep at least one foot in the door of the labour market makes them victims of modern exploitation? As part-timers, they enjoy no protection against dismissals; they are pushed to top productivity at minimum pay; theirs are the most monotonous tasks. More than the full-time worker, and similar perhaps to the factory hand during the first industrialisation, they seem to be at the mercy of their employer, without codified rights, without protection and without prospects (e.g. Gewerkschaft Handel, Banken und Versicherungen (HBV) 1982). Or is part-time working, as its advocates would maintain, an essential device to tap fully the resources of expertise in a society? Since part-time work is timed to meet peak demands, or to perform specific tasks, it is regarded as efficient and cost-effective for the employer, and as essentially satisfying for the employee (Hoff 1985). Moves to divide full-time positions between part-timers in job-sharing agreements are unlikely to be adopted as the model of the future. It was proposed by the government and also tested by some companies in order to meet the demand for part-time work without losing the continuity and responsibility embodied in full-time appointments.

Job-sharing and similar proposals of adjusting the working mode may never advance beyond an experimental stage. They point, however, to an important mobilisation of traditional role patterns and values. Society, politicians and institutions are beginning to respond to the expectations of West German women of the younger generation that their lives can be many-faceted, i.e. embrace homemaking, child-bearing, work, careers all at once or in sequences, depending on individual choice and socio-economic opportunity. The either/or prescriptions for home and work, for careers and motherhood, have been modi-fied and at times discarded by a multi-faceted approach whose dominant motives are choice and individuality. The reality of part-time working in West Germany, however, is one of lingering disadvantages which obstruct such a multi-faceted mode of living according to a woman's own choice and personal opportunities.

Part-Time Working and Women's Pay

The effects of part-time employment on women's pay and potential equality in the labour market is another such disadvan-tage. When West German labour legislation decreed in the Fifties that lower rates of pay for women contravened the spirit of the constitution, the principle of equality was accepted in law but did not prevail in the everyday working environment (Deutschmann et al. 1983). West German rates of pay are finely tuned to the exact tasks and duties of each post. Salaries or wages are determined by the nature of an appointment and its classification in a sliding scale from hard or essential to light or preparatory work. Women tend to occupy the work-places which attract lower pay. In manufacturing industry, for in-stance, women's wages amount to around 60% of men's. They have increased since the early Sixties and the gap has narrowed as women have bettered their pay from 65% to 72% of that earned by men (*QuintAB* 4, 1984: 33). A gap, however, does remain. It is largest in agricultural work and smallest in manu-facturing. In 1982, the income of women in agricultural employ-ment was only 40% of that earned by men in this sector. Even in

Table 5.12 Women's monthly income as a percentage of men's
income[a] (1982)

Occupation	Average income (in DM)		B as % of A
	(A) Men	(B) Women	
Farming/horticulture/forestry	1,367	540	40
Manufacturing/production	1,664	1,019	61
Technical occupations	2,415	1,327	55
Service sector occupations	2,052	1,200	59

[a]Men and women in paid employment: excluding self-employed and unemployed.
Source: QuintAB 4, 1984.

technical employment, women earn only 55% of men's salaries
on average (Table 5.12).

Generally speaking, men are concentrated in the upper half of
the income spectrum, women in the lower half. As already
mentioned, the discrepancies have decreased and women's pay
is closer to that of men today than it has ever been. However,
the differences have not gone away. In 1986, 80% of women at
work or in training earned less than DM1,800 take-home pay per
month; so did 37% of men (Table 5.13). Among men, the
majority of those with the lowest incomes were in vocational or
professional training; among women, the numbers in the lowest
income bracket were swollen by women who were in employment, most of them part-time. Part-time employment plays an
important role in depressing women's average incomes. A
survey conducted by the Organisation for Economic Cooperation and Development (OECD) in 1984 concluded that a deficit
in qualifications or work experience due to career breaks might
have a detrimental effect on women's earnings, but the main
reason for their lower income was the proliferation of part-time
working (OECD 1984; *Wirtschaft und Statistik* 7, 1986: 494). Currently, part-time working and low monthly income are closely
linked. However, a new type of part-timer is slowly emerging.
The statistical data for 1986 suggest that some top earners with a
take-home pay of over DM4,000 per month work part-time or
are in training: one in four top-earning men and one in three of
the few top-earning women. Here, it seems, can we find the
qualified expert, the career-orientated woman of the future who

Table 5.13 Monthly net incomes of men and women in paid
employment[a] (April 1986)

Monthly income in Deutschmark	Men %	Women %	All employed %
Under 600	7	16	11
600 – under 800	2	9	4
800 – under 1,000	2	11	5
1,000 – under 1,200	2	12	6
1,200 – under 1,400	4	11	7
1,400 – under 1,800	19	20	19
1,800 – under 2,200	25	12	20
2,200 – under 2,500	11	3	8
2,500 – under 3,000	10	3	7
3,000 – under 4,000	10	3	7
4,000 and over	9	1	6
Subtotals			
Under 1,800	36	79	53
Over 1,800	64	21	47
Top earners (over 3,000)	19	4	13

[a] Data include self-employed but exclude unemployed.

Source: Statistisches Jahrbuch für die Bundesrepublik Deutschland, Mainz: Kohlhammer, 1988: 102

is in managerial training, consultancy or employed in a professional capacity – capable of competing in the top salary bracket, but doing so part-time. Among men, many of the top-earning part-timers may be retired experts selling their know-how; among women one would expect to find the highly trained expert who is working part-time in her dual capacity as a working woman and as a family woman and part-time homemaker.

As well-qualified women enter the labour market in increasing numbers, and bring with them the expectation that their qualifications should be utilised in their work, the face of part-time employment seems set to change. Their motivation to obtain and update qualifications in order to meet the changing demands and developments in the contemporary working environment can be expected to change the quality and status of some part-time work itself. Already, part-time women professionals have come to the fore in accountancy, in teaching, in medicine and other fields. However, in most part-time working the traditional place of women at the bottom end of the labour market in terms of skills, managerial functions, pay and job security has remained sharply evident.

References

Aleman, Ulrich and Heribert von Schatz (eds), *Mensch und Technik. Grundlagen und Perspektiven einer sozialverträglichen Technikgestaltung*, Opladen: Westdeutscher Verlag, 1987

Baethge, Martin et al., *Zukunft der Angestellten*, Göttingen: Sozialwissenschaftliches Forschungsinstitut (SOFI), 1984

Baethge, Martin and Heribert Oberbeck, *Zukunft der Angestellten. Neue Technologien und berufliche Perspektiven in Büro und Verwaltung*, Frankfurt: Campus, 1986

Bednarz-Braun, Ines, *Arbeiterinnen in der Elektorindustrie. Zu den Bedingungen von Anlernung und Arbeit an gewerblich-technischen Arbeitsplätzen für Frauen*, Munich: Deutsches Jugendinstitut, 1984

Bernadoni, Claudia and Vera Werner, *Ohne Seil und Haken. Frauen auf dem Weg nach oben*, Munich: Saur, 1987

Bolte, Karl Martin and Hans Büttner (eds), Arbeitskräftestruktur 2000, *Mitteilungen auf der Arbeitsmarkt- und Berufsforschung 1*, Stuttgart: Kohlhammer, 1986

Boss, Alfred, 'Die Erwerbstätigkeit verheirateter Frauen in der Bundesrepublik', in Wolfgang Klauder and Gerhard Kühlewind (eds), *Probleme der Messung und Vorausschätzung des Frauenerwerbspotentials* (BeitrAB 56, pp. 69–81), Nuremberg, 1981

Brinkmann, Christoph and Hans Köhler, *Am Rande der Erwerbsbeteiligung: Frauen mit geringsfügiger, gelegentlicher und befristeter Arbeit*, Beiträge aus der Arbeitsmarkt- und Berufsforschung 56, Nuremberg, 1981

Büchtemann, Christian et. al., *Zur Sozio-Ökonomie der Teilzeitbeschäftigung in der Bundesrepublik Deutschland*, Discussion Paper IIM-LMP 86–165, Berlin: Wissenschaftszentrum für Sozialforschung, 1986

Dahrendorf, Ralf, *Society and Democracy in Germany*, London: Weidenfeld and Nicolson, 1967

Datenreport, ed. Statistisches Bundesamt, Bonn: Bundeszentrale für politische Bildung, 1987

Deutscher Gewerkschaftsbund, 'Fragen der CDU/Antworten des DGB', in *Frauenbeschäftigung und neue Technologien* (pp. 220–41), Bonn: CDU Bundesgeschäftsstelle, 1985

Deutschmann, Christoph et al., *Lohnentwicklung in der Bundesrepublik 1960–1978*, Frankfurt: Campus, 1983

Dobberthien, Marliese et al., *Frauen und neue Technologien*, Hanover: Landeszentrale für politische Bildung, 1986

Drostal, Werner, 'Mit Schirm, Chip und Konsole. Die Datenverarbeiter', *Materialien aus der Arbeitsmarkt- und Berufsforschung* 6, Nuremberg, 1987

Familie und Arbeitswelt, Schriftenreihe des Bundesministers für Jugend, Familie und Gesundheit vol. 143, Stuttgart: Kohlhammer, 1984

Frauenbeschäftigung und neue Technologien (Schriftliche Stellungnahmen zum Hearing der CDU am 29. Jan. 1985), ed. CDU Bundesgeschäftsstelle, Bonn, 1985

Gewerkschaft Handel, Banken und Versicherungen (HBV) (ed.), *Arbeitsheft Teilzeitarbeit. Nicht nur ein Problem für Frauen*, Düsseldorf, 1982.

Hegelheimer, Barbara, *In-firm Training and Career Prospects for Women in the Federal Republic of Germany*, Berlin: European Centre for the Development of Vocational Training (CEDEFOP), 1981

Hellmich, Andrea, *Frauen zwischen Familie und Beruf*, Schriftenreihe des Bundesministers für Jugend, Familie, Frauen und Gesundheit vol. 184, Stuttgart: Kohlhammer, 1986

Hofbauer, Hans, 'Zum Erwerbsverhalten verheirateter Frauen', *Mitteilungen aus der Arbeitsmarkt- und Berufsforschung* 2, Nuremberg, 1979

Hoff, Andreas et al., *Handbuch Teilzeitarbeit*, Forschungsbericht 127. Berlin: Der Bundesminister für Arbeit und Sozialordnung, 1985

Jenkins, Eva, 'Teilzeitarbeit: Eine Sackgasse', in Gerlinde Seidenspinner et al., *Vom Nutzen weiblicher Lohnarbeit*, Opladen: Leske & Budrich, 1984

Kehrmann Institute, unpublished report; summary of results in *Frankfurter Allgemeine Zeitung*, 18 April 1985

Kern, Horst and Michael Schumann, *Das Ende der Arbeitsteilung? Rationalisierung der industriellen Produktion*, Munich: Beck, 1984

Klauder, Wolfgang and Gerhard Kühlewind (eds), *Probleme der Messung und Vorausschätzung des Frauenerwerbspotentials* (BeitrAB 56), Institut für Arbeitsmarkt- und Berufsforschung, Nuremberg, 1981

Klug, Gabriele C. et al., *Teleheimarbeit. Chancen oder Risiken für die Frauenerwerbstätigkeit in Hessen*, ed. Der Bevollmächtigte der Hessischen Landesregierung für Frauenangelegenheiten, Wiesbaden, 1987

Krebsbach-Gnath, Camilla, 'Frauenbeschäftigung und neue Technologien', in *Frauenbeschäftigung und neue Technologien* (pp. 43–58), Bonn, 1985

—— and Ina Schmid-Jörg, *Wissenschaftliche Begleituntersuchung zu Frauenförderungsmaßnahmen*, Schriftenreihe des BMJFG, Bonn, 1985

—— et al., *Frauenbeschäftigung und neue Technologien*, Munich: Batelle Institut, 1983

Landenberger, Margarete, 'Aktuelle sozialversicherungsrechtliche Fragen zur flexiblen Arbeitszeit und Teilzeitbeschäftigung', *Zeitschrift für Sozialreform* 6, 1985: 321–36; 7, 1985: 393–415

——, 'Flexible Arbeitszeitformen im Spannungsfeld von ökonomischer Liberalisierung und sozialem Schutzbedarf', *Aus Politik und Zeitgeschichte* B 21, 1987

Lane, Christel, 'Industrial Change in the 1980s in West Germany and Britain'. Paper delivered at the Labour Process Conference, Aston University, 23 March 1988 (mimeo)

Mendius, Hans-Gerd et al., *Qualifizierung im Betrieb als Instrument der öffentlichen Arbeitsmarktpolitik* (Institut für Sozialwissenschaftliche Forschung, Munich), ed. Bundesminister für Arbeit und Sozialordnung, Bonn, 1983

Müller, Walter, *Strukturwandel der Frauenarbeit*, Frankfurt: Campus, 1980

——, 'Wege und Grenzen der Tertiarisierung', in Joachim Matthes (ed.), *Krise der Arbeitsgesellschaft?* Frankfurt: Campus, 1983

Myrdal, Alva and Viola Klein, *Women's Two Roles*, London: Routledge & Kegan Paul, 1956

OECD (ed.), *Working Party on the Role of Women in the Economy*, Paris, 1984

Rothkirch, Christoph and Inge von Weidig, *Die Zukunft der Arbeitslandschaft. Zum Arbeitskräftebedarf nach Umfang und Tätigkeiten bis zum Jahr 2000*, Beiträge aus der Arbeitsmarkt- und Berufsforschung 94.1 and 94.2, Nuremberg, 1986

——, *Zum Arbeitskräftebedarf nach Qualifikationen bis zum Jahr 2000*, Beiträge aus der Arbeitsmarkt- und Berufsforschung 95, Nuremberg, 1986

Scharfenberg, Günter, *Die technologische Revolution. Wirtschaftliche, soziale und politische Fragen*, Berlin: Landeszentrale für politische Bildung, 1986

Schwuchow, Karola, 'Frauenbeschäftigung und neue Technologie – bezogen auf die Deutsche Bundespost', in *Frauenbeschäftigung und neue Technologien* (pp. 243–53), Bonn, 1985

Steppke, Gisela, *Geschlechtszugehörigkeit und Interessenlage*, Doctoral Dissertation, Free University Berlin, 1980

Stooß, Friedemann, 'Wirkungen moderner Bürotechnik auf kaufmännische Berufe', *Materialien aus der Arbeitsmarkt- und Berufsfor-*

schung 8, Nuremberg, 1987

—— and Lothar Troll, 'Die Verbreitung programmgesteuerter Arbeitsmittel', Mitteilungen aus der Arbeitsmarkt- und Berufsforschung 15, Nuremberg, 1982

——, Lothar Troll and Hasso von Henninges, 'Blick hinter den Bildschirm. Neue Technologien verändern die Arbeitslandschaft', *Materialien aus der Arbeitsmarkt- und Berufsforschung* 1, Nuremberg, 1988

Stutenbäumer-Hübner, Annette, 'Femmes au travail en RFA', *Allemagnes d'aujourd'hui* 101, 1987

Troll, Lothar, 'Büroberufe im Wandel', *Materialien aus der Arbeitsmarkt- und Berufsforschung* 1, Nuremberg, 1984

Volkholz, Volker, *Frauenerwerbsarbeit im Jahr 2000*, Dortmund, 1987 (Unpublished expert report) (Gesellschaft für Arbeitsschutz und Humanisierungsforschung)

Willms-Herget, Angelika, *Frauenarbeit. Zur Integration der Frauen in den Arbeitsmarkt*, Frankfurt: Campus, 1987

'Zur Stellung der Frau in der Wirtschaft', *Wirtschaft und Statistik* 7, 1986: 489–99.

6
Women and Politics
in West Germany

The changes in the educational, vocational and occupational position of women and the changing expectations about personal lifestyles and the balance between homemaking, motherhood, and work have also had repercussions on the role of women in the political life of West Germany. The gender gap of disinterest, apathy and non-participation which seemed to make men the political sex and women the non-political bystanders has narrowed significantly. West German women turn out to vote in greater numbers today than in the founding years of the Federal Republic, and women have altered their electoral preferences to such an extent that they may be regarded as potential kingmakers in a political system where a small shift in the vote can demote a governing party to the opposition benches (Smith 1986; Padgett and Burkett 1987). Today, the agendas of all political parties have to address themselves to women voters and their expectations of equal opportunities. In the Eighties, parties have even been challenged into rethinking their practice of representation as women demanded better access to parliamentary seats and to decision-making bodies in the party organisations. The 'end of modesty'[1] points to a new assertiveness among politically motivated women who seem set to dismantle the traditional men's advantage in politics and reach for positions of responsibility and leadership. In this chapter, I shall trace the patterns of participation in elections, party organisations and parliaments and evaluate the extent to which the new emphasis on women's opportunities reduced the gender gap in contemporary political life.

---

1. *Das Ende der Bescheidenheit*. This phrase was coined by the Greens and used for their women's campaign after 1985.

Table 6.1 Electoral turnout of men and women, 1953–1987 (in %)

Elections	Turnout overall	Men	Women	Gender gap
1953	86.3	88.0	84.9	–3.1
1957	87.8	89.6	86.2	–3.4
1961	87.4	88.9	86.2	–2.7
1965	85.9	87.5	84.6	–2.9
1969	86.1	87.5	84.9	–2.6
1972	90.8	91.4	90.2	–1.1
1976	90.4	90.8	90.0	–0.8
1980	87.6	88.2	87.1	–1.1
1983	88.4	89.1	87.8	–1.3
1987	83.3	84.2	82.1	–2.1

Source: Compiled from *Repräsentative Wahlstatistik*, Wiesbaden, 1953 and ff.

Turning Out to Vote

In West Germany, voting is easily the most popular mode of political participation. Since the Federal Republic was founded, turnout in national elections has been well over 80% and at times around 90% (Table 6.1). Before looking at the voting as a mode of political participation among West German women, voting itself has to be discussed in its wider political context. Going to vote has a long tradition in German political culture. Even in the troubled years of the Weimar Republic and in Imperial Germany, close to 80% of the electorate tended to cast their vote (Falter et al. 1986). In the contemporary setting electoral turnout draws on two currents of motivation. On the one hand, elections have been regarded as the duty of the citizen *vis-à-vis* the state (Edinger 1986). That voters in West Germany have to present their identity cards before casting their vote has tended to underpin the semi-official status of voting. In this light, the high turnout would indicate that West Germans, as their forebears in non-democratic political environments, are willing to do what is expected of them. There is, however, another aspect: since the foundation of the West German state voting has emerged as a core element of democratic political behaviour. Voting allows the citizens to articulate preferences and influence the polity. It is perceived as an act of participation and a chance to bring individual influence to bear, while fewer

193

people perceive voting as, above all, an act of obedience to the powers-that-be.

Voting in West Germany is increasingly seen and valued as an opportunity to choose, an opportunity which also includes the choice not to vote (Jesse 1988; Klingemann and Kaase 1986). A number of social and economic factors come together to explain this change in expectations and attitudes. The post-war generations have been brought up to know and also to accept the principles and the institutions of democratic politics, including the place of the citizen in the overall process of representative government (Hoffmann-Lange 1987). The relative affluence and the educational mobilisation discussed earlier have mellowed class divides and produced a new confidence in the potential role of the individual in politics. Although many people of all ages and walks of life tend to voice their doubts as to whether the political leaders of the day or the political parties will ever listen to the ordinary 'man in the street', and although some have opted for non-conventional actions to express their discontent, elections are widely endorsed as a useful mode of political participation and are for many the major form of personal involvement in politics.

Generational Perspectives on Turning Out to Vote

Since German women won the right to vote in 1918, their turnout has tended to trail behind that of men. The 1919 elections to the National Assembly brought a partial surprise, when turnout among the youngest age cohorts was much higher among women than among men (Hofmann-Göttig 1986: 28). It seems that young women were eager debutante voters while the young men who had just returned from the war preferred to remain detached and defer participating in the new polity. Later elections established the pattern which has since become familiar: women vote less frequently than men. In contrast to the Weimar Republic, the Federal Republic commenced with a gender gap in political participation and its political history is, among other things, the history of reducing gender-specific electoral participation. In the Fifties, average electoral turnout among women was lower than that of men; by the Seventies electoral participation had nearly evened out. In the Eighties,

Table 6.2 Electoral turnout of women by age, 1953–1987

Age	1953	1957	1961	1965	1969	1972	1976	1980	1983	1987
18–20						84.3	83.2	79.2	83.2	74.9
21–24	77.4	80.3	80.0	77.5	77.0	85.0	82.9	78.0	80.6	71.9
25–29	81.8	84.0	83.7	81.7	82.5	88.0	86.8	82.6	83.7	75.2
30–34	86.0	87.6	88.5	85.7	86.0	91.3	89.7	86.6	87.4	80.3
35–39				87.3	87.0	92.3	92.0	89.2	89.7	83.9
40–44	88.4	89.4	89.5	88.0	88.5	92.8	92.6	90.4	91.3	86.3
45–49				87.5	88.5	93.5	93.3	90.8	92.0	87.9
50–59	89.0	89.4	89.2	88.1	88.2	93.3	93.0	91.6	92.2	89.4
60–69	85.9	87.4	87.3	86.4	86.7	92.2	93.0	91.3	91.5	89.7
70+	72.5	75.3	75.8	74.8	75.7	83.3	86.0	83.6	82.9	76.5
Total	84.9	86.3	86.2	84.6	84.9	90.2	90.0	87.1	87.8	82.1

Sources: Dieter Noetzel, 'Der Wandel des Wahlverhaltens der Frauen', *Die Frau in unserer Zeit* 3, 1986: 12; and Eckhard Jesse, 'Bundestagswahlen von 1972 bis 1987 im Spiegel der repräsentativen Wahlstatistik', *Zeitschrift für Parlamentsfragen* 2, 1987: 234.

turnout has fallen again in general and also among women. Table 6.1 presents a summary sketch of the gender gap as the difference between overall turnout of men and women: this decreased from three percentage points in 1953, the first post-war elections for which separate data for men and women are available, to under 1% in the Seventies. In the 1987 federal elections turnout fell among men and women to its lowest level since 1953, and the gender gap of electoral participation grew again. As we shall see later, young women were among the most reluctant voters in 1987.

Since the founding years of the Federal Republic, the social opportunities of women have widened as women have closed the conventional gender gaps of educational and vocational qualifications. As we have seen in the previous chapters, life-styles, social participation and personal expectations of equal opportunities have changed greatly in the post-war era; older generation women experienced an unprecedented scope to define their social role while younger generation women grew up to expect such a scope, since an environment of political democracy and relative personal affluence was all they had known. The profile of women's electoral turnout in Table 6.2 shows the participation rate of different age groups in federal elections since 1953 and allows us to follow the participation of age cohorts since the Fifties. If we look at the progress of the generation who were under thirty at the time of the 1953 elections it is evident that a cohort of initially reluctant voters became eager voters as they adjusted to the democratic environment and as their opportunities of equal chances in society broadened. When the under-thirties of 1953 were between forty and fifty, their turnout was higher than that of any other age group and it has remained high even into their old age. Women today are a keener electorate than they were in the founding years of the West German state, and many women who did not vote in the Fifties when they were young have become regular voters during their adult years. The political experience of this generation of women was the experience of being socialised into democratic political participation; to that extent the increased participation of women in elections is part of the consolidation of democracy and the emergence of a democratic political culture in West Germany.

In the contemporary setting of the Eighties, the trend towards electoral participation seems to have slowed down among young women. Are we witnessing, as some observers have warned, a return of the apolitical woman of yesteryear? (INFAS 1987.) At first glance, the young women of 1987 seem to have been even more passive than their mothers' generation had been over thirty years earlier. Compared with the 1983 elections, turnout among women under twenty-five was down by 10% (Table 6.2). Many young women who had voted in previous elections chose not to vote in 1987; for women in their early twenties, turnout was the lowest ever in the history of the Federal Republic (Jesse 1987). History, however, has not turned full circle: the traditional reasons for women's lower participation rate rest in their lower involvement with political affairs; as we shall see below, these continue to be relevant today. In addition, however, the political participation of women has been expanded by the choice to abstain: non-voting, then, may point to passivity but it may also point to dissent. For male voters, the two reasons have always been cited to explain non-voting; for women we can now also assume that non-voting reflects a political stand rather than a lack of political orientation. Non-voting can be akin to protest and imply that elections do not offer a meaningful set of policy choices or are not perceived as a meaningful way by which the individual can take part in politics. Much of the non-voting among young women belonged to this protest variety. By not voting these young-generation women wished to indicate that their preferences were not catered for by the political parties or in the parliamentary processes of the day. However, the majority of women of all generations regard elections as meaningful and would be willing to vote if an election were to be held next Sunday (*Frauen und Männer Europas* 1987: 43 and 44).

Interest in Politics and Changing Value Orientations

The changes in turnout broadly match the changes in political interest since the Fifties. Then the majority of women showed little interest in politics, and political issues rarely featured in their everyday conversations (*Frau und Politik* 1963). Two decades later, seven in ten women declared that they were interested in politics, and West German women were among the most politically orientated in Western Europe (Inglehart 1981: 304–6). In the Eighties, politics has lost some ground. Although it continued to be an important topic of conversation (*Frauen und Männer Europas*: 40) only 60% now stated that they were interested in politics while 40% showed little or no interest. Interest in politics itself seems to correspond with confidence that an individual can influence political decisions (*Datenreport* 1987: 516). Women in the Eighties were much less confident than men that their personal commitment could be effective. They were more hesitant to regard change as a desirable aspect of the socio-political process, and were more inclined than men to favour traditional structures and established value orientations.

Since Ronald Inglehart first observed a connection between socio-economic affluence, educational qualifications and political preferences, the study of political behaviour has focused on the similarities and differences between the three principal types of people: materialists, for whom the stability of the political system and the established political priorities are binding; postmaterialists, who set their own priorities and are guided by their search for individual satisfaction and their own

197

Table 6.3 Value orientations and political innovation, 1978–1984 (in %)

Value orientations	Overall			Men			Women		
	1978	1980	1984	1978	1980	1984	1978	1980	1984
Materialists	42	41	34	35	33	27	43	48	40
Mixed types	48	47	50	49	53	51	48	42	48
Postmaterialists	11	12	16	16	14	22	9	11	1
Political innovation[a]									
Keen to innovate	55	51		60	58		48	45	
Prefer tradition	37	42		33	38		40	47	
Don't know	10	7		7	5		12	9	

[a] No data for 1984.
Source: From the longitudinal study of attitudes (Wohlfahrtssurvey) conducted at the University of Mannheim; quoted in *Datenreport* 1987: 514.

notion of 'quality of life' (in political life, the postmaterialists would be advocates of innovative change); and a third group, so-called 'mixed types', who have absorbed many of the concerns of the postmaterialists for 'quality of life' issues without relinquishing their commitment to a stable institutional framework of the political system (Inglehart 1975; Klages and Kmieciak 1979). Empirical studies which have applied the analysis of value orientations and political types to political participation suggest that women have been more strongly represented among the materialist types than men, although men and women are changing from materialist towards postmaterialist and in particular towards mixed type orientations. Table 6.3 highlights these changes and also shows how women have remained more hesitant about political innovation than men.

In West Germany today, interest in politics and the importance attached to influencing political decisions increases with educational qualifications. One in three West Germans with higher educational qualifications interprets political participation as daring to be innovative and as turning one's back on tradition; the same is true for young-generation West Germans. In 1980, one in three in the 18–24 age cohort opted for innovation, only 2% opted for tradition while the remainder did not express a clear preference (Mohr 1984: 160). Women, whose advances in education have been relatively recent, do not appear to be drawn to new values, innovative zest and political participation as strongly as men in a similar position. Women today are more orientated towards political participation than their mothers had been in the past, and most combine their educational qualifications with a preference for traditional politics and a stable political system. There is, however, a second current which seems to be gathering momentum: some younger women appear to have translated their new value orientations into a preference for non-conventional politics, for non-hierarchical forms of participation, for individual politics outside the established institutional frameworks (Allerbeck and Hoag 1985: 11ff.). While conventional political participation would focus on elections, parties and parliaments as the meaningful venues for effecting change, non-conventional participation among these young women concentrates on action groups, so-called autonomous women's centres and facets of the women's movement as the focal points of political participation (*Jugend '81*: 674ff.).

Educational mobilisation appears to have worked in two ways: on the one hand, women have intensified their political orientations, although a deficit of political interest and confidence in the individual's role in politics has persisted; on the other hand, educated young women see electoral political participation and interest in the established politics of parties and parliaments as out of step with their own identity as women, and with their priorities for participation. The high-point of electoral participation and political interest which had been reached in the Seventies did not last, but the participatory trend has not moved back to that of the Fifties. In the mid-Eighties, non-participation and not-turning-out in elections have assumed political overtones for women and reflect a critical intent, although the apparent retreat into an apolitical sphere mirrors the traditional realm of passivity and 'private virtues' (Dahrendorf 1967: 299) from which women have begun to emerge and which the post-war generations at least claim to reject.

Between Tradition and Choice: Party Preferences of Women

When Lipset and Rokkan evaluated democratic party systems and the origins of party preferences in the mid-Sixties, they found for West Germany that little had changed since the Twenties: the social cleavages in electoral behaviour, i.e. the strong links between specific social groups and political parties, continued to dominate post-war society; they were, as they put it, 'frozen' (Lipset and Rokkan 1967). The working class, notably the segment organised in trade unions, had supported the Social Democratic Party (SPD) and continued to do so while religious traditionalists, notably Catholics, supported the centre–right Christian Democrats (CDU) (Klingemann 1985). For women, the apparently static pattern of party preferences was particularly evident. Although women cannot be regarded as a social group and the gender divide not as a social cleavage, the electoral choices of women in the first two decades of West German political history fitted the frozen structure: they voted along the same cleavage lines of class and denomination as they had done in the Weimar Republic. Since unionisation was low and the working-class environments had been disrupted through National Socialism and the Second World War, SPD support among women was low. Regardless of whether they were Protestants or Catholics women have been more active churchgoers than men. In the founding decades of the Federal Republic the majority of women opted for the CDU/CSU and this still holds true for women over the age of fifty (Noetzel 1986). The CDU/CSU has also been regarded as the party for the better-off, committed to political and economic stability rather than contemplating innovation and reform. Although contemporary conservatism is more innovative than this popular view would suggest, the party has tended to attract voters who wanted to preserve their personal standard of living, and to win votes in times of economic uncertainty through its image as the party of stability. In other words, the CDU/CSU is in an advantageous position to utilise the materialist value orientation and traditional approaches to politics which we noted as an important dimension of women's contemporary participation in West German politics.

That the majority of working women have been employed in white-collar occupations also militated against their political orientation towards the left, at least while it was inconceivable that respectable people – *bessere Leute* – would vote anything but Conservative or further to the right. All these factors combined

Table 6.4 Party preferences of men and women 1953–1987 (%)

Election	CDU/CSU		SPD		FDP		Greens[a]		Others[b]	
	m	f	m	f	m	f	m	f	m	f
1953	38.9	47.2	32.5	27.6	11.7	10.4	—	—	16.9	14.8
1957	44.6	53.5	35.3	28.9	8.6	7.4	—	—	11.5	10.2
1961	40.3	49.6	39.7	32.9	13.6	12.2	—	—	6.4	5.3
1965	42.0	51.7	44.0	36.2	9.7	9.2	—	—	4.3	2.9
1969	40.6	50.6	45.6	40.4	6.1	5.3	—	—	7.7	3.7
1972	43.0	46.0	46.8	45.7	8.8	7.7	—	—	1.3	0.7
1976	47.2	48.8	43.6	43.1	8.1	7.6	—	—	1.2	0.5
1980	44.2	43.7	43.1	43.9	10.8	10.8	1.6	1.2	0.6	0.3
1983	47.7	49.2	38.4	39.4	7.2	6.3	5.9	4.8	0.7	0.3
1987	42.5	45.1	38.5	37.8	9.2	8.3	8.3	7.7	1.6	1.2

[a] The Greens competed for the first time in the 1980 elections, and entered the Bundestag in 1983.
[b] The category 'others' includes all other parties which participated in the respective election. Between 1949 and 1961, some had Bundestag representation. The most important ones are the refugee party BHE in 1953, and the German Party (DP) from 1949 to 1961. None of the 'other' parties – left or right – is strong enough today to obtain seats in the Bundestag.
Source: Joachim Hofmann-Göttig, *Emanzipation mit dem Stimmzettel*, pp. 109–10; Eckhard Jesse, 'Repräsentative Wahlstatistik 1972–1987', *Zeitschrift für Parlamentsfragen* 2, 1987: 237.

to underpin the conservative orientations of women which carried over from the Weimar Republic into the Federal Republic. Until the end of the Sixties, it seemed almost inevitable that the CDU/CSU enjoyed a women's bonus in elections and scooped the majority of their votes (Table 6.4). Throughout the Fifties and Sixties, the party won on average 10% more votes from women than from men while the SPD suffered a lingering women's deficit (Hofmann-Göttig 1986). Until 1969, the majority of SPD voters were male and the electoral gender gap between CDU/CSU and SPD was never less than 11% (1969) and had amounted to 25% in 1957.

From 'Stimmvieh' to Mobile Voter

To explain the change of electoral preferences and generational perspective, we have to look at the broader context of social and political mobility in West Germany. The economic prosperity and proliferation of comfortable living standards across social groups which commenced in the Fifties sufficiently mellowed overt social differences for the majority of West Germans, who began to see themselves as middle class. To be more precise: the notion of class – *Klasse* – faded altogether and people regarded themselves as mainstream, as in the middle politically and socially. In the Seventies, eight out of ten West Germans classified themselves as belonging to the middle (Feist et al. 1979: 179). The changes in self-perception reflected changes in the employment structure, the emergence of new occupations, new labour processes, new working environments and a new middle class. As mentioned earlier, these were people who worked in administrative or technical capacities. In our context it is important to stress that this new middle class did not have fixed party affiliations. It fitted neither the traditional conservative orientation nor, indeed, did the new middle class identify with the labour movement. Although each person may have come from a politically defined background or parental home, their own living situation no longer matched conventional political orientations and had created room for independent, individual political choice. A growing segment between the two traditional camps of the socialist left and the conservative right, the new middle class was in principle non-aligned. Rather than acting upon inherited loyalties, people could develop their own or change between parties to suit their interests (Chandler 1988).

The decline of partisan alignment also played an important role in making the political choices of women more flexible. Partisan alignment means that political parties or groups present themselves and are perceived by their followers and by the public at large as committed to a specific ideology, socio-political interest or class (Mintzel 1984). The traditional division into left-wing and right-wing politics uses the parliamentary seating order to underline more fundamental differences of political orientation. One of the main developments in West German politics since the Fifties has been the decrease of political ideologies with a sharply left or sharply right focus (Baker et al. 1981). Political parties without partisan alignment aim for a broad political appeal and tend to serve an integrative function. The first party of this type to develop in West Germany was the CDU/CSU. It had been founded as a potential catch-all party of Catholics and Protestants of all social origins and classes, a

Volkspartei. In West Germany, the broad appeal corresponded to the blurring of class lines in the wake of socio-economic affluence. The SPD embarked on a similar process of moving towards the centre after it lost all federal elections during the Fifties and could not see a chance of government if it remained a left-wing opposition with a Marxist outlook (Becker et al. 1983). The Godesberg Programme of 1959 signified the demonstrative abandonment of partisan politics on the left, and paved the way for the emergence of a Social Democratic *Volkspartei.* Women, who may in the past have hesitated to turn to a seemingly Marxist party, now began to perceive the SPD as a force of reform and political innovation. The partisan de-alignment of the West German party system helped to reduce the women's deficit which had plagued the SPD since the days when women were first allowed to vote.

Young-Generation Choices: SPD and Greens

The new orientations of women towards the SPD are closely linked to political generations. In the Seventies, younger women voters opted for the SPD while older women tended to retain their conservative focus. In particular, the generations born since 1940, whose political socialisation occurred during the lifetime of the Federal Republic, broke the tradition of women voting to the right. Among these age cohorts, the SPD could consolidate its position in the Seventies while the CDU lost support. For both major parties, the electoral support of women has become a prime issue, and none could or can rely on a loyal female electorate. The CDU/CSU saw the unquestioning support from women in the Fifties crumble as younger women perceived other parties as electoral alternatives. The SPD, which reaped the benefits of the new electoral mobility of women in the Seventies, found in the Eighties that its capacity to integrate younger women has recently been challenged from two sides. The first challenge is occupational: the use of new technology has moderated traditional working practices and party affiliations (Feist and Krieger 1987). There are no data specifically for women and the impact of new technology on their electoral preferences. Given that the gender gap in voting has narrowed greatly, the general data can be read as applying to men and

203

women. The new hi-tech blue-collar worker, the technical expert in production, has strengthened his or her SPD affiliation. New technology in manufacturing and production had the same effect as specialist skills in the past: to enhance unionisation and an identification with the SPD. For white-collar employees who work with new technology, the political repercussions are less clear, and leanings to the CDU appear to predominate. Since white-collar working, low unionisation and relatively unskilled use of high technology characterise the situation of women in this area, the new working environments are likely to reduce the electoral drift of women towards the SPD.

The second factor to challenge the electoral appeal of the SPD to women has been the emergence of the Green party. It originated in the Seventies as a new party on the left of the political spectrum. Contrary to the established parties, the Green party did not aim for the middle ground but saw itself as an agent of the extra-parliamentary in parliamentary politics, and as the electoral party for the young generation, the adherents of post-materialist values (Smith 1987; Bürklin 1988). Drawing on the participatory political culture of the Seventies the Greens have to be seen in the context of issue-based initiatives and movements with their focus on nuclear power, the environment, women's rights or peace (Kolinsky 1987a). As a political party, they attracted an educated, urban, new middle-class electorate, predominantly under the age of thirty-five. Electoral support among women for the Greens has been slightly below average although – as we shall see later – the party has placed a special emphasis on women's rights and equal representation. In West Germany, women have always been reluctant to vote for small parties and preferred mainstream politics. In the light of this electoral trend, the Greens have done well in the past and seem set to reverse the women's deficit among the under-forties (Table 6.5). In the 1987 elections, one out of three women under the age of twenty-four voted Green. Among women in this age group, the Greens were the strongest party, closely followed by the Christian Democrats. The SPD, which might have expected the young women's vote a decade earlier, had fallen to third place. Among the youngest voters, more men than women voted SPD in 1987 (see Table 6.5). The Green vote has been a young vote and also an urban vote. Table 6.5 also summarises

Table 6.5 Party preferences of young women in the 1987 federal elections

Young voters 18–24[a]	CDU/CSU	SPD	FDP	Greens
All	32.4	27.4	5.6	33.0
Men	30.2	32.7	5.3	29.8
Women	36.0	21.0	5.9	37.0

Changes of the Green electorate in cities with 200,000 or more inhabitants[b]

Women aged 18–25: change since 1983	+ 4.6%
Women aged 25–35: change since 1983	+ 9.9%
Women aged 35–45: change since 1983	+ 7.1%
Overall change: Green vote men 1983–1987	+ 1.3%
Green vote women 1983–1987	+ 4.6%
Electoral deficit: women/men 1983:	− 1.7%
1987:	− 1.3%

Sources: [a]*Die Welt* 13 Jan. 1987, Pre-election survey; [b]Wolfgang Bick and Joachim Hofmann-Göttig, 'Die Wahlurne übt auf junge Frauen nur geringen Reiz aus', *Frankfurter Rundschau* 5 Feb. 1987: 12.

the electoral results in cities with over 200,000 inhabitants. Here, women increasingly turned to the Greens, in particular those age groups which previously had voted for the SPD – women between the ages of twenty-five and forty-five. Although the gains of the Greens in the cities were larger among women than among men, the party overall retained a women's deficit of just over 1%. The potential attractiveness of the Greens for women voters in the younger age groups is challenging the place of the SPD as the electoral party for the 'new woman' and has given women additional influence on the overall balance between political parties, and ultimately between government and opposition.

Issue Competence and Electoral Choice

The electoral landscape today shows new divides. Traditional cleavages of class or denomination have begun to recede. Age and education have emerged as prominent factors and the electoral preferences of women are similar to those of men in comparable socio-economic circumstances. The mobilised electorate of young educated, qualified, motivated women tends to opt for parties to the left of centre. In the Seventies, the SPD held the monopoly here; now the allegiance of this group of women is split between SPD and Greens. Women over the age of thirty-five, often less educated, active churchgoers, women who feel they belong to the better-off strata in society and look for a political guarantee of their secure socio-economic situation, constitute the CDU/CSU electorate. The CDU/CSU has retained a firm hold on this segment of the electorate, and on the party preferences of older voters of both sexes. In contrast to the three other parties, the FDP (Free Democratic Party) does not specifically aim at mobilising female voters, nor have changes in the gender balance swung its political fortunes in the past.[2]

In the contemporary political environment, women hold a key position in the electorate. The experience of the Seventies and Eighties has shown that women are now willing to change their party preferences and regard elections as a matter of personal choice, not as endorsing traditional allegiances. In the Seventies, the SPD benefited sufficiently from these changes to score its best ever result in 1972, and to remain in government throughout the decade. The previously male-dominated party has come to depend on women for more than half of its electoral support. In the Eighties, the Green party could make some gains among women, although the women's deficit which has been characteristic for small parties is still visible. The Christian Democrats, who built their dominant position in government on their women's bonus in the electorate in the Fifties and Sixties, continue to win majority support among older women and women with traditional value orientations. They have, however, failed to convince younger-generation women that conservatism could work innovative change and address what have been perceived as women's interests.

The volatility of women's preferences is particularly pressing in the camp left of centre, where SPD and Greens are competing for the electoral support of the 'new woman'. Among the factors

2. In the 1980 elections, the FDP gained support from Protestant women who had voted Conservative in the past but did not wish to give their unreserved support to the CDU/CSU with Strauß as chancellor candidate. The shift of Conservative women voters towards a moderate-Conservative middle ground prepared the ground for the FDP's change of coalition partner two years later.

Table 6.6 'Which political party represents the interests of women most effectively?' Answers mentioning specific party as most effective

	All women over 18	Women aged 18–29
CDU/CSU	11	7
SPD	13	9
Greens	24	26
FDP	1	*

*No data available.
Source: Unpublished Infratest survey (April/May 1985), *Development of the Women's Issue*, Bonn: Archiv beim Parteivorstand der SPD.

influencing party preferences, issue competence has acquired a special significance in the Seventies and Eighties. Electoral choices have, of course, always been linked to the perceived competence of political parties in selected policy domains. In the past, these tended to cover traditional fields such as the economy, employment, international relations and defence. In the Seventies, environmental protection, social policies and secure pensions also ranked among the top ten or so issues in which parties had to prove their competence if they wanted to stand a chance of winning an election. These issues continue to be regarded as valid measures of competence which might determine electoral choice (Schulze 1987). What has changed is that specific groups have begun to single out specific issues, and judge the competence of political parties not against the broad band of traditional policies but against their point of concern. With regard to women, the commitment of political parties to equal opportunities has become a core issue of this type. Here, the Greens have been able to gain recognition as the party most committed to women's issues and most likely to be effective in women's policies. Table 6.6 shows that regardless of age about one out of four women looked towards the Greens to represent women's interests. Young women were hardly more inclined towards the Greens than women overall, but they were less certain than older women that the Christian Democrats or the Social Democrats could be relied upon to advance the causes of women. Among young women, the Greens enjoyed a clear competence bonus compared with the more established political parties.

Choosing a political party continues to involve expectations about economic performance, social stability or the international standing of the West German state. But it also involves, to a greater extent than in the past, a choice about the position women should have and wish to have in society, in economic life and in the political process itself. While the gender gap of party preferences has diminished, gender itself has become a focal point of policy formulation and party choice.

Party Membership: An Overview

Next to taking part in elections, joining a political party can be regarded as indicative of active political participation. The Basic Law recognises the key function of political parties as articulating the political will of the people through their policies and programmes and, of course, through representing the electorate in parliament, and constituting governments and oppositions. Although political parties in West Germany do not have a formal monopoly of political representation, independent members of parliament or non-party forces play no part at regional and national level, and a minor part only in communal assemblies. West German political parties have tended to interpret their role expansively as a party privilege of parliamentary representation. In practical terms, party membership provides access to policy formulation, party posts, parliamentary seats, government offices and political positions in the administrative structure of the localities, the regions or the federal state. Through their control over the nomination of candidates for political office, political parties are, above all, bodies for elite recruitment. Party membership allows the individual a voice in elite selection and also access through the party to elite positions (Herzog 1982). While the issue politics of the Seventies, when various initiatives and movements articulated certain themes or grievances, has modified the function of parties to formulate political goals and initiate change, the role of the political party in elite recruitment has not diminished (Flanagan and Dalton 1984). It is here that party membership can obtain a special significance for the individual and for society.

Although political parties are widely accepted in West Germany as core institutions of political democracy, joining them has remained a minority exercise. In the founding years of the post-war state, people used to emphasise that they had burnt their fingers once – by joining the National Socialist Workers Party – and were unwilling to risk a second disappointment. In fact, party membership reached record levels in 1948 when membership in an approved and democratic party could be used to demonstrate detachment from National Socialism, when the shortage of goods and services made any network of connections desirable, and when refugees and dislocated people looked towards party membership to facilitate their social and economic integration. The popularity of political parties in the first hour was short-lived, and membership fell by at least 50% immediately after the currency reform and the stabilisation that followed in its wake. In the Fifties and Sixties, party membership stagnated at the one million mark, and with an average of 15% women among party members. The Social Democrats retained their Weimar profile of about 18% women in their membership; the Christian Democrats (CDU) counted 13% women among their members; for the Bavarian CSU and the Free Democrats, the proportion of women in the membership amounted to less than 10% (Fülles 1969: 25; 37).

Today, just under one in four members of the political parties which are important enough to have parliamentary representation are women. In the Greens, one in three, in the CDU, SPD and FDP about one in four members are women; the Bavarian CSU has the lowest participation rate of women with 14%. From about 180,000 at the end of the Sixties, female membership has more than doubled to about 440,000 in 1987 (Table 6.7).[3] In the same period, party membership overall has doubled and the increased participation of women in political parties has to be seen within a wider context of an increased willingness of West Germans to take an active part in politics, and to look to political parties as the preferred framework for their contribution to politics.

Within this broad pattern, the place of parties as membership

3. All except the Greens store their membership files on computer and have provided the author with the relevant print-outs. The Greens estimated their membership figures on the basis of party congress reports from the regions and delegate entitlements. The percentage of women among the Greens is presumed to be one in three; regional differences have not been divulged.

Table 6.7 Party membership of women, 1969–1987 (in 1,000s and in %)

Year	CDU	%	CSU	%	SPD	%	FDP	%	Greens	%
1969	39.8	13	5.3	7	134.9	17	7.0	12	n/a	
1974	93.1	18	12.8	11	195.5	20	12.2	17	n/a	
1976	128.7	20	17.4	12	215.3	21	15.0	19	n/a	
1980	145.6	21	22.0	13	227.8	23	19.5	23	10.0	30
1983	159.4	22	25.5	14	226.8	25	17.3	24	11.0	33
1985	158.1	22	25.4	14	232.4	25	15.7	24	13.0	33
1987	157.4	22	25.6	14	229.9	25	14.5	23	14.9	33

Sources: Data were supplied to the author by the federal party offices (Bonn) of the CDU, SPD, FDP and Greens; by the CSU head office in Munich.

organisations for women has changed greatly. At the beginning of the Seventies, nearly eight out of ten women who belonged to a political party belonged to the SPD. As an organisation based on mass membership the SPD always included the largest number and also the highest proportion of women. While this continues to be the case the gap between the SPD and its Conservative rival has closed. In 1987, 42% of all women party members belonged to the Christian Democrats – taking CDU and CSU together – and 44% to the Social Democrats. In the CDU, more so than in the CSU, women have played a major role in the transformation of the party during the Seventies from a small, club-like assortment of local dignitaries and businessmen with few organisational structures and a marginal role only for party members to a modern party organisation, an 'apparatus party' as Mintzel has called it, which attracts members and has to respond to their interests in its organisational practice (Mintzel 1983). While women constitute just 22% of the CDU membership, one in three new members are women; given the special political role of the CSU in Bavaria and the socio-political conditions in a Catholic environment with a strong and state-centred party, the Bavarian wing of West German conservatism has been less attractive to women, and continues to lag behind the general membership developments.

For the Free Democrats, membership developments during the Seventies and Eighties have been troubled by the after-effects of coalition changes. The first half of the Seventies saw major membership fluctuations as established members left the party and new members were recruited in the wake of the FDP shift towards the left, and a governing coalition with the SPD (Kolinsky 1984). Among the newcomer members, women were strongly represented, and an internal study of membership developments emphasised in 1976 that the party had an unexpectedly high number of young women members for whom a role ought to be found in the party.[4] After a further change of coalition in 1982 – this time in the opposite direction – the party again lost members. There are no official and detailed figures on these developments, but information provided by the party head office in Bonn points to membership losses of 20,000 overall, among them many younger women members for whom the move to the right was not acceptable.[5] Despite these ups and downs, the FDP today has nearly twice as many women members as it had in 1969; as we shall see later in this discussion, women and their status in the organisation have gained a new topicality and elicited new responses in the party.

The Greens, the latest addition to the party landscape, are a difficult party to assess in the context of membership developments. Being a party with an emphatic commitment to organisational informality and grass-roots participation, the party has not, until recently, kept membership data on file. It appears that computers have now been put into operation and data have been collected and analysed in a similar fashion to other parties, but these data are not freely available within the party or to interested researchers. The figures included in Table 6.7 are based on the information provided by the business manager of the Greens at the party head office in Bonn; he in turn based his calculations on the dues paid by regional parties to the central organisation. Regional parties have to contribute a fixed sum per number of members, and their rights to party congress delegates are calculated on the basis of these returns. This adminis-

4. In 1976, the party commissioned an empirical survey of its membership to determine the interests of its members, especially those who had joined since the SPD/FDP coalition in 1969. This survey drew attention to the new women members in the party, most of them under the age of forty. The survey has not been published and is accessible in the archives of the Friedrich Naumann Foundation, Gummersbach; some of the findings have been incorporated into Kolinsky 1984: 101ff.

5. This information was provided by the head of the Abteilung Politik, Dr Dierke, during an interview with the author in January 1987.

trative tie-in is, of course, no guarantee of their accuracy; this is particularly evident in the numbers given for the membership of women. The party has assumed that no less than one in three Greens are women, and we have to accept this statement until more detailed figures become available. We can conclude, however, that the Greens have not attracted a significant enough number of women to increase their share among the membership; although regarded as the party which is competent to address itself to women's issues, membership developments do not indicate that women have flocked to join the Greens and shape it into a women's party (Kolinsky 1989).

The SPD, which has lost its place as the only mass organisation for women, still includes the largest number of women of all the parties. In 1987, the party had about 230,000 women members, one in four of the party membership (Table 6.7). However, SPD internal data on membership development show that the gender balance in the party is tipping towards women. Among new members, 40% are women. Between 1970 and 1987, the SPD registered a net membership gain of 10,000 men but 90,000 women. In 1976, the new importance of women for the party received symbolic recognition when SPD membership briefly surpassed the one million mark: the party celebrated a woman as the one millionth member. With minor exceptions (in 1983 and 1987) the number of women in the SPD has increased continuously since the mid-Sixties. If membership trends continue along similar lines, the SPD will be heading towards an equal number of men and women in the organisation – if not in the party as a whole then at least among the new party members. The SPD, it seems, is no more than one step ahead of a broader trend in West German society: women are narrowing the gender gap in political parties, and party membership is increasingly regarded as a useful and accessible mode of political participation not just for career-minded men who aim for political elite positions, but for women as well.

Membership Motivations

The increased interest of women in joining a political party reflects the increased willingness among the post-war generations to participate in political affairs, which has moulded the political culture since the late Sixties. It can also be linked to the advances in education, qualifications and occupational mobility which opened choices to women which may not have been seen or which may not have existed in the past. On paper, women have been free to join political parties ever since parties admitted them as members. The Social Democrats built up a special women's section from the 1890s to win the newly expanding female labour force into the party, and also to bring the wives and daughters of active party members closer into the organisation and familiarise them with its aims. Until 1908, however, women did not enjoy full membership status since they were not permitted by law to attend public meetings. Once the law permitted women to mix with men in public meetings, party membership and a constructive role for women in the party could gradually emerge. The obstacles which did remain were cultural rather than legal or organisational: from the very beginning, women have complained that parties made their participation virtually impossible since meetings tended to be held in smoke-filled rooms, often the back room of a pub. Early SPD party congresses regularly heard reprimands about this and the comment of a woman politician in the late Seventies about the venue for party meetings has a familiar ring to it: 'there is no reason why party meetings continue in the traditional way. Taking women into consideration seems to be a luxury. Party meetings are invariably held in smoke-filled men's boozers which are reeking of beer. This in itself is repulsive to many women' (Berger 1979: 82). A second cultural obstacle can be traced to social customs: until the Sixties, women would not normally go out by themselves, something which was considered unsuitable for someone respectable. Attendance at a party meeting, then, depended on an escort – normally the husband, another family member or friend. For women to enter a public house alone has until recently been frowned upon. Although these customs have lost some of their persuasive force, they linger on. Today, women may not hesitate to attend meetings without company but they often feel uncomfortable about the tone and venue of the local party culture.

Why, then, do women join political parties? Is it in conformity with their family tradition and social background or in obedience to their husbands, and how do membership motivations of women differ from those of men?

From Political Spouse to Potential Leader

Traditional patterns of dependency and female uncertainty about a personal membership motivation have not fully subsided. Women have been party wives just as much as party individuals. In the Fifties, women would frequently follow the political preferences of their husbands in voting and also in joining a political party. Even thirty years on, husbands have retained their place as influential persuaders. The only detailed survey of women in political parties has been conducted in Bremen, but other case studies of party organisations suggest that the findings are more widely relevant (Hoecker 1987). In Bremen, 15% of women mentioned that they joined at the request of their husbands while few husbands (0.7%) had joined to please their wives. Overall, three in four married women members belonged to the same party as their husbands; one in three of married male members to the same party as their wives. Family ties have remained important for women and influence their membership motivation more strongly than they do for men.

However, other motivating patterns have emerged in the Seventies and have reshaped membership motivations. Women now expect to gain something other from their party membership than merely strengthening the family commitment, confirming conventional orientations in their background or class, or similar supportive and circumstantial reasons. Women today hold specific expectations about personal gains they wish to derive from party membership and articulate personal motivations for taking up such membership. Generally speaking, the politically active women who join a political party are as educated and as qualified in vocational terms as their male peers. Since joining a political party is still less accepted among women than among men – in the mid-Eighties, 19% of men and just 8% of women declared they might join a political party or had already done so – those women who do join tend to be particularly interested in politics. The most active women are as active as men in their respective party while slightly more women

(27%) than men (20%) can be found among those for whom party membership means little more than paying the monthly due (Hoecker 1986: 72). Across the parties, nearly one in three women and men are keen or willing to hold a party office. A study of motivations for party membership in the early Eighties showed for Bremen that the main reason for joining was the desire to put specific political goals into practice. Party political differences in motivation were slight: CDU members tended to emphasise that they would work with like-minded people; FDP members underlined the individual nature of their goals and of the contribution they would wish to make; SPD members tended to underline their desire to effect changes in the overall course of politics; the Greens were not included in the survey but their goals have been closely linked to specific issues and a general posture of opposition which should innovate party politics and the parliamentary process itself (Roth and Wiesendahl 1986: 60ff.).

Although the membership motivations of men and women today are broadly similar within each party, some interesting gender differences have remained. Women, it seems, are more likely to relate party membership to their personal situation and regard the party as a gathering of potential friends. In the Bremen study, women and men were asked to list the reasons which persuaded them to join. For men, putting political goals into practice or limiting the power of other parties topped the list. Among women, variants of the traditional theme of party loyalty were mentioned most: a sense of belonging, mixing with like-minded people, giving support to the policies of one's party (Appendix VI). Given the emphasis in their replies, women join in order to register support, not in order to change, mould or redirect. In their reflections on membership motivations, women like to present the party of their choice as a congenial environment permeated by political consensus. Even if party political realities are different and women experience political parties in a more controversial way, it is important to note that the ideal notion of membership – the self-presentation of original motivations – assumes a harmony between individual preferences and organisational orientations. While women focus on such a harmony, men list more conflicting factors and intentions to explain their membership motivations. Men, it seems, name more overtly political points, women more personal views and feelings when attempting to explain in retrospect why they became members of a political party.

As a mode of political participation, party membership provides social contact, political debate and various opportunities for personal involvement, but it also constitutes an entry point to influencing the composition of the political elite, or joining it through holding an office in the party organisation or in parliament. Since the conventions of the contemporary political culture militate against openly stating political ambition, survey data can only hint at motivations, not generate a reliable and quantitative profile. Political ambition tends to be veiled as concern for the communal best, as a form of service, as something one never intended to take on but had been asked to do (Falke 1984). Women in particular have been reluctant to focus directly on a career path or to admit openly that careers matter to them. The conventional notion that the competitive world of careers and advancements is male-oriented and at odds with femininity has left its traces even among career women. Even those who made it to the top appear to be unwilling to ascribe their success to intent, to ability, or to determination; women prefer to give the impression that the major agents of their rise to the top and their achievements were chance, luck or coincidence beyond their personal control (Bernadoni and Werner 1985). The conventions not to admit to personal ambition nor to political ambition or interest in leadership make it difficult to penetrate the camouflage of overt reasons and detect the extent to which membership in the political elite motivates people – men and women – to join a political party. The data which emerged from the Bremen study probably underestimate the leadership motivation, but they clearly show that leadership motivation is important for women. Holding a party office is just as much a woman's goal as a man's goal in the contemporary party environment (see Table 6.8).

Two strands of membership motivation among women are relevant in contemporary party organisations: on the one hand, there is the woman for whom political work and office holding are core aspects of her party membership; in her motivation she hardly differs from men. Where she differs is her relative lack of success in holding an important office. This discrepancy be-

Table 6.8 Party membership and career motivations of men and
women
'How do you personally feel about this: Are you
interested in rising in the party and holding an office?'

	All members %	Women %	Men %
Yes, political activity is very important to me and I am aiming for important positions	4.5	5.4	4.2
Yes, I am interested but cannot find the time at present due to other obligations	27.6	21.4	29.8
No, I would not have the confidence to take this on	11.9	23.7	7.8
No, I have other interests	37.1	37.4	37.0
No, after a number of unsuccessful attempts I have stopped trying	0.9	—	1.1
I have already achieved important positions and am not aiming for further ones	9.9	3.4	12.1
Other reasons	8.1	8.7	8.0
N[a]	560	197	363

[a] The study draws on membership surveys of the three main parties in Bremen
in the early Eighties: CDU, SPD and FDP. It does not include the Greens.
Source: Beate Hoecker, 'Frauen in der Politik', *Zeitschrift für Parlamentsfragen* 1,
1986: 73.

tween motivation and opportunity has inspired the current
debate on women's quotas and will be discussed below. On the
other hand, there is the woman who looks familiar from the
past: she is either not interested in holding party posts, or she
lacks the confidence to aspire to them. The lack of confidence
which nearly one in four mentioned in the Bremen study sets
women sharply apart from men, for whom confidence is less of
a problem in considering whether or not to take on political
responsibility. Among women – even among those sufficiently

interested in politics to join a political party – remnants of conventional women's roles with their focus on modesty and a supportive role in the background continue to cast their shadow and conflict with their motivations to play a more active, assertive and influential part in the organisational environment of their party and political life as a whole.

Expectations of Equality and Experiences of Party Culture

Compared with the founding days of the Federal Republic, women in the Eighties constitute a larger share of party memberships, but they also constitute a potentially more active, competitive, politically motivated group. In the past women tended to prefer specifically female roles in their party, or they acquiesced to these roles if other opportunities did not present themselves. Today, women's expectations are less gender-specific: an increasing number of women, in particular younger women with advanced levels of education and effective communicative skills, compete with men for the positions of political representation, leadership and elite involvement their party has to offer. Two examples of political experiences in the SPD can illustrate the changes in climate and in motivation. In 1966, Ursula Pausch-Gruber, who has since built her career in the SPD women's association and in the party organisation, was interviewed on television as the youngest ever female delegate to the SPD party congress. She was thirty-three at the time, a product of the post-war era in her political motivation and the results she expected from it. She stunned her interviewer and her audience when she rejected women's groups and dismissed their activities as non-political. Who were these women and why had they joined the SPD, and why did she take a different view of politics?

> They were elderly and old female comrades, who had felt close to the SPD through their husbands since the National Socialist years. Many had lost their husbands in the war or through resistance to National Socialism. They had come together in the post-war period since they had common interests: the material deprivations suffered by single women with children. . . . Most remained at work until well past the official retirement age since their meagre pension would not have allowed a decent living. They were distrustful of a young woman

comrade who came from a well-to-do middle class background, even if they liked her as a person. Their loyalty to the SPD was rooted in their feelings and their experiences of the years before 1933, and the traditions which they preserved in their own families and which continued to influence them. . . . They knew that the party and its women's groups needed younger members, but they did not want anything to change. They attended party meetings, but they hardly ever spoke. If there was a vote, they would support the executive, even if they did not fully agree with it. . . . The choice of pub as a venue and the size of the meat salad which was served there seemed to be more important for their party participation than any aspirations to make a political impact. (Pausch-Gruber 1981: 73–4)

Ten years later Anke Martiny, who has since married the former party manager Peter Glotz and narrowly failed in her bid to lead the Bavarian SPD, formulated the experiences of her generation of able, motivated and ambitious women with the party establishment, and the obstacles which women have to tackle before hopes of holding political office can become reality. She sees the SPD dominated at the local level by a type of functionary whom she calls 'Comrade Obstruction'. Since all party work and potential political careers have to commence at the local level, he is strategically placed to make or break party political aspirations and opportunities for women:

Comrade Obstruction is especially numerous at the level of the local and district executive. He administers his office in a patriarchal and authoritarian fashion and believes in hierarchies. Professionally he came up the hard way, often via trade union and party courses, which turned the former worker into a white collar employee, the man in the boiler suit into one wearing a clean shirt and tie. . . . Comrade Obstruction is easily offended even by rationally delivered criticism; because he serves the cause of the party for the sake of his own person he has not learned to deal with criticism in a rational manner. Comrade Obstruction likes to be the centre of attention, and sees himself as a courteous friend of the female sex. His personality permits him only to see women as 'little women' and view any political aspirations of women with misgivings. He is not capable of acknowledging female achievement, and he always feels threatened by it. (Riedel-Martiny 1975: 733).

In other parties, similar obstacles confront the changed aspirations of younger women. Participation today implies an involvement of women at all levels of activity in the party organisation and in electoral politics. Gender-specific political roles – be it silent attendance at meetings or channelling the activity of women away from the main party work into women's organisations – are no longer accepted as the socio-economic situation and the political preferences of women themselves cease to be gender-specific. The new climate of participatory intent is supported by a sharpened awareness in German society about patterns of inequality, and an increased acceptance of women in positions of leadership and public responsibility (*Frauen und Männer Europas* 20; 33ff.). All parties have been challenged to accommodate women's expectations of achieving political office, and to create new openings for them in the party organisation and also in parliamentary politics. For party women to demand more say and better representation is, of course, nothing new. In 1947, for instance, CDU women built their claim for representation at all organisational tiers of the fledgling party on the notion that women had special qualities as 'carriers of life and as guardians of peace' which should be incorporated into all levels of political work (Frauenvereinigung 1987: 1). They were rebuked by the party chairman and later prime minister of Rhineland Palatinate who had envisaged that women in the Christian Democrats should be mothers in politics rather than women leaders jostling for a place at the top:

> We need women who care in a motherly way for the well-being of the people, not women who sit there with their pencil busily calculating that more women than men vote for the CDU and that therefore the majority of the new members of parliament should be women or whatever other version of women's rights they underwrite. It is futile for a couple of suffragettes to get together and formulate an opinion, which in no way reflects the views of our CDU housewives. (Frauenvereinigung 1987: 3)

While the hopes of politically active women for more substantive integration into their party and a more sizeable share of political influence are not new, the scope for the parties or for the 'Comrades Obstruction' to respond to them has changed: they can no longer afford to ignore them altogether. The women members are more motivated towards leadership than in the past, and the fact that none of the parties can comfortably rely on women's votes has shattered organisational complacencies. As we shall discuss later in this chapter, all parties have introduced formal women's quotas or try to develop other ways of giving women a bigger and more equal share of posts and political influence. Before examining the prospects of participation based on women's quotas, we have to turn to the most public area of participation: that in parliaments and in public office. The discrepancies between the expectations of young-generation women about the political role they should play in society and the realities of limited representation have, perhaps, been the most powerful catalyst in the organisational changes towards an equal participation for women in West Germany.

Women in Parliament

One of the miracles of German political history has been the strong representation of women in parliament as soon as they gained passive voting rights. The early promise of parliamentary politics as a career for women was not met by political reality: in 1919, women constituted 10% of the National Assembly delegates; it took until 1983 for women to reach the same proportion of seats in a national parliament for the second time, and until 1987 to surpass it (Table 6.9). Not only did women's representation in the Bundestag fail to reach the target set at the threshold of the Weimar Republic, it actually declined at the very time when women's interest in politics and motivation to participate increased. In the mid-Fifties, forty-eight women were members of parliament. The majority had been active in the various women's movements of the Weimar Republic or in political parties, and continued their political career which had been interrupted or diverted by National Socialism. In the first Bundestag, relatively few women gained seats; in the Fifties, the Christian Democrats expanded to win an absolute majority in 1957. As more candidates were elected for the CDU/CSU more women were elected, although their share of the parliamentary group remained at 8%. In the SPD, the second Bundestag elections brought the veterans of the socialist women's movement back into parliamentary politics and the number of female

Table 6.9 Women members of the Bundestag 1949–1987[a]

Year	All	% of BT	CDU/CSU	%	SPD	%	FDP	%	Others	%
1949	28	7	11	8	13	10	0	—	4	5
1953	45	9	19	8	21	13	3	6	2	4
1957	48	9	22	8	22	12	3	7	1	6
1961	43	8	18	7	21	10	4	8	—	—
1965	36	7	15	6	19	9	2	7	—	—
1969	34	7	14	6	18	8	2	5	—	—
1972	30	6	15	6	13	5	2	5	—	—
1976	38	7	19	8	15	7	4	8	—	—
1980	44	8	18	8	19	8	7	13	Greens	—
1983	51	10	17	7	21	10	3	12	10	36
1987	80	15	18	8	31	16	6	13	25	57

[a] The numbers refer to the beginning of a legislative period, i.e. reflect the election results. Since the Federal Republic does not have by-elections, vacant parliamentary seats are filled from party lists which normally increases the number of women members of parliament.

Sources: Schindler, *Datenhandbuch*; Kürschners Volkshandbuch vols 10 and 11.

SPD parliamentarians rose despite the party's poor electoral fortunes. The FDP and other small parties had some women parliamentarians but not enough to look towards them as trailblazers of gender equality (Funke 1984).

The return of the Weimar veterans of women's politics hampered a rejuvenation of women's policies or organisational initiatives in the two major parties: as the dust of a new democratic beginning had settled, West German politics appeared to return in the Sixties to a parliamentary practice which included very few women. In 1972, when a lifestyle of choice and socio-economic opportunities had· shaped a young generation who expected equality, the number of women in parliament fell to its lowest point since 1949. In fact, in 1972 the Christian Democratic parliamentary group included more women than that of the SPD even though the SPD was widely regarded as the party which would transform West German society and put equality of opportunities into everyday practice. This discrepancy between women's expectations, in particular those young women who had joined the party, and the weak place of women in SPD political representation laid the seeds for the controversy of today about a fair place for women and the introduction of compulsory quotas (Kolinsky 1989). The 1987 elections to the

Bundestag were finally governed by an overt concern about the representation of women and a commitment at least to increase the share of women in parliamentary politics. The Green party, which entered the Bundestag in 1983, has contributed significantly to increasing the parliamentary place of women. In 1983, ten of their twenty-eight members of the Bundestag were women; 20% of all women in the Bundestag belonged to the Greens. Four years later, the Greens had adopted a quota system by which no less than half the Green members of the Bundestag should be women. Of the eighty women who were elected as members of the Bundestag in 1987, close to one in three belonged to the Green parliamentary group.

In the *Länder* a similar process is evident, and access of women to parliamentary politics accelerated in the 1980s after an uneven start in the post-war years and a decline in the Sixties and early Seventies. While the city states and Berlin in particular always had a larger contingent of women among their parliamentarians than the larger *Länder*, the representation of women at regional level is remarkably similar to that in the Bundestag. In the first *Land* elections held in the 1950s an average of 8% of the seats were won by women; for *Land* parliaments elected between 1985 and 1988 the share of women's seats had risen to 16%. Representation ranged from one-third of parliamentary seats in Hamburg to just over 7% in Baden-Württemberg. In all parliaments in which the Greens hold seats they also have the largest share of women in their respective parliamentary groups. Although the SPD tends to have a larger number of women members of parliament, the Greens have the larger proportion. In Hamburg, the regional Green party – the Green Alternative List – even entered an all-woman list to fight the last two *Land* elections.

A New Type of Woman Parliamentarian

The numerical changes are only the most evident aspect of a further reaching transformation of the political participation of women. In the founding decades of the Federal Republic parliamentary politics seemed to be a career for single or childless women. In the late Fifties, one in five women in the Bundestag were married and had children, while 60% were single (Table

6.10). In the 1980s the proportions have nearly been reversed with one in three of parliamentary women single, and close to half married with children. The career motivation of young-generation women in political parties carries over into parliamentary representation. In the past, the single career woman in parliament tended to be in her late forties or early fifties; today's women parliamentarians are some ten years younger. In 1987, four of the ten youngest but only two of the ten oldest members of the Bundestag were women (*Kürschners Volkshandbuch* 1987: 238).

Candidate Selection

One of the key devices for controlling access to parliamentary careers has been the system of candidate selection (Henkel 1975; Schröder 1971). Here, women have been disadvantaged throughout the history of the Federal Republic. In the West German electoral system, half the members of parliament win their seats outright as constituency candidates for their respective party while the other half is chosen from party lists of candidates for each region (Stöss 1985). Depending on the proportion of the total vote any one party has received and the number of direct seats it has won, list candidates can enter parliament until the proportion of seats is in line with the share of the total vote won by a party. Safe seats tend to be safe direct seats, or nominations at the front end of an electoral list. Women have held very few safe constituency nominations; the majority of those who have been elected entered via *Land* electoral lists, or during a legislative period to fill a vacancy. The majority of women whose name appears on an electoral list have tended to populate the tail end where electoral chances are nil (Schindler 1984: 190). Again, things have begun to change, albeit slowly. In 1987, women were more strongly represented as direct candidates and on electoral lists than ever before (Kolinsky 1987b). For the SPD, one in three candidates were women, for the CDU one in four, for the Greens more than half while the FDP and CSU refused to give special consideration to the electoral chances of women and adjust their nomination procedures. Although women's success in entering parliament still fell behind their numerical presence among the candidates

Table 6.10 Women members of the Bundestag by marital status, 1957–1987 (in %) (In brackets: % men in same category)

	1957–61	1961–65	1965–69	1969–72	1972–76	1976–80	1980–83	1983–87	1987–90
Single/widowed, without children	60 (8)	58 (9)	50 (8)	53 (6)	50 (5)	50 (6)	30 (8)	27 (8)	30 (5)
Married, without children	19 (48)	16 (33)	14 (24)	9 (17)	7 (13)	13 (12)	25 (10)	8 (10)	8 (8)
Married, divorced, widowed with children	21 (44)	26 (58)	36 (68)	38 (77)	43 (82)	37 (82)	46 (82)	57 (82)	55 (87)

Sources: Peter Schindler, *Datenhandbuch* 192; *Kürschners Volkshandbuch* vol. 10: 245; vol. 11: 245.

and on the party lists, the round of elections since 1987 saw clear increases in women's representation for the SPD, for the Greens and depending on context and locality for some of the other parties (Table 6.9). The increases reflect the career motivation of today's women in politics but also, and more pragmatically, the impact of changed nomination procedures and various quota regulations. As we shall discuss later in this chapter, quotas have been considered or introduced by West German political parties as they compete for the electoral loyalty and the political participation of the younger generation of women.

Women and High Government Office

Women have become more numerous among the parliamentary membership and more visible among the leadership. Although there is no sign in West Germany that a woman would run the country as chancellor or be nominated by her party as potential chancellor candidate, governments since the early Sixties have included at least one woman minister. In the forty years of democratic government in West Germany, ten women have held ministerial offices in Bonn. Some were members of the government in more than one legislative period; but overall, the little group of women ministers has remained very select indeed. Normally, women administered women's portfolios: health or the amalgam of family affairs and youth which today includes health and also women. Only two women administered portfolios outside the traditional women's realm: in the mid-Seventies, Marie Schlei became Minister for Economic Cooperation and Dorothee Wilms has been Minister for Education and Science since Helmut Kohl displaced Schmidt as chancellor. Marie Schlei, who served as parliamentary secretary to the chancellor, Helmut Schmidt, has written an account of her appointment outside the female track:

> My constant efforts to advance equal opportunities for women in their social environment and in society as a whole did not succeed fully due to resistance which persisted not only in the chancellery but also in a number of ministries. At the reconstitution of his government after the 1976 elections, Helmut Schmidt offered me the Ministry for Youth, Family and Health. Our intelligent Katharina Focke had left her office as Minister for Family Affairs. Since I believed and

still believe that family policies are not only women's affairs, I declined and suggested that a man be appointed to this office or that a second woman be invited to join the cabinet. If, however, Helmut Schmidt wanted to see me in a ministerial office I was prepared to accept the Ministry for Economic Cooperation which remained vacant due to the departure of Egon Bahr. The chancellor preferred to offer the Ministry of Family Affairs to a woman, but I became, as I had wanted to, Minister for Economic Cooperation. (Schlei 1984: 100)

Marie Schlei's period of office was short-lived. In 1978 she was dismissed apparently after refusing to accept staff cuts and a curtailment in the scope of her ministry. She may, however, also have attracted the displeasure of the chancellor by giving priority to improving the social and economic situation of women in the Third World rather than more traditional areas of economic policy making (ibid. pp. 103–4). Since she acceded to the ministry as a reliable member of the Schmidt entourage when the newly elected chancellor cleansed the government of appointments made by his predecessor, Brandt, Marie Schlei may also have shown more independence of intent than a woman, or indeed a minister in that administration, was allowed to entertain.

The second incumbent of a non-female ministry does not appear to have faced similar difficulties. Dorothee Wilms was appointed Minister for Education and Science in October 1982 when a change of coalition brought the CDU/CSU back into government after thirteen years in opposition. Following the 1987 election victory of the CDU/CSU and FDP coalition, she was put in charge of the Ministry of Inner German Relations. In the first part of her ministerial career, Dorothee Wilms was the only woman in the cabinet; in 1985, Rita Süßmuth became the second woman with ministerial office in the Conservative government. She took over the conventional portfolio which had been renamed the Ministry of Youth, Family and Health when the politics of the Seventies focused on young people rather than on families. In 1985 the ministry was renamed again and 'women' were added to its special responsibilities. After the 1987 elections, Rita Süßmuth was confirmed in office. An excellent election result in her constituency in 1987 and consistently high popularity ratings in public opinion polls have shown her to be one of the best liked West German politicians. Her popularity, appeal to women and generally liberal image also made her an ideal candidate to help the government out of a tight spot: in November 1988 the President of the Bundestag, Philip Jenninger, resigned after having delivered a controversial speech during a memorial session of the Bundestag in honour of the victims of the so-called 'Night of the Broken Glass' in 1938. Rather than remembering the victims, Jenninger focused on explaining why Germans had liked Hitler and had followed him, and he used the language, terminology and categories of the Nazis to explain their impact to his audience. In its embarrassment, the government invited Rita Süßmuth to become President of the Bundestag, after Annemarie Renger the second woman to hold this office. In her place, Kohl appointed an expert gerontologist from the University of Heidelberg, Professor Ursula Lehr, to take the vacant ministerial chair and assume responsibility for women's affairs in the Federal Republic. Thus, the contingent of two women in the cabinet was maintained and seemed assured for the lifetime of that particular government. In a cabinet reshuffle in April 1989, a third woman was appointed to ministerial office: Gerda Hasselfeldt from the Bavarian CSU became Minister of Urban Planning and Housing.

Most ministries have yet to appoint a woman to a top position. The current ministry responsible for youth, the family, women and health – itself an amalgamation of two separate ministries for family affairs and health – has offered the best opportunities for women. Nine of the ten women who held ministerial office at federal government level since the inception of the West German state were appointed to these areas. Two of the eight women who held the top political appointment just below ministerial level and served as parliamentary secretaries were appointed to the youth/family/women/health portfolio. Katharina Focke was the first woman to hold a post at parliamentary secretary level when she was appointed to the chancellor's office under Willy Brandt in 1969. For her, the post was a stepping-stone to ministerial office in 1972. In a similar way, Marie Schlei progressed from parliamentary secretary in the chancellery to her ministerial post (Economic Cooperation), and Anke Fuchs advanced from being parliamentary secretary in the ministry for labour to run the ministry of youth, family and health in the final months of the SDP/FDP coalition government from April to October 1982. Perhaps the most interesting top appointments for women have been in Foreign Affairs, which had a female parliamentary secretary in 1976, and in Defence, which appointed a woman parliamentary secretary in 1987. Foreign Affairs, of course, has been run by the FDP since 1969 when the party, and indeed Hans Dietrich Genscher, retained the portfolio even after the change of coalition. The appointment of a woman to a top post in this ministry offers the prospect of top-level involvement to female FDP politicians in a party in which government participation has been a lifeline of political mobilisation and, indeed, survival. The top job for a woman can be seen as an incentive aimed at FDP women members of parliament, and also at the female electorate who should be persuaded that the FDP offers women opportunities at the top leadership level.

The appointment of Agnes Hürland-Büning as parliamentary secretary in the Ministry of Defence has been seen in connection with the political discussion in West Germany of whether or not women should be called upon to serve in the armed forces. The Bundeswehr is a conscript army and is based on compulsory military service of young men. The combined influences of a numerical decrease in the age cohort of eighteen-year-olds and the increased readiness of young people to refuse military service and opt for the so-called *Zivildienst* or seek exemptions have raised concern in conservative circles that the Bundeswehr would be short of people. Military service of some kind for women did not spring from an interest in equal opportunities but from an interest in maintaining the defence capacity of West Germany. The prospect of military service for women has been strongly rejected by women themselves, by the women's movement, the SPD and the Greens. The appointment of a woman into the Defence portfolio has to be seen as an attempt to neutralise the controversy by bestowing responsibility in the field of defence on a woman, and also to aim for a political consensus in the matter of conscription and the place of women.

Parliamentary Leadership

In West Germany, as in other parliamentary democracies, the

229

parliamentary groups or *Fraktionen* articulate party policies, turn them into parliamentary and public actions, and allow members to make their mark as spokesmen on core issues. Playing a prominent role in the parliamentary group renders members of parliament into strong contenders for government posts at national level and also in the regions. In West Germany, the Bundestag *Fraktion* in particular can act as a springboard to political leadership. Members of the executive can influence policy issues and personnel decisions of their party in opposition and in government. Since each of the parliamentary groups runs committees to prepare policies and to shape the parliamentary business, the chair of such a group has a significant voice in politics and parliament. To gain access to the leadership of the parliamentary party is, therefore, a landmark of political equality for women, and a recognition of their political acumen. In the Eighties, women have made some inroads into the power structure of all parliamentary groups in the Bundestag.

Of the four parties with Bundestag representation in the mid-Eighties, the FDP has the worst record for electing women to key positions in the parliamentary party. Between September 1949 and February 1987, the beginning of the eleventh legislative period of the Bundestag, no women had been elected to a parliamentary group office in the FDP, and the only woman to serve on the parliamentary group executive did so *ex officio* in her capacity as deputy chairman of the party organisation (Liselotte Funke). The Christian Democrats did somewhat better. As far back as 1957, the CDU/CSU established a tradition of electing a prominent representative of the women's association as one of the deputy chairmen of the parliamentary group. Recently, the range of positions for women in the executive of the CDU/CSU parliamentary party has broadened. Women have been elected deputy business manager (from 1980) and also to the chair of working parties and committees whose core function is policy formulation in relation to parliamentary legislation. The working parties with women in the chair have been in the traditional realm of women's affairs. More interesting is the appointment of a woman to the chair of the influential CDU/CSU foreign affairs committee. On closer inspection, the apparently impressive step towards the equality of political influence for women loses some of its sparkle: Michaela Geiger, who holds the position of expert in foreign policy for the CDU/CSU parliamentary group, entered the Bundestag as replacement candidate for Franz Josef Strauß, then chairman of the Bavarian wing of the Christian Democrats, who has since died (Geiger 1984: 320). Could it be that the heiress to Strauß's constituency won influence and high office with such alacrity as the mouthpiece of Strauß's political ambitions, and as such could expect to have a voice in foreign policy without even being a member of the Bundestag, let alone the relevant committee of the parliamentary group? Even after Strauß's death, the CSU retains a strong voice in articulating the foreign policy of the CDU/CSU parliamentary party.

In the SPD parliamentary group, women found it hard to enter the executive. During the Fifties and Sixties, they played no part in the parliamentary leadership of the SPD during a time when the party regarded women as supplementary rather than essential to its political thrust. The onset of the social-liberal era in 1969, when Willy Brandt led the first government with the SPD as senior partner, changed the prospects for women. Although the parliamentary party has never been chaired by a woman, the party elected women as deputies and party managers and into other positions on the executive. As women in the SPD expected to participate in the leadership, the party had to broaden access. In 1969, the SPD parliamentary group had one woman on the executive; in 1987, eight women held positions on the parliamentary group executive. One of them was Annemarie Renger. She had made her way into politics as the private secretary to the first chairman of the post-war SPD, Kurt Schumacher, became the first woman president of the Bundestag and has since retained a position on the executive of the parliamentary party. In 1973, Helga Timm joined the executive as parliamentary group business manager. The promise of more say for women in the SPD which the early Seventies seemed to hold out was not fulfilled in line with expectations. Only two more women came to prominence in the SPD parliamentary group at that time, and in both cases the positions seemed designed to pacify them over loss of influence rather than to extend their power base: Marie Schlei had, as mentioned earlier, been eased out of her ministerial office, and Elfriede Eilers had been voted out of heading the SPD women's associations in the autumn of

1977. The real change of tone and of political intent among women in the SPD parliamentary party is evident from 1983, when a younger generation found their way into the executive; it gathered momentum in 1987 when the parliamentary group had three women deputies, two women parliamentary managers, and three women chairing committees. From the 'old guard' of SPD women, only Annemarie Renger remained on the executive of the parliamentary party in her capacity as Deputy President of the Bundestag. The new deputies and chairpersons of committees belong to the post-war generation of educated, politically motivated women who interpret their role in political life more expansively as one of equality than had been customary for SPD women in the past.

The new opportunities of women to play a visible role in parliamentary politics have been greatly advanced by the impact of the Greens on the membership and the leadership of the West German parliaments. As discussed earlier, the proportion of women in parliament tended to rise noticeably where the Greens gained seats. In many instances the number of women in the small Green groups came close to the number in the much larger CDU and SPD. In the Bundestag, 31% of the eighty women members who were elected in 1987 belonged to the Green parliamentary group, which held 8.3% of the seats (Table 6.9). From the outset, the Greens fielded women in prominent positions as joint leaders of the parliamentary party, and as taking the chair at the parliamentary committee to which the party was entitled under the West German regulations of parliamentary cooperation in proportion to party strength. Green women have been regular contributors to plenary sessions on all aspects of policy, not only on traditional women's issues. Since the entry of the Green party into West German parliamentary politics, more has changed than just the number of women who stand as candidates and succeed in elections: women have acquired a voice as regular participants in everyday parliamentary proceedings – that a woman takes the floor as the leading spokesperson of her party on a specific policy issue has become common practice since the advent of the Greens in parliamentary politics. In 1984/5, an all-woman team headed the Green parliamentary party in the Bundestag and women held never less than half the available positions at executive level.

The women's opportunities in Green parliamentary groups to hold front-bench positions in all fields of policy expertise and parliamentary business have acted as catalysts of equal opportunities for women elsewhere in the party system. Thus, the two large membership parties, the CDU and SPD, in particular have responded to the participatory zeal of women in their organisations and to the uncertain loyalties of the female electorate and have agreed quota regulations for the representation of women. The appeals for more say and the pledges to heed them, which were as old as the participation of women in political parties, have been superseded by plans for action. Although each party generated its own model of equality, its own set of regulations on how to implement it, and its own cluster of obstacles, West German politics seems to be moving towards a new era of opportunities for women.

Quota Regulations and Organisational Adjustments

The discrepancy between the motivation to participate in politics on equal terms with men and women's actual chances of achieving positions of influence and leadership is at the heart of the contemporary debate on the use of women's quotas in political life, and the efforts to introduce and implement them. After the USA set out to curtail discriminatory practices through affirmative action programmes which require companies to recruit their workforce in proportion to the ethnic mix in their vicinity and line of business if they wish to compete for government-sponsored orders, and after Norway seemed to overcome its deficit of women in politics through a compulsory women's quota of no less than 40%, women's quotas have been a buzz-word of West German political discourse, and a much disputed goal of organisational reform (Janßen 1987). Nobody is altogether sure whether a quota of some kind would be a good thing or whether women should make their impact through calibre and quality alone. The mere quota woman, the woman who made it because a specified number of posts had to be filled, would not only be second class; her circumstantial entry into politics would reduce the value of that office, and the quality of political representation and leadership.

233

Despite some uncertainties about quotas and their effect on the status of women and the opportunities of men in political life, the four West German parties with electoral prospects have begun to scrutinise their organisational practices and explore ways of widening the avenues of participation for women. Even where a quantitative formula of women's representation has not been considered, the place of women in party organisations and political positions has become a focal point of interest and a target for change.

The Women's Statute of the Greens

The Greens were the first party to move from a discussion of equal opportunities and policy commitments to organisational regulations. In November 1985, the federal party congress decided to amend the organisational statutes of the *Bundespartei* by including a special section on the representation of women. The Greens had, of course, started out in politics with a broad commitment to equal opportunities but the 'good intentions' had not been as effective as the party founders had envisaged: 'It is plainly visible that only few women occupy positions in the Greens which are important within the party or in public life' (*Präambel*). To rectify this anomaly but also to create an organisational reality in their own party which could anticipate a social order in which equality had been achieved, the Greens decided on a 50% quota across all electoral and organisational positions: 'in order to ensure parity, electoral procedures have to be defined in such a way that men and women are elected separately. Electoral lists have to name men and women in alternation, whereby the uneven places should be reserved for women' (for full text see Appendix VII). The only exception from the 50% rule was that all-women electoral lists and party organisations should be permissible.

Women's Quotas and the Free Democrats

Although the Green answer to equal opportunities for women was too radical for the other parties, none could ignore the challenge. The first to respond were the Free Democrats. At their congress in Hanover in May 1986 the party endorsed a programmatic statement 'Putting Equal Rights into Practice' (Appendix VIII) which contained three key decisions: to advance career chances of women in all areas of economic life and increase flexibility in employment; to reject any kind of quota regulation in political life; and to change electoral legislation in such a way that the voter could select from the electoral lists those candidates – men or women – who inspired most confidence. In this way, those who were the best in the eyes of the citizens, not in the judgement of the party functionaries, would have the best chances of entering parliamentary politics. A similar proposal had already been voiced by the CDU one year earlier as one possible way to increase electoral chances for women. In its 1986 programmatic statement the FDP stressed that quality rather than gender should guide the selection of the political elite and women who seek recognition should compete with men and prove themselves. In 1987, however, and under pressure from the political climate and the women members, the party executive decided on a *Frauenförderplan* (Plan for the Advancement of Women) in the FDP which set the party firmly on a path towards better opportunities for women without relinquishing its rejection of quota regulations (Appendix IX).

SPD Promises and Quota Resolutions

The next party to rise to the challenge of quota regulations was the SPD. At its federal congress in Nuremberg in August 1986, the party endorsed a three-stage plan of transition towards equality: congress agreed that by the 1990s women should be represented at all levels of the SPD party organisation and in parliaments in proportion to their share of the population or at no less than 40% (Appendix X). Congress deferred altering the party statutes and asked the SPD executive to take the matter in hand, and to word within twelve months a recommendation on quota regulations and the transitory stages of putting them into practice. The slow pace of party bureaucracy is not untypical. By the time women's quotas were accepted in principle in 1986, the original SPD resoluton to improve equal opportunities for women was already seven years old (*Parteitag* 1979: 1589). It had been reinforced at the 1984 SPD congress with a decision that women were to receive special access to leading positions in the party and to training programmes for party functionaries, and that regular reports on the state of equality in the party had to be presented to congress for information and discussion. A first report of this type was to have been submitted in 1984, but little happened since the districts claimed that no women had come forward to compete for relevant offices and nothing new had occurred which called for a report. In September 1985, the Party Council took the matter in hand and instructed district and regional parties to give preference to women in the nomination of candidates for the 1987 elections:

> The Party Council notes: the goal which is on the agenda now is to increase the proportion of women members of the SPD parliamentary group in the Bundestag for the 1987 elections. The Party Council knows full well how difficult it can be to change personnel structures, which have changed over time. But the point in time for an energetic effort is favourable. The SPD has a good chance not only to improve on its 1983 election result but to become the strongest political force in the country. This means that many vacant places in the constituencies and on the regional electoral lists can be filled in 1987. If we want to make optimal use of our electoral chances we have to fill the vacant (and well positioned) places with female candidates. (Party Council, resolution 16 Sept. 1985)

Between 1985 and August 1986, equal opportunities and the possibility of quota regulation were considered throughout the SPD; some local and regional parties favoured them and wrote them in their statutes, some rejected them. At its annual congress in Hanover in October 1985, the Arbeitsgemeinschaft Sozialdemokratischer Frauen (ASF) agreed an action plan of equality in stages with quotas as a central component and threatened to agree women's lists or similar types of political pressure if the party were to stall unduly (Appendix XI). In the past, quotas had always been rejected as detrimental to women's claim that their abilities and quality as politicians were equal to men's and should not need protective measures; now the SPD women embraced the formula with an alacrity born from years of futile pleading but also from fears of being overtaken by the Greens (*Organisationsprobleme* 1988).

The mainstream SPD organisation proceeded more cautiously. To clarify the constitutional and legal implications the party obtained a specialist report which found that quotas could be operated within the law of equal access and opportunities if they remained below 40%. The report also stressed the problems encountered in small wards where an inflexible quota could destroy the fabric of grass-roots politics. A joint meeting of the SPD executive party council in Mannheim in October 1987 followed these recommendations and decreed that small organisational units should be exempt, and that the transition towards a 40% participation of women should follow a different pace for the party organisation and for parliamentary seats, with target years of 1994 and 1998 respectively (Appendix XII). In May 1987, the working group on equal opportunities had already presented a document outlining which paragraphs in the party statutes would have to be amended and how the various party formations should implement the women's quotas. The group also announced that the whole text of the SPD statutes would have to be rewritten to remove the gender bias from its vocabulary (Wettig-Danielmeier 1987).

After more than a decade of internal debate and a firm recommendation to agree a 40% women's quota and proceed with implementing it, the 1988 SPD congress in Münster finally decided to do so. In the prevailing political climate of internal pressure from SPD women and the flagging electoral fortunes of a party whose former female voters were now looking towards the Greens, the SPD had no alternative than to embrace the 40% quota. Congress itself honoured the new climate and elected ten women into the party executive – the highest number of women ever to be voted into the SPD leadership (*Das Parlament* 23 Sept. 1988). The more radical political practice of the Greens has set benchmarks of participation. Within the SPD, women now expect better opportunities where in the past they had been hived off into a politically powerless coffee-morning culture; among the young and potentially mobile women voters, the SPD would lose credibility if its verbal commitment to equal opportunities failed at the first hurdle, that of its own party organisation. Since SPD and Greens are competing for a broadly similar electorate and their members share many political attitudes and views, the SPD has come under pressure of innovation from overall changes of expectations and political values and also from the decisive focus on women within the Greens.

The continued support from women under the age of forty-five – the SPD core electorate of today – appears to hinge on the women's issue and the question of participation. In its own organisation, the SPD now has to meet the challenge of redressing the gender balance within the party organisation. The elections for the party executive at the 1988 congress provided a first taste of controversies to come. According to the new regulations, fourteen men and an equal number of women had to be elected in the first round. In fact, the women were elected; but only six men received enough votes to qualify for a place. For the first time in the party's history, established politicians and members of the executive had to compete in two and even in three electoral rounds for a place on the executive, and veterans like the former Finance Minister Hans Apel and the former business manager of the party, Peter Glotz, failed to gain enough votes to remain in the party leadership. Of the forty-one members of the executive who were elected in September 1988, fourteen are women. Two women, a deputy chairperson and the business manager of the party, are among the small group of seven who run the party; the remaining twelve women (24%) belong to the extended executive. In his address to congress, party chairman Vogel compared the move towards women's quotas with the historical move seventy years earlier when women gained the right to vote:

> In the women's question, the Social Democratic Party has brought a long historical process to its temporary conclusion and has agreed on a set of regulations and statutes which obligates the party to give women – i.e. the majority of the people – step by step that kind of representation at all levels of party offices and parliamentary participation which is in line with their overall importance. (Hans Jochen Vogel, at the Münster congress of the SPD)

Functionaries or Mothers? Quota Pressures and the Christian Democrats

Although the Christian Democrats draw on a different segment of the electorate than SPD or Greens, the party could not evade the issue of equal opportunities in political life and had to pledge improved practices (Geißler 1986). Inside the party, the CDU was less exposed to pressures for a change in women's representation than SPD or Greens had been, whose female members were inspired by the women's movement and its concepts of a female perspective on politics and society which was no less valid than that of men, and needed no less of a voice. In the CDU, conventional ideas about the role of women in the family and alongside men continue to be widely accepted. If the party began to rethink its approach to the participation of women it responded to the erosion of the female electorate, and a need to offer a place for women which was in line with contemporary views and expectations. Internal pressures from the CDU women have also been less forceful since the party has always allowed its women's association a voice at the top leadership level. While women's groups or the ASF in the SPD were dependent on the executive and did not have a right to initiate policies or party congress resolutions, the CDU Frauenvereinigung – recently renamed Frauenunion – enjoyed these rights. The chair of the women's associations is an *ex officio* member of the party executive; the holder had also normally been elected into the Bundestag and joined the executive of the parliamentary group there. In this way, the concerns of women could be articulated at core policy formulation levels of the party, while the women's association in the SPD with its more rebellious notions of equality and its motivated clientele could be effective only through especially created channels such as the Equal Opportunities Commission. Although the numerical balance between men and women in the CDU leadership never corresponded to membership figures, women have been able to wield influence and the women's association has been recognised as an important tier of party organisation. When the ASF was created in the early Seventies, the women wanted more say and political recognition in line with their calibre and ambitions while the party executive wanted to retain firm control from the top over its women's working group, its aims and activities. The CDU Frauenunion, by contrast, was created to show emphatically the core place of women in and for the CDU. This format worked smoothly until the issue of equal participation in politics challenged the equilibrium that women should have limited, albeit prominent, influence in the CDU. In the Bavarian sister party, the function of the women's association was similar to that in the CDU, but true to the centrist spirit of the CSU and its character as a well-structured party machine (Mintzel 1983), the party women have acquiesced in the political environment and the opportunities available to them.

Not so in the CDU. At its thirty-fourth federal congress in Mainz in 1986, the CDU tackled the question of women's participation in the party organisation and in political life. Congress passed a resolution stating that women should be involved at all levels of party organisation and have political representation in accordance with their share of the party membership (Appendix XIII). Quota regulations have been ruled out, and the recommendations about women's participation will not be written into the party statutes. Some younger CDU women appear to favour a firmer commitment and would welcome a quota system of representation in relation to membership strength, but overall opinion in the party and among CDU women opposes quotas as an unsuitable device in politics which depends, above all, on personality, on ability, and on the luck of being in the right place at the right time.[6] The gist of CDU women's policy has, in any case, originated at the top. The problem is not, as in the SPD, to accommodate grass-root pressures but to market the concept developed at head office and generate local and regional support for it.

The CDU concern about women is much wider than internal party representation or membership of women in parliamentary groups. The demands for better representation of women in the party were formulated by a policy planning group headed by the CDU general secretary Geißler as part of a package of guidelines which were to launch the CDU as the major party of

6. The different positions emerged clearly in interviews with CDU politicians: in an interview on 11 April 1988 Otti Geschka, a prominent member of the Frauenunion and the *Land* parliament and since 1987 head of the women's bureau in Hesse, and holding the rank of Staatssekretärin, expressed strong support for women's quotas and was doubtful whether the declarations of goodwill and intent which had been accepted in the CDU would have any substantive effect on practical representation at all levels of party organisation and parliamentary work. In contrast, interviews with Rotraud Hock (FU) and Elvira Bickel MdL (Mainz, 12 April 1988) indicated that CDU women dismiss quotas as an impediment of quality, and believe in personal ability and in chance as the main factors in women's political success. Within the Frauenunion, most of the active membership and body of functionaries are older women, who neither share the ambitions of their younger colleagues nor would endorse means such as quota regulations to obtain them. Internally, the CDU seems a long way removed from compulsory quotas.

policy innovation and practical reform in the field of equal opportunities (Appendix XIV). Under the heading of 'Women in Employment, Family and Politics' the party advocated a 'new partnership' approach, and used its party congress in March 1985 in Essen to publicise its ideas and claim a new image of the CDU as a party for young, modern women, not just for families and mothers. Surrounded by a glare of publicity Geißler had invited five hundred women from all walks of life and political camps, who mingled with the regular delegates and with party dignitaries and were asked to discuss the role women should play in the contemporary world. The congress in Essen repeated a format which had first been tried in 1981 when the CDU invited seven hundred youngsters to attend the party congress in Hamburg in the hope that a more youthful CDU image might shore up the party's dwindling support among young voters. Four years later, the party had an eye on the crumbling support among younger women for whom conventional Conservative role models of homemaking or motherhood had lost their exclusive appeal. The 'new partnership' advocated a new flexibility between roles, while encouraging motherhood through offering financial incentives and through keeping working conditions flexible. Women should be able to take turns with men in being 'mothers', they should be able to create their own pattern of combining roles, and they should be able to return to secure employment after a career break by having a job kept open or by taking part in retraining programmes.

In the context of these broader political ambitions, participation of women in the CDU is an important but not a centre stage issue. Since orders came from the top to accomplish women's participation in accordance with their membership share, and since the conservative factions in the party, notably the Bavarian CSU, strongly oppose the 'new partnership approach' and its notion of choosing between work, family or a combination of both, the party has yet to test whether there is sufficient internal goodwill to make room for women in the organisation, in party functions and in parliaments.

Towards an Age of Organisational Equality?

Disadvantage of women in political life, which has been the

241

hallmark of party political and parliamentary history, seems set to become a mishap of the past as party leaderships gear up to coax or coerce their organisations into the age of equality. The willingness of women to change their electoral preferences, and the salience of equality as an electoral issue for many young women, have forced the parties into practical adjustments. Credibility as a political force seems increasingly tied to a party's ability to break some or all of its internal gender barriers. Women under forty and especially those on the left of the political spectrum favour quota regulation and a socio-political transformation of the party structure towards equal representation and equal opportunities. They look to the Greens or to the SPD as agents of this change who should make it happen internally and who might promote it in society. Women with conservative views prefer to talk about personal qualities rather than quotas, but neither FDP nor CDU can afford to ignore the demands of their women members for party posts and political responsibility. After a century of providing back-room support or serving in the chorus of politics, women are set to step into the footlights.

What Does It All Add Up To?

At the time of writing, it is too early to assess the impact of women's quotas or their equivalents on the participation of women in political parties and their opportunities to hold a party office or a parliamentary seat. In 1985 Helga Wex, the chairperson of the CDU-affiliated women's association, sounded a note of warning that women's expectations and party political realities were no longer in tune: 'many well qualified women turn their backs on political involvement, because of their unequal opportunities inside political parties' (*Neue Ruhr-zeitung* 27 Sept. 1985). Her answer, and that of her counterparts in the other political parties, was that parties needed to adjust to the new motivations and capacities of women by opening party hierarchies and bringing leadership positions in reach of women, which should boost membership numbers and change the gender balance of German politics. The focus on women's quotas and the varied steps to make party offices accessible to women are just beginning to take shape and their full effects will only be apparent in a decade or so. However, the evidence which is to hand so far hardly suggests that the discrepancies have been resolved between women's expectations of participating in politics and the avenues of participation which parties are able to offer. The picture is far from uniform, since each party presents its own organisational obstacles and motivations vary between women of different political persuasions as to the role they would wish to play in their parties and in West German political life.

Profiles of Party Change

In the SPD, the discrepancies have been sharpest between women's political motivations and the opportunities within the party to hold responsibilities. The SPD more than any other party activates the educated middle class, the professional women whose political ideas border on the Greens in some respects and tend towards the conservative in others. SPD women are often social risers compared with their parents, with better education, employment, career prospects and earnings, and many come from SPD-affiliated environments. For these women, the potential conflict between career motivation in employment and finding time for additional political work is a potent one. While the older generations of mothers and grandmothers joined the SPD since the party needed women to create the social and personal environment in which the next generation of social democrats could flourish, these new women want to make a contribution in their own right and compete with men on an equal footing. The history of the SPD since the early Seventies has been a history of failing to respond to these new expectations and to build on them. Only the dependence of the party on women voters and the danger of losing support to the Greens changed the climate in such a way as to acknowledge the right of women to participate in a leading capacity. The quota regulations could reassure politically minded women that party work might lead to a career and thus fit their broad achievement motivations, rather than distract from it as a leisure-time hobby without serious prospects. Women's quotas in the SPD could also win back from the Green circuit those women who aspire to political office but who do not fully share the fears of organisational hierarchies which prevail in the Green party.

In the SPD, prospects for women in politics look better than they ever did in the past. In the last five years, women's representation has risen at all levels of party politics, with the exception of the top leadership in the regions and at federal level. Although the ASF women insist that a female chancellor is a possibility and that the association can call on enough highly qualified and competent women to staff all the top positions in the party, women have yet to conquer the hot seat of party chairman at any of these levels. Lower down, however, representation has increased. At the party council, the party executive, the party congress, the European parliament, and even at the executive of the powerful parliamentary group in the Bundestag, the proportion of women has increased sharply in the Eighties, and reached between 20 and 30% in 1986. Table 6.11 is taken from an account prepared by the women's association ASF to demonstrate the slow pace of change in the party; it does that but it also demonstrates how change has accelerated as the issue of women's representation began to head the political agenda, and that all party levels are now equally amenable to giving women a chance of leadership (Table 6.11). Inroads for women have been more modest at the grass-root levels of party organisation than at the top: in 1988, none of the district chairmen were women, although women have increased their seats on the respective executives; at sub-district and local level, the traditional power bases of SPD politics, women have strengthened their position on the executive, but few hold the chair. Women have found it easier to gain access to party responsibilities above the district level, with the party council and membership in various specialist commissions especially important. The executive recommendation that small local branches should be exempted from a women's quota is likely to consolidate this pattern: opportunities for women in the SPD arise above the grass-root level, and seem most readily attained at the higher levels of party council, membership in special committees, the regional executive or the party presidium. In most cases, however, women occupy (as they have always done) supportive rather than leading functions. A detailed report for Hesse showed for the period 1986 to 1987 that women found it easiest

Table 6.11 Women office holders and parliamentarians in the SPD, 1982–1988 (selected offices)

Office	Year	Women total	As % of office	Difference 1982–1988 (in %)
Congress delegates	1982	55	13	
	1984	83	19	
	1988	106	24	11
Executive	1982	6	15	
	1984	7	18	
	1988	10	25	10
Presidium	1982	1	9	
	1984	1	9	
	1988	3	27	18
Local branch chair (9,666)	1984	595	6	
	1988	659	7	1
Local branch executive (58,362)	1984	10,599	19	
	1988	10,018	17	–2

Sources: Compiled by the author from party congress reports; *Bericht über die Gleichstellung der Frauen* 1986: 5, 19; *Stuttgarter Zeitung* 28 Aug. 1986; *Zweiwochendienst Frauen und Politik* 15, 1987: 17.

to gain new representation as delegates to party congress or as elected members of the Bundestag. Here participation rates increased by 14% and 12% respectively. The experiences in Hesse suggest that progress towards equality has been more evident in the federal party organisation than at regional, district or local level, where women made only modest gains in posts and opportunities (*Bericht über die Gleichstellung* 1986; 1987). The internal organisational transformation of the SPD in accordance with its quota decision at the party congress in September 1988 promises to be one of the most far reaching and interesting processes of party political change in the post-war period, and one without precedence in intensity and intent.

Parliamentary nominations and electoral lists have emerged as a major and effective device to increase the role of women in the politics of their party, and women have made more visible

gains here than in many of their local or area party organisations. Paired with the programmatic emphasis in the SPD on
women's quotas, the slow pace of change at local level can no
longer produce the required gender balance of political representation in electoral lists and parliaments. It seems that
patterns of recruitment are changing. Either supportive functions on the local executive, which in the past were of little
consequence, will gain in political weight, or the very concept of
office-holding as a precondition for advancement in the party
will have to change. The so-called *Ochsentour* (the 'hard way up',
such as an ox might have to take) through a succession of party
offices has, of course, been a major deterrent for women who
already held the dual responsibility of their careers and families.
The straight route to positions in the federal party hierarchy
seems a promising device for enhancing inner-party mobility
since it would free women from some of the pressures to hold
numerous positions in the party before politics as a career comes
within reach. Women have, in any case, been under pressure to
take on multiple political roles in the women's association ASF
and also in the party organisation. Although the ASF has played
a major part in formulating the SPD women's policies and
insisting on quota regulations, ASF office holders do not enjoy a
recognised place in the party and command little power, unless
they also hold an office in the mainstream party organisation.

The Free Democrats, who had been reluctant to produce' a
numerical definition of equal opportunities, nevertheless had to
respond to the salience of the women's issue and to the climate
of the quota debate by measuring the state of their party against
target figures of women's representation. In a small party, shifts
of personnel and gender distribution can be accomplished more
rapidly than in a large party with a vast organisational network,
and mobility in the FDP may be rapid once the party encourages
women to hold leading posts. The scale of party imbalance can
be gauged if we consider that the SPD has nearly as many
members of local branch executives as the FDP has party members overall. Yet, the pattern of women's participation is similar
between parties: increases have occurred at the very top, in the
federal executive, in the parliamentary group executives and in
parliamentary representation in the Bundestag and in the regions. The mainstays of party organisation – in the FDP the

Table 6.12 Women office holders in the FDP in Hesse

Office	Office holders			
	All	Women	%	Target figure
Land executive	25	3	12	6
Members of the Bundestag (for Hesse)	4	1	25	1
Members of the Landtag	9	2	22	2
Delegates to party congress	44	7	16	11
Delegates to *Land* congress	300	43	14	75
District chairpersons	26	2	8	6
Deputy district chairpersons	55	7	13	14
Local council mandates	624	79	13	156
Chair of FDP groups in assemblies/parliaments	111	6	5	30

Source: Report compiled by Ruth Wagner, Deputy Chairperson of the FDP in Hesse, dated 11 January 1988; unpublished.

regional and the district offices – tend to be dominated by men, with women additional, often non-voting executive members. Since the FDP does not have a women's association, political careers of women depend on the party organisation alone, and this has remained overwhelmingly male at the key organisational levels. The FDP in Hesse published a detailed report on the representation of women, matched against the target figure that one in four posts should be held by women; this target figure should apply to all aspects of the party from membership to leadership (see Table 6.12). In January 1988 when the report was compiled, women constituted 24% of the FDP membership. With over 20%, they came ·close to their target figure in the parliamentary representation of women in the Bundestag and in the *Land* parliament in Hesse, and also in chairing local branches. None of the regional party organisations and just 8% of the districts in Hesse (10% in West Germany as a whole) were chaired by a woman. At the second level of deputy chair and members of the executive women did hold more posts but with 14% their share fell short of the target figure of 24%.

For the CDU, details of changes in the participation or office-holding of women have also been reported and discussed although in a lower key manner than in the SPD. There is some evidence that at core points of the party organisation, notably at the district level, women do not hold any leadership positions while their number has increased among parliamentary candidates and as non-leading members of district and regional executives. In particular, the CDU has created special office holders with responsibility for women's affairs to initiate policies and to oversee their implementation at local and regional level. Office-holding in the CDU appears to be more closely linked to active involvement in the women's association than in the other parties, and openings for women tend to arise for proven activists from the Frauenunion. However, two of the top positions which have been offered to women since the mid-Eighties were not allocated to reward loyal service in the party, but were given to women who had not been active previously and were not even members of the Frauenunion. The two cases concern the Ministry for Youth, Family, Women and Health. Rita Süßmuth was selected from outside the party track. As director of a research institute for Women and Society in Hanover, and as a university professor, she enjoyed considerable prestige before her appointment and seemed to have the calibre to put the new focus on women and the liberal conservatism which characterises CDU policies on women at present into practice. Her appointment was not liked but was accepted since Rita Süßmuth gained instant recognition across all parties, and, as mentioned earlier, became a darling of public opinion polls. Her replacement in the ministry – on her move to become President of the Bundestag – was also an outside appointment. In a climate of intensified expectations that party work should pay off for party women with top jobs, the choice of the gerontologist Ursula Lehr was regarded and resented as a snub. This time, more than ever, the Frauenunion activists felt that the traditional commitment to their role had been cancelled, and their work or qualified candidates for the office ignored. Even without a track record in the party organisation, the so-called *Quereinsteiger* ('entering from the sidelines') like Süßmuth and Lehr tend to be given the top position over the heads of the Frauenunion; again at the expense of regular and loyal activists, they gain coveted posts and leadership opportunities which do not normally result from regular and even outstanding party work.

The new emphasis on women in the CDU has already in-

creased the significance of the Frauenunion as a potential training ground for political leadership; this at least is the view of the
women who are active in it. The party and especially the
government have yet to acknowledge its role as a career track
from local to national politics for women and link top appointments to a background in traditional CDU women's politics. The
prospect that positions might be allocated to women in proportion to their party membership may be a deterrent for the
male-dominated districts to go on recruitment drives (Grafe
1986: 206) but it is a clear incentive for the women's association
to intensify their activities and broaden their support. Since
1987, the CDU has also begun to create women's working
parties in regional parliaments and at local level, all of them
headed by women who rose through the Frauenunion and
whose newly prominent position serves to underpin the importance of women's activities in the party.

New Politics and the Limits of Quota Participation

It would be a simplification to expect that the scramble for
women's quotas or promises to improve opportunities could
now unleash a participatory potential among women which had
been dormant in the past and was only waiting to be tapped.
The organisational adjustments in the parties feed on political
intentions from the Seventies and hope to win the women of
today and tomorrow. The women who fought and won the
battles about equal opportunities in the West German parties
belong to the generation of women who joined their respective
parties in the late Sixties or early Seventies: their expectations of
political involvement reflected the high pitch of political interest
at the time and a broad confidence in the effectiveness of
political parties as agents of political change. Since then, interest
has changed in two ways: it is less intense than it had been in
the early Seventies, in particular among the young generation;
and interest in politics is more likely than in the past to be
channelled into political activity outside established party
organisations.

The changes of attitudes and orientations from materialist to
postmaterialist values which have occurred in West Germany,
as in other advanced industrial societies, have moderated the

views and behaviour of many West Germans, who absorbed new issues and embraced new priorities. Earlier in our discussion, we noted that the so-called 'mixed types' constitute the largest group, flanked by those with predominantly materialist and postmaterialist concerns. For the changed interest in politics and styles of participation among the young generation the emergence of postmaterialist values has been the more important. They tend to go together with critical views of West German democracy, its policy priorities, its avenues of participation and its institutions (Fuchs 1987; Dalton 1984). They also go together with preferences for styles of participation which are not indebted to the hierarchical and formalised practices of traditional party organisations (Barnes et al. 1979). The essence of quota politics, that women should obtain a share in the established power structure of parties, parliaments and governments, conflicts with the sceptical assessment that this very power structure would inhibit rather than facilitate the reorientation of issues and action which has been called the New Politics (Baker et al. 1981).

In West Germany, the new social movements which added an important extra-parliamentary dimension to the contemporary political process in the Seventies and Eighties (Pulzer 1987) could draw on the critical potential of postmaterialism. While each of the new social movements focused on a specific issue – nuclear power, the environment, nuclear missiles to name just a few broader ones – they shared a contempt for visible organisational hierarchies and an emphatic concern about grass-root participation and a personal linkage between political actions or decisions on the one hand and individual involvement on the other (Roth and Rucht 1987; Roth 1985). The new women's movement which emerged in the Seventies, with a positive focus on the self-realisation of women against pressures of social conventions and a negative focus against restricting abortions, belongs to the culture of postmaterialist values and new politics. The movement itself, as we know, soon splintered into local groups and projects. The participatory style, however, of personal involvement and self-realisation as the core of political activity has continued to shape the expectations among many young, educated, politically motivated women as to the nature and effects of their activities. These kinds of expectations are hardly met by a quota allocation of posts in a traditional party environment but envisage that the environment itself should change to honour the subjective and personal qualities of women.

The Green party as the party most closely aligned to the new politics and the value orientations which sustain them also seemed to offer the most congenial environment for women with postmaterialist and new politics preferences. In fact, most of the women who initiated women's policies in the party and advocated the quota system of parity between men and women gathered their first political experiences in the women's movements or related projects. Even within the Greens, whose 50% commitment has aroused the envy of women in other parties, the place of women in the party, in parliaments and in elite positions remains unsettled. Access has been removed as an obstacle through the quota commitment. However, the focus on self-realisation which is prevalent among Green women conflicts with the practicalities of party political work. The expectations of changing the nature of the political process, which form the core of women's new politics and are the legacy of the new women's movement to the Greens, have not been met in the Green party culture.

Although leadership positions have been accessible in the Green party from the outset, and a 50% quota has been in effect since 1985, it has proved impossible to recruit more women members, or even to find enough women for party posts other than parliamentary mandates[7] (Kolinsky 1988). Among potential Green members, in particular among women, interest in politics which might be conducive to party membership often goes hand in hand with a distrust of party organisations and a preference for informal patterns of political action and small groups. While the Green party intends to mobilise those women who regard themselves as close to the women's movement, and

7. The business manager of the Greens in Rhineland Palatinate, Konrad Will-Schinneck, stressed the point during an interview on 9 April 1988 in Mainz that it was near impossible to find women who would be prepared to take on an unpaid party office, but that the quota regulations had created a climate of intense rivalry and horse-trading over the paid positions, whether as elected members of parliament or as fully paid-up employees in one of the parliamentary parties. In Will-Schinneck's view, women were only interested in political functions if they could earn a respectable income through their work.

as committed to new modes of equality, the aversion towards organisational work amongst this very clientele makes the party an unloved institution. Many of those who have joined and have taken an active part attempt to preserve their ideas of non-hierarchical political work in the day-to-day operations they perform. At all levels of Green politics, women have been disappointed that attitudes and practices which prevail in the party do not match the notions of equal, gender-neutral communication which they would wish to experience (Richardsen and Michalik 1985). Personal tensions and bickering have been perennial problems in the Greens. The deliberate informality of the organisation tends to encourage personal styles and foster accusations of chauvinism in one direction and all-too-strident feminism in the other. The emphatic pursuit of quota politics occurred in a party without a settled organisational tradition and with a multifarious network of personalised centres of power. Given the uncertainty as to how the Green party commitment to grass-root politics should be implemented, the concern with gender gave rise to additional personal tensions and political mistrust. The Green party culture seems dominated by a male-against-female camp mentality which has been exacerbated rather than smoothed by the commitment to quotas. It is unlikely to win reluctant feminists into the organisation, or broaden the party's appeal towards more conventionally minded women.

For Party Women Only?

Many of the young women whom the quota-type regulations hope to attract are looking beyond the parties to new forms of politics or have opted not to participate. Even the Greens, who seemed to forge ahead to establish a party culture of women's opportunities have only succeeded in establishing a climate of gender divides. The political drive of the Sixties and Seventies generation of women to take part in mainstream politics and play an equal and significant role is no longer evident among the youngest. A general dissatisfaction with or disinterest in the West German political environment have bred apathy or protest against the presumed futility of party politics or elections. The assumption that prospects of office-holding and access to elite positions in politics may activate young West German women and bring them into the political parties does not fully match social and political realities of present-day West Germany. The experiences of the Green party show that encrusted hierarchies of party organisation or entrenched leadership cliques are not the only obstacles to party membership and participation. The all-party target group of the new emphases on women, the educated, qualified, motivated women with career ambitions, are also the very women for whom the age-old questions of multiple commitments have yet to be solved.

As we have seen earlier, young women of today at all levels of skill hope to build a career in employment and also to have a family and children. They do not wish to choose between roles, they wish to combine them and be career women, mothers, wives, all in one. The notion of partnership is gaining ground among the younger generations but practical modalities of sharing duties and bearing responsibilities are still heavily tilted towards traditional role patterns. It is here that quota regulations may not become the participatory incentive which party women expect them to be. Unless the political parties can offer more full-time paid positions to women, which can serve as the starting block for a parliamentary career or an economically secure life as a party functionary, politics remains difficult to enter. The mothers and grandmothers of the present-day generation of leading party women joined political life as housewives, unpaid, as a meaningful pursuit in their free time, not as 'a career. For the present-day women, at least those outside the Conservative party, this niche of women's participation is no longer regarded positively. In order to create new foundations for careers in politics, quota regulations are not enough, nor are small measures such as crèche facilities during congresses. The very focus on women's participation, and the determination to define channels, targets and measures of implementing women's participation, have begun to tackle the gender gap in politics. The discrepancies of the Seventies, when motivated and qualified women sought a newly active role in political parties and found their opportunities blocked by encrusted hierarchical structures and patterns of control, are beginning to crumble in the Eighties. Only in the contemporary political climate has the participatory zeal of young women waned sufficiently to suggest that the parties will be clearing a backlog of pent-up expectations of office-holding among the over-thirties, but will be slow to break into a new reservoir of female support with the organisational promises they hold out at present.

References

Allerbeck, Klaus and Wendy Hoag, *Jugend ohne Zukunft*, Munich: Piper, 1985

Baker, Kendall J., Russell J. Dalton and Kai Hildebrandt, *Germany Transformed. Political Culture and the New Politics*, Cambridge Mass.: Harvard University Press, 1981

Barnes, Samuel et al., *Political Action. Mass Participation in Five Western Democracies*, Princeton: Princeton University Press, 1979

Becker, Horst, Bodo Hombach et al., *Die SPD von innen. Bestandsaufnahme an der Basis der Partei*, Bonn: Neue Gesellschaft, 1983

Bericht über die Gleichstellungs der Frauen in der SPD, unpublished typescript, prepared for the party congresses in Kassel, 1986 and Alsfeld, 1987

Berger, Liselotte, 'Als Bundestagsabgeordnete in Bonn', in Liselotte Berger (ed.), *Frauen ins Parlament*, Reinbek: Rowohlt, 1979

Bernadoni, Claudia and Vera Werner (eds), *Erfolg statt Karriere. Einstellungen erfolgsorientierter Frauen zum beruflichen Aufstieg*. Bonn: Deutsche Unesco Kommission, 1985

Bürklin, Wilhelm, *Wählerverhalten und Wertewandel*, Opladen: Leske & Budrich, 1988

Chandler, William M., 'Party System Transformations in the Federal Republic of Germany' in Steven B. Wolinetz (ed.), *Parties and Party Systems in Liberal Democracies*, London: Croom Helm, 1988

Dahrendorf, Ralf, *Society and Democracy in Germany*, London: Weidenfeld and Nicolson, 1967

Dalton, Russell J., 'The Persistence of Values and Life Cycle Changes', *Politische Vierteljahresschrift* Sonderheft 12, 1981

—— 'The West German Party System between Two Ages', in Russell J. Dalton et al. (eds), *Changing Electoral Forces in Western Democracies*, Princeton University Press, 1984

Datenreport 1987, ed. Statistisches Bundesamt, Bonn: Bundeszentrale für politische Bildung, 1987

Edinger, Lewis, *Germany*, Boston: Little Brown, 1986

Falke, Wolfgang, *Die Mitglieder der CDU*, Berlin: Duncker & Humblot, 1984

Falter, Jürgen et al., *Wahlen und Abstimmungen in der Weimarer Republik 1918–1933*, Munich: Beck, 1986

Feist, Ursula, Manfred Güllner and Klaus Liepelt, 'Structural Assimilation versus Ideological Polarisation: on Changing Profiles of Political Parties in West Germany', in Max Kaase and Klaus von Beyme (eds), *Elections and Parties*, London: Sage (German Political Studies 3), 1979

Feist, Ursula and Hubert Krieger, 'Alte und neue Scheidelinien des politischen Verhaltens', *Aus Politik und Zeitgeschichte* B12, 1987

Flanagan, Scott C. and Russell J. Dalton, 'Parties under Stress', *West European Politics* 1, 1984

Frau und Politik. Ergebnisse einer sozialwissenschaftlichen Untersuchung in einer westdeutschen Großstadt, INFAS, Bad Godesberg, December 1963 (unpublished report: results of an empirical survey in a West German city)

Frauen und Männer Europas im Jahr 1987. Nachtrag zu 26 Frauen Europas, ed. Commission of the European Community, Brussels, 1987

Frauenvereinigung der CDU: 40 Jahre Rheinland Pfalz, ed. Rotraud Hock, CDU, Mainz, 1987

Fuchs, Dieter, 'Trends politischer Unterstützung in der Bundesrepublik', in Dirk Berg Schlosser and Jakob Schissler (eds), *Politische Kultur in Deutschland*, Opladen: Westdeutscher Verlag (PVS Sonderheft 18), 1987, pp. 357–77

Fülles, Mechthild, *Die Frau in der Politik*, Cologne: Wissenschaft und Politik, 1969

Funke, Liselotte (ed.), *Die Liberalen. Frei sein, um andere frei zu machen*, Stuttgart: Seewald, 1984

Geiger, Michaela, 'Bayerin in Bonn für Bayern sein', in Renate Hellwig (ed.), *Die Christdemokratinnen*, Stuttgart: Seewald, 1984

Geißler, Heiner (ed.), *Abschied von der Männergesellschaft*, Frankfurt and Berlin: Ullstein, 1986

Grafe, Peter J., *Schwarze Visionen. Die Modernisierung der CDU*, Reinbek: Rowohlt, 1986

Hellwig, Renate (ed.), *Die Christdemokratinnen. Unterwegs zur Partnerschaft*, Stuttgart: Seewald, 1984

Henkel, Joachim, *Die Auswahl der Parlamentsbewerber*, Berlin: de Gruyter, 1975

Herzog, Dietrich, *Politische Führungsgruppen*, Darmstadt: Wissenschaftliche Buchgesellschaft, 1982

Hoecker, Beate, 'Frauen in der Politik', *Zeitschrift für Parlamentsfragen* 1, 1986

——, *Frauen in der Politik*, Opladen: Leske & Budrich, 1987

Hoffmann-Lange, Ursula, 'Eliten als Hüter der Demokratie? zur Akzeptanz demokratischer Institutionen und freiheitlicher Werte bei Eliten und Bevölkerung', in Dirk Berg-Schlosser and Jakob Schissler (eds), *Politische Kultur in Deutschland*, Opladen: Westdeutscher Verlag (PVS Sonderheft 18), 1987

Hofmann-Göttig, Joachim, *Emanzipation mit dem Stimmzettel*, Bonn: Neue Gesellschaft, 1986

Huber, Antje (ed.), *Die Sozialdemokratinnen. Verdient die Nachtigall Lob, wenn sie singt?* Stuttgart: Seewald, 1984

INFAS, Analyse der Bundestagswahl zum 11 Bundestag an 25. Januar 1987. Bad Godesberg, 1987 (mimeo)

Inglehart, Margaret, 'Political Interest in West European Women', *Comparative Political Studies* Vol. 14 No. 3, Oct. 1981

Inglehart, Ronald, *The Silent Revolution. Changing Values and Policy Styles among Western Publics*, Princeton: Princeton University Press, 1975

Janßen, Mechthild, *Halbe-halbe. Quotierung in West Europa*, Berlin: Elephantenpresse, 1987

Jesse, Eckhard, 'Bundestagswahlen von 1972 bis 1987 im Spiegel der repräsentativen Wahlstatistik', *Zeitschrift für Parlamentsfragen* 2, 1987

—— *Wahlen*, Berlin: Colloquium, 1988

Jugend '81, Jugendwerk der Deutschen Shell (eds), Opladen: Leske & Budrich, 1982

Klages, Helmut and Peter Kmieciak (eds), *Wertwandel und gesellschaftlicher Wandel*, Frankfurt: Campus, 1979

Klingemann, Hans-Dieter, 'West Germany', in Ivor Crewe and David Denver (eds), *Electoral Change in Western Democracies*, London: Croom Helm, 1985

—— and Max Kaase, *Wahlen und politischer Prozeß. Analysen aus Anlaß der Bundestagswahl 1983*, Opladen: Westdeutscher Verlag, 1986

Kolinsky, Eva, *Parties, Opposition and Society in West Germany*, London: Croom Helm, 1984

——, 'The Transformation of Extraparliamentary Opposition', in Eva Kolinsky (ed.), *Opposition in Western Europe*, London: PSI and Croom Helm, 1987(a)

——, 'The SPD and the Second Fräuleinwunder'. Paper delivered at the Sixth International Conference of the Council for European Studies, Washington DC, October 1987(b)

——, 'The West German Greens – a Women's Party?' *Parliamentary Affairs* 1, 1988

——, 'Women in the Green Party', in Eva Kolinsky (ed.), *The Greens in West Germany: Organisation and Policy Making*, Oxford: Berg, 1989, pp. 189–221

Kürschner's Volkshandbuch, Deutscher Bundestag, Rheinbreitbach:

Darmstädter Neue Verlagsanstalt, vol. 11, 1987 (published after each Bundestag election)

Lipset, Seymour and Stein Rokkan, *Party System and Voter Alignments*, New York: Free Press, 1967

Mintzel, Alf, 'Die Christlich–Soziale Union', in Richard Stöss (ed.), *Parteien Handbuch*, Opladen: Westdeutscher Verlag, 1983

——, *Die Volkspartei*, Opladen: Westdeutscher Verlag, 1984

Mohr, Hans-Michael, 'Politische und soziale Beteiligung', in Wolfgang Glatzer and Wolfgang Zapf (eds), *Lebensqualität in der Bundesrepublik*, Frankfurt: Campus, 1984

Noetzel, Dieter, 'Der Wandel des Wahlverhaltens der Frauen', *Die Frau in unserer Zeit* 3, 1986

Organisationsprobleme in der SPD, discussion paper prepared by the ASF, Bonn, 1988

Padgett, Stephen and Tony Burkett, *Political Parties and Elections in West Germany. The Search for a New Stability*, Hurst, 1987

Parteitag (Proceedings of the Party Congress) 1979, Bonn: Neue Gesellschaft, 1979

Pausch-Gruber, Ursula, 'Es mangelt an Solidarität', in Luc Jochimsen et al., *Frauen heute. Eine Bestandsaufnahme*, Reinbek: Rowohlt, 1981

Pulzer, Peter, 'Life after Dahl', in Eva Kolinsky (ed.), *Opposition in Western Europe*, London: PSI and Croom Helm, 1987

Richardsen, Elke and Regina Michalik, *Die quotierte Hälfte. Frauenpolitik in den grün-alternativen Parteien*, Berlin: LitPol, 1985

Riedel-Martiny, Anke, 'Genosse Hinderlich und die Frauen. Die Situation weiblicher Mitglieder in der SPD', *Neue Gesellschaft* 22, 1975

Roth, Reinhold and Elmar Wiesendahl, *Das Handlungs- und Orientierungssystem politischer Parteien*, Analysen und Berichte der Forschungsgruppe Parteiendemokratie, University of Bremen, 1986

Roth, Roland, 'Neue soziale Bewegungen und politische Kultur in der Bundesrepublik', in Karl-Werner Brand (ed.), *Neue soziale Bewegungen in West Europa und den USA*, Frankfurt: Campus, 1985

—— and Dieter Rucht (eds), *Neue soziale Bewegungen in der Bundesrepublik Deutschland*, Bonn: Bundeszentrale für politische Bildung, 1987

Schindler, Peter (ed.), *Datenhandbuch zur Geschichte des Deutschen Bundestages*; vol. 1, 1949–82; vol. II, 1982–84, Baden-Baden: Nomos, 1984, 1986

Schlei, Marie, 'Verdient die Nachtigall Lob, wenn sie singt?' in Antje Huber (ed.), *Die Sozialdemokratinnen*, Stuttgart: Seewald, 1984

Schröder, Heinrich Josef, *Die Kandidatenaufstellung und das Verhältnis des Kandidaten zu seiner Partei*, Berlin: Duncker und Humblot, 1971

Schulze, Rainer-Olaf, 'Die Bundestagswahl 1987 – eine Bestätigung des Wandels', *Aus Politik und Zeitgeschichte* B12, 1987

Smith, Gordon, *Democracy in Western Germany*, Aldershot: Gower, 1986 (3rd edn)

——, 'Party and Protest: The Two Faces of Opposition', in Eva Kolinsky (ed.), *Opposition in Western Europe*, London: PSI and Croom Helm, 1987

Stöss, Richard (ed.), *Parteien Handbuch*, 2 vols, Opladen: Westdeutscher Verlag, 1983

——, *Kandidaten und Abgeordnete. Zur sozialstrukturellen Repräsentation und Zirkulation*, Berlin: Freie Universität, Informationen aus Lehre und Forschung 4, 1985

Wettig-Danielmeier, Inge, 'Arbeitsgruppe Gleichstellung: Darstellung und Begrüdnung des vorgelegten Satzungsentwurfs', May 1987 (mimeo)

Conclusion

Much has changed since the promise of equality in the West German constitution prepared the path for women to overcome the shackles of the National Socialist mothers' cult and the related doctrine that it was women's biological destiny to care, serve and support others without ever thinking of themselves. In the recast polity of post-war Germany, one of the major currents of political culture change concerned the legitimate place of the individual versus the state, and the scope for political or personal influence he or she may command. The troubled democracy of the Weimar years had been too divided into ideological camps to allow scope for individual choices, and most camps had been too hostile to the political system to produce democratic citizens who favoured equal opportunities and participation. Women fitted the political mould and remained on the conservative right of the Weimar spectrum. In the early Thirties many swung to vote for the National Socialist German Workers Party.

Building a democratic political culture, and the climate of equal opportunities which corresponds to it, began in earnest only after the Second World War. Even then, the first decade of post-war development brought a retreat into the private sphere. After the upheavals and disruptions of personal environments in and through the war, home and family seemed to offer security and something resembling normal everyday living. Women, who had in many cases taken up employment in men's areas and had to master an unprecedented degree of independence and self-reliance in their private lives, looked to homemaking as a desirable way of life for anybody who could afford it. Going out to work continued to bear the stigma of compulsion; only women in low income groups or with no other means of support would go to work. Marriage, family life, child-rearing and a comfortable, well-furnished home became symbols of a good and affluent life after years of uncertainty and hardship.

One of the effects of socio-economic stability and the improvements in living standards which accompanied it was the emergence of choice as a salient factor in social and economic life. Where hardship and shortages had determined activities in the past, West Germans now were affluent enough to indulge in choosing certain aspects of their lifestyle: in what and how much they wanted to eat, going on holiday, taking up leisure time activities, and buying consumer goods and status symbols from cars to television sets. For the first time in generations, the Fifties offered a surplus of training places which allowed young people to choose careers and build their working lives more directly on inclinations and preferences. A shortage of labour also meant a choice of employment for those with the right qualifications. Rather than leading a life from hand to mouth and having to make do with unsuitable training or poor employment opportunities, all groups and classes of the West German population saw improvements in their personal environments which allowed them to choose careers, qualify beyond the minimum, utilise their potential, follow their inclinations and win greater social and economic mobility than the generations of their parents or grandparents would ever have thought possible.

In this climate of socio-economic mobilisation women could also begin to explore new roles, modes of participation and socio-economic choices. In the Fifties an increasing number of women remained in employment after marriage and motherhood, and more girls than in the past sought vocational and professional qualifications. Women looked beyond the private sphere and regarded training and employment at least as an insurance policy for the future in case their marriage should break up or other circumstances forced them to earn a living. The single working woman was no longer pitied as the spinster whom nobody wanted or cared for, but envied as the successful career woman who may have lost out on marriage but who could afford a lifestyle and luxuries which the homemaker-housewife was rarely able to match. The new tone also reverberated in the women's press of the late Fifties: working was presented as an option alongside others, and homemaking not as a life of duty spiced with self-sacrifice, but as another type of work, parallel to paid employment. Coinciding with the legislation to revise the civil code in the mid-Fifties, a number of magazines published accounts which added up how much a husband would have to pay for the various services delivered daily by his homemaking wife. In the short term, the petty accounting may have served as ammunition in divorce cases; in a longer-term perspective, it can be regarded as just one of the signs that values and orientations were changing to give women more choice. As notions faded away that women should by nature render service and be subservient they were encouraged to relate their own way of life to other aspects of society and look towards more participation and better opportunities in addition to and beyond the traditional grooves of family existence.

Education more than any other avenue of social participation brought equal opportunities within reach. It was a by-product of economic success and of the perceived need to exploit fully the intellectual potential and technical expertise in a given age cohort. Generally speaking, broadening access to education was a facet of equalising opportunities for all social groups in a democratic environment. Girls could benefit from it since well-to-do parents minded less if their daughters remained longer at school and many parents were now economically better off than in the founding days of the Federal Republic. After the educational reforms of the Sixties and Seventies created more places in secondary schools and in universities, the *Fräuleinwunder* of educational motivation and qualifications got truly under way. Educational achievements have frequently been a main route whereby socially disadvantaged groups gain equality of opportunities and rise to positions of influence and leadership. Women made use of education as eagerly as some immigrants have tended to do in their host societies, or as has been shown for the children of German refugees who have overtaken their peers as far as educational achievements are concerned. Today, the gender gap has disappeared in schools, and has decreased sharply at higher levels of education and in vocational training. In the mid-Eighties, nine in ten women under the age of thirty held vocational qualifications; in 1970, four in ten had done so. The motivation to qualify is also evident in universities, where women have noticeably increased their successes in final examinations; the high drop-out rate and poor orientation towards formal examinations which had characterised women academics in the Fifties are a thing of the past. If it was ever true that one of the reasons for young women to attend university thirty or more years ago was to move in socially advantaged circles and find a suitable husband, and that many only wanted to pass the time between school and marriage without serious intentions of training for a career, this *höhere Töchter* ('young ladies') approach to tertiary education has faded in contemporary society. West German young women at all levels of vocational training from apprenticeships to universities are looking for ways to extend their educational achievements into the world of work. At all levels, however, they have encountered obstacles of opportunities, transition and recognition. The problem at present is less the motivation of young women, but the perceived discrepancy between their motivations, the expectations built on them and the opportunities for women in training and employment.

Women have responded to the bottlenecks of opportunities in two distinctive ways: the first group – and numerically the larger one – has attempted to optimise vocational chances by obtaining multiple qualifications, by selecting careers in which women are known to have prospects, or courses of study which are well defined in content, vocational purpose and of short duration. Although women's occupational choices tend to be concentrated in a limited number of fields or subjects of study, vocationally motivated women have begun to diversify in search of labour market integration. That the most enterprising – the young women who trained in traditionally male areas – obtained excellent qualifications but often failed to find employment to match these qualifications highlights how entrenched the bottlenecks of opportunities are. Overcoming them is not merely a question of women broadening their horizons, but also one of women being accepted on the strength of their qualifications rather than being classified on grounds of gender.

The second type of response to the bottlenecks of opportunities consists of an interesting blend of expediency and a relapse into a traditional female marginality to the world of work. Women of this group tend to choose their specialism although they know that employment may not be available after training. At the apprenticeship level, such placements are frequently the only ones women can find; in higher education, choices are more open and women prefer not to avail themselves of them. While the vocationally motivated group would look for other fields, the second group embarks on training despite the uncertain rewards in the future. At the lower end of qualifications, these women tend to solve their problem of transition by opting out of the labour market and into marriage. Although many had originally planned to combine home-making and employment, the traditional women's role of home-making is still available as an option in itself, and preferable to the uncertainties of unemployment. At the higher end of qualifications, the academically trained women of this type tend to opt out of the competitive world of employment, in which they cannot find a ready foothold, and favour alternative lifestyles and orientations. This is not the women's road back to the home but the women's road out of the competitive climate of employment into an environment which does not appear to be dominated by the constraints and regulations of the world of work. One could argue that the inclination of academically trained women towards alternative lifestyles and activities is the contemporary successor to the *höhere Töchter* syndrome of the Fifties with qualifications and examinations of little relevance and traditional female roles in place to fall back on. Today, stepping outside the competitive spirit of qualifications and employment into alternative lifestyles means stepping into the sub-culture of West German feminism rather than into marriage and domesticity.

Drawing almost exclusively on academically educated women the feminist movement provides an ideological framework for individual experiences of the mismatch between personal inclinations and occupational opportunities. These experiences appear as inevitable products of a systemic disjunction of the patriarchal structures and practices which are said to dominate contemporary society, and of women's nature. The perceived discrepancies between women's preferences and qualifications on the one hand and the occupational opportunities open to them on the other constitute the socio-economic basis of the protest potential, which has inspired the West German women's movement. Alternative living is envisaged as a non-competitive environment and a counter-world to the patriarchal realities of contemporary society. As such it bears striking similarities to the fictitious 'women's world' of happy privacy in the past.

The gender gap of equal opportunities calls for more immediate remedies than a new set of social values with a central place for women. Despite the vocational motivation of women and despite improved qualifications at all levels of expertise, equality of employment has not yet been achieved. Young women find it harder to obtain training places; they are less likely to receive private offers from an employer in their locality, are more likely to be rejected several times and forced to accept training in fields they did not intend to choose. In order to be competitive at all, young women need better school results than young men. The odds are stacked against their successful transition from school through training to qualification and full employment. Many young women who fail to qualify today do so not by choice but because they were unable to overcome the obstacles of disadvantage.

For women, employment and qualifications are badly aligned. The practice of employing women in occupations where tasks are supportive and repetitive rather than managerial and innovative has kept even highly qualified women in white-collar and administrative functions from climbing to the top of the career ladder. Retraining programmes and the incorporation of new technologies have rendered fewer advantages for women than might have been expected: given the nature of women's tasks, new technologies have heightened the risk of deskilling. Programmes of additional training have been less effective in advancing women into managerial positions than they have been for men. Women, of course, find it difficult to engage in additional training and extend their normal working commitment if they are also mothers and wives, who spend a good deal of their time looking after their families and homes.

To date, women have borne the dual burden of employment and homemaking nearly single-handed. Partnership has gained ground as an ideal among the under-thirties but everyday practice provides little evidence that chores are shared and responsibilities shouldered by men and women. Childless couples where the woman is in full-time employment come closest to the ideal of running a partnership household. Women with children, whose entry into the labour market has been the most significant change since the early Fifties, have to find their own solutions to the dual burden. The majority of women move in and out of employment or between full-time and part-time working in order to accommodate the disparate demands on their time and person. It is the pattern of women's working lives, more so than specific discriminatory measures, which accounts for the disadvantaged position of women in employment. Few have the kind of uninterrupted employment on which a high-flying career might be built; few are free to undertake training after hours and have to jeopardise their chances of in-firm advancement. Most men consolidate their careers when they are in their thirties and forties. At that time of their lives, the majority of women can devote only some of their time and attention to employment and careers. With child care and homemaking still largely women's domains, the gender gap of opportunities in the world of work also persists.

There are some signs that attitudes among the younger generation of men and women are losing a little of their gender-specific slant with men taking a more active part in the household and child care arrangements, and women viewing their employment and careers as integral aspects of their personal lives. A reorientation of values which would eliminate the gender gap of opportunities, however, is at best a long-term process and would vary depending on the social, regional or educational backgrounds and the living environments of the people concerned. More immediate results may be derived from a different type of change: the recent legislation allowing women to return to their employment without loss of income or seniority after a career break promises to modify the adverse effects of family commitments on women's careers. Although the everyday distribution of household chores cannot be re-arranged by legislation, the broader question of socio-economic recognition for women in line with their qualifications can be adjusted in this way. The choice to resume employment after a break gives women more flexibility to adjust the balance between their private sphere and their career to suit their personal circumstances. The draft legislation had envisaged that women should have a right to return to the exact job which they had occupied before their maternity and child-care leave; under pressure from employers, the government retracted and promised equivalent employment. Although second-best, it is the first time that women can envisage combining family and work without being forced to work beneath their level of qualification in unskilled positions without prospects. In the long term, legislation of this kind should reduce the gender gap of opportunities as women need not punctuate their careers with breaks and ensuing demotions.

There are also signs that society can no longer afford to squander women's expertise and qualifications by blocking opportunities but will have to create conditions which open career opportunities for women no less than for men. Demography may be a more potent precursor of women's equality than appeals, ideologies or qualifications could ever have been. The baby-boom generation, which reached their twenties in the mid-eighties, has been the generation of educational expansion, vocational motivation and increased qualifications. When it entered the labour market, recession and unemployment made a transition from school to work doubly difficult. Women were hit by the shortage of training places and employment before they could have established a foothold at the level of employment for which they had just begun to qualify. The generation which grew up in the Seventies and which is entering vocational training and further education today is small by comparison: for the first time in decades, training places have remained unfilled and the supply of opportunities exceeds demand. This surplus situation is bound to benefit young women who will find it easier to obtain qualifications and whose skills will be in demand.

Forecasts of future labour market developments have shown that people with completed apprenticeships in the dual system, with technical, managerial and administrative expertise, will be in high demand, as will university graduates. Given the numerical decrease of the age cohort, West Germany cannot afford to bypass the skills and qualifications of her women. If the educational reforms of the Sixties were jolted into gear by the Sputnik effect – the realisation that the country had to educate everyone to full potential to remain competitive against the technological strides of the Eastern bloc – something of a Sputnik effect seems imminent for the 1990s: to make sure that the country commands a labour force of sufficient size and expertise to remain a leading industrial power, the employment potential of the whole population, men and women, needs to be developed and utilised to an optimal level. Women, it seems, are no longer knocking at the door of the labour market begging to be given a chance, but they are an invaluable resource of man-power/womenpower which must not be lost. The recent legislation on the child-care breaks (for men or women) and a guarantee of employment afterwards is but a first step towards making the gender gap of opportunities an issue of the past and allowing women to live the life young women today already would wish for themselves: to obtain vocational or professional qualifications, to follow a full career and to have a family, husband and children without facing the need to set one against the other.

In West German politics, the gender gap of participation and opportunities has already been challenged openly. Since 1985, the four main political parties – Christian Democrats, Social Democrats, Liberals and Greens – have moved towards women's quotas for party offices, for parliamentary seats and ultimately for positions of public leadership in government and opposition. If the present-day party resolutions can be implemented, women should be represented within ten years at all levels of political life at least in proportion to their strength in the membership of their party. SPD and Greens are aiming at women's representation of 40 or 50% across all political activities. By the turn of the century, the gender gap of political participation and opportunities should have been closed. First indications are that the endemic women's deficit in parliaments and in the leadership of party organisations has been reduced a little, and that more women hold top ministerial offices than had been customary in the past. Dismantling the political gender gap is, however, occurring at a slower pace than the authors of women's quotas had intended, and not without stirring up a good deal of conflict within all political parties, as established male politicians seek to defend their posts and as ambitious male members jostle to launch their political careers.

The contemporary focus on the rightful place for women in West German parties and political life is essentially a generational perspective on political participation. The generation of young, educated and qualified women who joined political parties after the late Sixties did not share the views of their mothers or grandmothers that women's political specialism was to proliferate atmosphere, hold coffee mornings, and contribute to future politics by instilling the relevant values or ideologies into their own children. The female children of post-war democracy have come to see themselves as equal citizens, as potential leaders and as competent party members. They had joined a political party because they were interested in extending their own political participation beyond voting and beyond conventional women's roles. Parties offered opportunities to hold office, and to compete for positions in the political elites; the new generation of women members in the political parties wanted to make full use of all of them. The dominant experience of the Seventies consisted of frustrated expectations: bids for equal opportunities within the established organisational channels brought very few results; despite their motivation to participate, and despite their competitive educational and professional backgrounds, party women encountered a gender barrier of political opportunities. In the eighties, pent-up discontent and frustrated expectations of having their political calibre recognised, shifted the agendas from appeals to prescriptive quotas.

None of the political parties might have been responsive to their women's claim to a slice of power, had it not been for a new topicality of gender in West German politics. Until the mid-Sixties, gender was a dormant political issue since the conservative parties commanded the majority of the female vote. That most women would vote for the centre–right seemed one of the home truths of West German politics and a built-in disadvantage for parties of the left. The entry of the post-war generation of women into electoral politics changed all that: young women, in particular those who had enjoyed more advanced education and higher vocational qualifications than their elders, developed a degree of electoral mobility, even volatility, which was unprecedented for women. They began to choose parties according to perceived policy competence, and were willing to change preferences between elections. Among the younger generations of women none of the parties has a secure footing, and all have to prove that they are competent to develop equal opportunities. The mobilisation of women through education, qualifications and party political involvement has reduced the gender gap in the contemporary social environment and brought women one step nearer to being nothing special:

just citizens in a democratic polity with equal opportunities for all people with similar skills, background and inclinations to shape their personal lives or make a bid for power.

Appendices

Appendix I

The Top Ten Choices for Women's Vocational Training

Ranking 1975 (in % of female apprentices)

1. Sales assistant[a]	12	6. Dentist's assistant[a]	5
2. Hairdresser	10	7. Sales assistant (food)	4
3. Business administrator	8	8. Banking	4
4. Doctor's receptionist[a]	7	9. Lawyer's/solicitor's	
5. Industrial sales/admin.	6	assistant	4
Subtotal 1–5	43%	10. Wholesale merchant	4
		Total 1–10	65%

Ranking 1977

1. Sales assistant[a]	12	6. Industrial	
2. Hairdresser	12	sales/administrator	6
3. Business administrator	6	7. Dentist's assistant[a]	5
4. Doctor's receptionist[a]	6	8. Sales assistant (retail)[a]	4
5. Sales assistant (food)	6	9. Banking	4
Subtotal 1–5	41%	10. Wholesale merchant	3
		Total 1–10	63%

Ranking 1984

1. Hairdresser	9	6. Industrial	
2. Sales assistant[a]	9	sales/administrator	5
3. Sales assistant (food)	7	7. Dentist's assistant[a]	4
4. Business administrator	6	8. Banking	4
5. Doctor's receptionist[a]	5	9. Sales assistant (retail)[a]	4
Subtotal 1–5	36%	10. Clerical assistant	3
		Total 1–10	57%

[a] Training programmes of 2 years' maximum duration.
Sources: Berufsbildungsbericht 1986: 42; *Berufsbildungsbericht* 1977: 16; Walter R. Heinz and Helga Krüger, 'Berufsfindung unter dem Diktat des Arbeitsmarktes', *Zeitschrift für Pädagogik* 1981, no. 5.

Appendix II

The Ten Most Popular University Subjects Among Female and Male Students, 1961 and 1986

(a) Female students 1961 and 1986 (summer term)

Rank	1960/61		1985/86	
	Subject	Total	Subject	Total
1.	Medicine	6,643	Management/ Economics	48,380
2.	German	4,704	German	35,505
3.	English	3,816	Medicine	33,978
4.	French	3,224	Law	30,786
5.	Pharmacy	2,402	Education	30,786
6.	Management/ Economics	2,248	Biology	18,576
7.	Law	1,802	English	16,642
8.	Latin	1,023	Architecture	15,422
9.	Biology	973	French	14,790
10.	History	946	Politics/Sociology	14,606
	Total (1–10)	27,781	Total (1–10)	261,810
	All subjects	39,130	All subjects	481,867
	First ten as % of all subjects	71	First ten as % of all subjects	54

(b) Male students 1961 and 1986 (summer term)

Rank	1960/61		1985/86	
	Subject	Total	Subject	Total
1.	Management/ Economics	16,476	Management/ Economics	106,017
2.	Law	15,039	Electrical engineering	76,771
3.	Medicine	12,362	Mechanical	

(b) Male students 1961 and 1986 (summer term)

	1960/61		1985/86	
Rank	Subject	Total	Subject	Total
			engineering	57,776
4.	Mechanical		Law	51,541
	engineering	9,140		
5.	Chemistry	6,802	Medicine	44,255
6.	German	6,626	Information science	27,171
7.	Physics	6,434	Physics	26,488
8.	Electrical		Civil engineering	25,329
	engineering	6,360		
9.	Civil engineering	5,091	Chemistry	24,828
10.	English	4,045	Architecture	24,210
	Total (1–10)	88,375	Total (1–10)	455,386
	All subjects	134,034	All subjects	779,954
	First ten as % of all subjects	66	First ten as % of all subjects	58

Source: Lothar Mertens, 'Die Entwicklung des Frauenstudiums in Deutschland'. Paper delivered at the conference of the Gesellschaft für Deutschland-forschung, Tutzing, March 1988 (mimeo).

Appendix III

The Changing Structure of Employment: Projections for the 1990s

	1970 %	1990 %
Occupational areas with an expected increase in importance (total workforce)		
Personal services	9	12
Task-related services	9	10
Distribution, administration, planning	32	36
Work, not related to specific product or industry	6	6
Occupational areas with an expected decrease in importance		
Machine assembly/servicing	19	17
Producers of raw materials and investment goods	7	6
Producers of consumer goods	8	6
Producers of natural products and minerals	9	4

Source: QuintAB 1, 1975: 25.

Appendix IV

Women's Main Occupational Groups

(a) The top twelve

Group	Group as % of female labour force	% of women in each occupational group
1. Office workers (semi/unskilled)	24	65
2. Office staff (skilled)	20	61
3. Sales personnel	13	63
4. Health service personnel	8	88
5. Cleaning	6	86
6. Agricultural workers	4	78
7. Teachers	4	48
8. Labourers (unskilled)	3	37
9. Textile workers incl. dressmakers	3	92
10. Accountants; data processing experts	3	59
11. Social work	3	82
12. Testers; despatch workers	2	55
Interim total	91	65
Other occupational groups	9	10
Women at work overall	100	38

(b) Occupations with the highest proportion of women

Occupation	% of women
Doctor's assistant (receptionist)	99
Dressmaker	98

(b) Occupations with the highest proportion of women

Occupation	% of women
Housekeeper	98
Cleaner	97
Copy-typist	97
Nursery nurse	96
Seamstress	95
Laundry worker, presser	91
Nurse	85
Sales assistant	84

Note: Percentages have been rounded to the nearest number; 'Interim total' is
percentage of women at work employed in these groups.
Source: Frauen in der Bundesrepublik 1986: 22, and *Frauen in Familie, Beruf und
Gesellschaft,* ed. Statistisches Bundesamt, 1987.
Data relate to 1983.

Appendix V

Part-Time Working Women in Selected Occupations[a] (%)

Occupation	%	Occupation	%
Child care/Nursery nurse	15	Banking merchant	15
Hairdresser	18	Seamstress	21
Tailor	21	Nurse/midwife	22
Wholesale/retail merchant	24	Office administrator	27
Unskilled worker	28	Cook	29
Doctor's receptionist	31	Packaging/despatch control	32
Stenographer, typist	33	Waitress/stewardess	38
Primary/special school teacher	38	Postal distributor	38
Sales assistant	45	Accountant	53
Housekeeper/home help	55	Domestic/commercial cleaner	74

[a] Three in four women are employed in these occupations.
Source: Frauen und Arbeitsmarkt, *QuintAB* 4, 1984: 30.

Appendix VI

Motivations for Party Membership

Q: 'Joining a political party is not an everyday and ordinary decision. Everyone has special reasons for becoming a party member. Please name the reasons which influenced your decision to become a party member.'

	Overall	Women	Men
Putting political goals into practice	65	49	71
Preventing power for other parties	60	48	64
Desire to be politically active	57	54	58
Mixing with like-minded people	57	54	58
Supporting the party's current policies	56	56	56
Feeling of belonging to the party	48	56	44
Dissatisfaction with other parties' policies	46	39	48
Citizen's duty	43	38	45
Ideological/religious convictions	38	33	38
Family/family tradition	25	33	22
Friends/relatives in same party	17	26	14
To meet nice people	16	16	16
To face a new challenge	13	17	12
Influence of other organisations	12	7	15
Something to do in one's spare time	12	12	12
Changes in private situation/work	7	12	6
Looking for social/occupational advantages	6	6	7
Intention to take on political office	6	3	6
Multiple answers; N=	560	197	363

Source: Beate Hoecker, 'Frauen in der Politik', *Zeitschrift für Parlamentsfragen* 1, 1986: 72.

Appendix VII

The Women's Statute of the Green Party (Passed September 1986)

The Green Party agreed detailed regulations on the representation of women in the Party. The following excerpt presents the main provisions for the federal party organisation (*Bundespartei*); similar statutes have been agreed for the regional party organisations.

To allow the reader some insights into the conceptual and organisational approach of the Greens to the issue of women's equality, the following text presents more than the bare numerical regulations and electoral procedures.

A major aim of the Greens is to put the rights and interests of women into practice. Here, expectations and reality differ sharply. As in the traditional political parties the internal structures of the Greens are a mirror image of the exterior patriarchal society. But mindful of their pledge to match expectations, ideas and actions the Greens have to develop a specifically 'Green' behaviour towards women which is not without contradictions. In the desire to find new behaviour styles in everyday life, to embrace new issues and to avoid conventional mechanisms of repression, many men do not oppose the demands for emancipation which are raised by women. On the other hand, there are tendencies of conscious or subconscious regression when men adopt traditional modes of thinking and follow practices of male dominance.

It is plainly visible that only few women occupy positions in the Greens which are important within the party or in public life. In this way, women in the Greens are barred from the right of decision making to which they are socially entitled.

Women and men in the Greens know that a change cannot be accomplished by hoping and an expression of goodwill. Therefore, concrete measures have to be developed and used on many different levels in order to strengthen the position of women.

The Greens make a further step towards change in adopting a women's statute. The women's statute identifies concrete measures designed to correct familiar structures and to facilitate new developments and experiences. A core element in this is to create conditions of parity. It is our aim that women will not only claim their formal rights but that they will realise their own interests in all aspects of their lives.

The women's statute is only a first beginning since it can only address the problems at an organisational and formal level. The

281

measures contained in this statute are not our aim but the means to realise women's interests. The statute should, above all, set further changes in motion and facilitate them.

I. Elections

In order to ensure parity, electoral procedures have to be defined in such a way that men and women are elected separately. Electoral lists have to name men and women in alternation, whereby the uneven places should be reserved for women (parity for minorities). If no woman candidate has come forward for a place allocated to women or is not elected, the electoral assembly decides on any follow-on procedures. The women who are present at the electoral assembly do enjoy a right of veto (see section II).

In order to ensure parity, even if rotation takes place within a legislative period, the lower section of an electoral list should include more women than men. Women-only lists are permissible.

II. The right of veto

In cases which touch upon the right of self-determination or which affect women especially, women are entitled to vote if prior to the main vote a separate vote among women only should be held. If the results of these votes differ, the women's right of veto defers a decision. The questions on which the vote took place have to be referred for further discussion to the party membership [*die Basis*]. This procedure is designed to ensure that questions which touch upon women's right of self-determination are being discussed more fully in the party. Requests to put this procedure in motion will be decided at the next congress of the party [*Bundesversammlung*] or in cases of urgency by the party's main committee [i.e. the party executive and regional representatives: EK] . . .

3. Party congresses [*Bundesversammlung*]

The presidium has to include an equal number of men and women. Discussions will be chaired in alternation by a female or male member of the presidium. The presidium has to ensure that women are entitled to half the time allocated for speech making; if necessary, separate lists of speakers should be opened.

4. Internal structures

Congress is in favour of annual women's conferences . . . and will allocate the necessary funds. . . . .

5. Appointments

The Greens as an employer will ensure equality between men and women. Therefore at least half the posts at all levels of qualification have to be filled with women. In areas where women are poorly represented, women have to be appointed in preference to men until the anomaly has been rectified and parity been reached.

(*Source*: *Satzung der Bundespartei. Frauenstatut. Die Grünen*, Bundesgeschäftsstelle, Bonn.)

Appendix VIII

The FDP Position on Equal Opportunities

The Liberals (FDP) passed their resolution on equal opportunities at their congress in Hanover in May 1986. The text combines a broad statement on socio-economic change with specific recommendations concerning the situation of women. The following are excerpts from a fuller programmatic text.

Introduction

The Basic Law has been in force for thirty-six years: it demands equal rights for men and women. But everybody knows that gaps remain between intentions and reality. Some things have been achieved, much remains to be done. And women are becoming increasingly impatient.

Women today have other expectations than earlier generations. They expect, as a matter of course, to be able to participate in political, social and economic decision. Liberal policy aims for more freedom and self-determination in all areas of life. An indispensable precondition of this is to put demand for equal rights which is formulated in the Basic Law into practice. In order to achieve this, we want to generate a joint effort of all forces: a concerted action for women is the answer to the challenge.

There is not enough awareness of the many small acts of discrimination; chances are uneven in many areas. Some people are clearly prepared to question traditional views and to change them in the light of equality. However, the will to reinforce intent through action has to become stronger. The attitude of many men is quite understandable: is there anybody who willingly gives up advantages which he enjoyed for decades? The challenge also extends to women themselves.

Liberals consider it a mistake to believe that special rights and protective clauses can create equal participation. On the contrary: the world of work has proved that protective clauses have made it more difficult for women to take part.

For women it has to be clear: equality is not available at zero rating. Whoever wants chances has to accept risks. Whoever obtains rights also has duties. Whoever wants to change something has to contribute actively to the process. The path from demand to realisation is a long one.

Industrial society is undergoing profound changes: new technologies

284

create new opportunities. Women are especially affected: positively since new technologies increase flexibility and make it easier to combine family duties and employment and also give rise to new, qualified places of work; negatively since many traditional women's posts are being disestablished and there is a danger of losing the contacts outside the home which women wish for. To make use of the opportunity afforded by new technologies is up to every individual; to reduce the risks is a matter for the state which defines the framework for this.

These challenges demand new political answers. . . . Now the 'fatherless family' and the 'motherless society' have to be replaced by a period of partnership in all areas of life. . . . The kind of division of labour which allocates men the office and women the honorary office has to be replaced by a just distribution of tasks.

[In the programme, the party develops its answers in three core areas: family, employment and participation in political and social decision making. In our context, the focus on participation is of interest:]

To extend participation of women in political and social decision
The first Bundestag had more female members than the Bundestag today [in 1986: EK]. The situation then stemmed from the strong involvement of women during and after the war. In the Fifties, the number of women in public life declined. Although a reversal of this trend has to be accompanied by supportive political measures, it can only be accomplished by women themselves: they have to join political parties, they have to become candidates, and they have to support other women. Women have to accept the challenge. . . .

The electoral law has to be changed
Every citizen shall not only be able to choose his preferred party but should be allowed to change the order of candidates presented on the party lists.

The FDP rejects quota regulations
Liberal women face competition. But if qualifications are comparable, women have to enjoy equality of chances not only in law but also in real life.

Make self-help for women a success
Self-help groups occupy a firm place in the necessary net of decentralised care and social support. Most of these groups want to work without state interference and in doing so they have proved to be more effective than the clumsy organisations of many charities and state-run bodies. It has to be a task for communities and districts to support these

groups since they contribute to social provisions there.

A women's equality officer with an ombuds-commission has to support the effort to put equality into practice
About forty years after the demand for equality in the Basic Law it is clear: success has to be fought for, and it has to be organised. The FDP asks the government to create the post of an independent federal woman officer for the equality of men and women. She shall investigate infringements of the law and demand that they be stopped, and she shall provide assistance to fight court cases. She shall organise hearings and initiate model projects. She shall report to the Bundestag on a regular basis.

The concerted action for women can only succeed if men and women give it their support. More equality can only be achieved if men really accept their new role and the concept of partnership. Solidarity among women is desirable, since jointly we are stronger. But we shall only succeed as a society.

(*Source:* FDP (Die Liberalen), *Gleichberechtigung durchsetzen. Wir wollen eine Konzertierte Aktion für Frauen*. Resolution passed at the 37th regular Federal Assembly of the FDP in Hanover, 23–25 May 1986. The resolution has been adopted as the women's section of the FDP electoral programme for 1987–1991. Published as a separate brochure by FDP Bundesgeschäftsstelle, Bonn, 1986.)

Appendix IX

Plan for the Advancement of Women (Frauenförderplan) in the FDP

The following is the text of an executive decision of 6 April 1987 which specifies how the commitment to equality should be put into practice. It has been the basis for the report compiled by Ruth Wagner and the discussion within the FDP about target figures and *de facto* participation of women (see Chapter 6).

1. It is the aim of the FDP to increase within the next five years in a first step the share of women in decision making functions in such a way that it is in line with their share of the membership (at present 25 per cent).

2. The FDP will

— create and support special groups, initiatives and committees at federal, regional and communal level;

— create an equality office [Gleichberechtigungsstelle] at the head office of the party as soon as finance has been agreed;

. . .

— adjust dates and organisation of party congresses and other party events in such a way that they are more readily combined with family obligations.

3. The chairpersons at districts, regional, *Land* and federal level report annually at their respective congresses on

— membership developments and the proportion of women in the FDP

— number and proportion of women delegates at the congress in question

— the share of women on party electoral lists (especially top places) and in party executives.

The FDP continues to underwrite the concept of personal responsibility and therefore dispenses with inflexible quotas based on parity.

(*Source: Freie Demokratische Korrespondenz fdk*, Anlage 1, edition no. 89, 7 April 1987.)

Appendix X

Equality [Gleichstellung] for Men and Women in the SPD

The following text presents the main points of the resolution on equal opportunities which was passed at the Nuremberg congress of the SPD in 1986 and which prepared the ground for the 1988 quota decision. In essence, the arguments had been rehearsed by the SPD women's association ASF since the mid-Seventies, and carried into the main party through the work of the equality commission which has been attached to the party executive since 1977 and prepares policy initiatives in this area.

In order to make democracy a reality, men and women should participate equally in the political life of a country.

Therefore, the SPD fought for women's voting rights and has promoted equality before the law for men and women in marriage and in society at large. To grant women full equality within its own ranks has now become a question of credibility for the SPD. . . . All male and female comrades are increasingly aware of the fact that we only practice what we preach if we enable women to make their own decisions: but we also have to incorporate female perspectives on life and female experiences into our political concepts if we want to make full use of the chances inherent in social democratic policies. Only in this way shall we be able to increase the share of women in our membership.

. . . it is the firm goal of the SPD to increase the share of women in elected parliamentary seats, in offices and functions in such a way that in the 1990s women are basically represented in all functions and electoral posts in accordance with their share in the population.

We assume that this goal can be reached in three steps: first we have to increase the proportion of women in party functions to their proportion of our membership, but to no less than 25 per cent. Then we have to ensure that every third post in the party is held by a woman. A third step will finally ensure that the participation of women at all levels of office holding corresponds to the proportion of women in the overall population.

The party will endorse the goal of internal equality – if this has not already happened in the various sections – by changing organisational statutes, electoral procedures and other regulations accordingly and make equality obligatory.

(*Source: Politik Informationsdienst der SPD* no. 14, September 1986: 2.)

Appendix XI

ASF Resolution: Women in the SPD

The ASF took the initiative in October 1985 and passed a resolution at its federal congress in Hanover (4–6 Oct. 1985) which spelt out in considerable detail the different measures which needed to be taken; of particular interest were the preparations for the 1987 elections, and the composition of electoral lists and distribution of constituency places among men and women.

Equality in the party

The SPD has a great many very highly qualified women who are suitable for all political posts and public offices. This means that female Social Democrats are also available as candidates for the office of chancellor and that they shall also register this claim for the future. For the 1987 federal elections we demand that the electoral team and the future cabinet will include equal numbers of men and women. . . .

Quotas

The organisational statutes will be changed to include the requirement that all decision making bodies, party offices and parliamentary seats shall include no less than 40 per cent both of men and women.

Equality of women in the SPD

In reality, equality in the SPD is lagging behind substantially. Appeals and congress resolutions have not had any effect so far. Changing the internal structure of the party has yet to be accomplished at all levels of the party. . . . The ASF executive are called upon to prepare specific actions which should include strategies of refusal and, for instance, separate women's lists in the party as well as public solidarity campaigns in the event that the party does not put its own resolutions on women's equality into practice.

(*Source: Frauen in der SPD. Schwestern zur Sonne, zur Gleichheit! Sozialdemokratischer Informationsdienst* no. 24, November 1985: 6–7, 9.)

Appendix XII

Quota Regulations: The SPD Position

On 20 October 1987 Anke Fuchs, the SPD party manager, summarised the recommendations which had been reached by a special executive meeting in Mannheim, and which were to form the basis for the party congress decision of September 1988 to incorporate quotas into the party statutes.

In accordance with the request from congress, the party executive has now formulated the following proposal for discussion:

1. A general quota regulation will be incorporated into the organisational statutes as a compulsory component, which prescribes a minimum participation of 40%. However, local party branches with a membership below 50/100/150 (the precise figure has yet to be decided) will be exempted from compulsory quota regulations. For these local branches, quotas will merely be recommended.

(a) Compulsory quotas apply to all elections of delegates (e.g. at district and regional party congresses) and of executive bodies with more than one member (e.g. party executives). These quotas also apply to the federal party congress, regardless of whether the delegates have been elected by district congresses or, as is permissible in the statutes, by sub-district congresses. The districts have to ensure that quotas are being adhered to.

(b) Obligatory quotas will be introduced in two stages: from 1988 onwards, 33%; from 1994 onwards, 40%.

2. Quotas also apply to candidacies on electoral lists for European, federal, regional and communal elections. Quotas apply to the lists in total, and also to the number of places on the list which were successful in the preceding election. For candidacies at local and regional elections, districts are asked to formulate their own statutes and procedures.

These quotas will be introduced in three stages: 25% in 1990; 33% in 1994; and 40% in 1998.

3. The electoral procedures shall be changed in such a way as to ensure compliance with the quota regulations.

(*Source: SPD Mitteilungen für die Presse*, 20 Oct. 1987: 1–2.)

[Within the ASF, the notion of exemptions for small party branches was received with misgivings:]

Troubles with quotas
. . . it is clear that in the long run nobody can gain acceptance in the SPD if he ignores the women. The women's question has become too much tied up with a test of credibility for the SPD. Yet, the recent decision on quota regulations by the SPD executive in Mannheim has caused considerable annoyance with regard to its time span and also because small branches of 50, 100 or 150 members shall be exempted from compulsory quotas. Some 52% of SPD branches have less than 100 members, and for these the gender quota would not be compulsory. If the upper limit were to be 150, even more branches would be exempted.

(*Source: ppp Hintergrund Dienst* 19 Oct. 1987: 4.)

[In her speech to the federal congress of the ASF on 16–18 October 1987, the chair, Inge Wettig-Danielmeier, presented a good summary of the history and the current situation:]

The troubled path towards equality
It has been a long story. In 1971 the protective clause of electing at least four women into the party executive was abolished. The young women believed at the time that women should be able to gain positions and participate on equal terms without special protective measures. In the following year, only two women were elected into the party executive instead of the previous four. In 1977, the ASF demanded that a Commission for Equality should be created, with an equal number of male and female members. Willy Brandt supported the demand, and agreed to chair it jointly with the ASF chairman, Elfriede Hofmann. The Commission prepared the concept that equality should develop gradually through special women's plans, and that each party congress should receive progress reports.

Willy Brandt and Egon Bahr, the business manager of the SPD, were even then in favour of a system of protective quotas. In 1979, the SPD congress in Berlin accepted the proposals about equality for men and women in the party. Until 1982, nothing much happened. Therefore, the party women once again demanded a working group on equality, which should not only develop proposals for congress but also focus on the question of how proposals could be implemented. The working group on equality has since been in permanent session; it included an equal number of members of the women's group and the party executive. Chairmen with equal rights are the chair of the ASF and one of the deputy party chairmen. For two years, Peter Glotz had taken on this task.

291

The party congress in Essen in 1984 made the proposals more concrete and committed all tiers of the party organisation to suggest more women for party posts and for electoral mandates: 'The aim of equal representation of men and women has to be reached in recognisable and planned steps'. There have been clear signs of progress in electing women to positions in the party executive, but in elections the proportion of women remained low. Therefore, the ASF in 1985 and the SPD congress in 1986 decided that a firm minimum to protect the position of women (and men) was required.

. . . It is time that women have more influence in the political process, and that they can achieve political success at local level and in party committees which is in line with their needs and those of their families. Political work does not have to be boring, it does not have to be detrimental to health or laden with stress; it could, more than at present, involve the whole person. The SPD is well advised to change its statutes and make it clear that it needs new members, not only to pay their party dues, but especially to participate in making policy.

(*Source*: Archive of the SPD Parteivorstand, X 21-ASF P.)

Appendix XIII

CDU Resolution on the Equality of Men and Women

In 1985, the CDU launched a new initiative on women. Headed 'The New Partnership' and inspired by the party business manager and then also Minister of Youth, Family and Health, Heiner Geißler, the CDU held a special women's congress in Essen. In a public jamboree with some 500 women as special guests and under the full glare of television cameras, the party launched its partnership programme (see Appendix XIV) which was followed one year later by a more mundane document on inner party adjustments and organisational equality. This, however, has been regarded as the key to rights of representation by the women in the Frauenunion who consider it as an institutional promise. This emerged in a number of interviews the author conducted with CDU women between January 1987 and April 1988.

Resolution on Equality of Men and Women passed at the 34th CDU party congress in Mainz, October 1986

1. A consistent implementation of equal rights of men and women . . . presumes equal chances in politics. Through the guidelines on the new partnership between men and women which were accepted at the Essen party congress, the political equality of women has become a topic for the party. The CDU committed itself to formulating clear targets for women's participation and to putting them into practice step by step in a deliberate, and intensive fashion. . . . The CDU . . . contributes its share to the equality of men and women. The share of women among office holders, elected positions and party functions will be increased by the early 1990s· to match the share of women in the party membership.

2. The CDU undertakes to put the principle of equality into practice at all organisational levels in the party and its divisions.

(a) In order to reach this target it is necessary to consider women for favourable positions on party electoral lists or as constituency candidates. This applies to all communal, regional, federal and European elections.

(b) This principle shall also apply to leadership positions in parliamentary groups, and for government posts.

(c) A report about equality in the party shall . . . be presented annually at the party congress. The party organisations at the *Land*, district and local level are asked to do the same. These reports inform

293

about the proportion of women among the membership, office holders, members of parliaments and elected assemblies as well as in commissions, special working groups and associations of the party and among full-time paid party employees.

Appendix XIV

CDU Guidelines on 'New Partnership'

The *Essener Leitsätze* – the guidelines entitled 'The New Partnership between Men and Women' – anticipated the CDU legislative programme which was designed to make it easier for women to combine employment with raising a family; this aspect has been discussed in Chapter 2. The guidelines also define the framework for the CDU internal discussion of the role of women. The guidelines are a prime example of the new flexible conservatism of the CDU which attempts to make a pragmatic adjustment to changed attitudes in order to retain or even increase its electoral appeal. The concept of new partnership and the acceptance of non-family roles for women has been strongly attacked within the CDU by representatives of the Catholic Church and other conservative circles, and also by the Bavarian CSU. The younger women in the party, however, regard it as the core policy which they can support, and which the party ought to advocate in a more assertive fashion.

The New Partnership of Men and Women (sections on women's participation in politics)
Every democracy depends on the participation of its male and female citizens. Partnership in politics means that men and women recognise each other's expert knowledge, life experiences and ability to judge issues and regard this as an essential precondition for arriving at political decisions. The strong call on women's time through raising children and through housework or the dual obligations of employment and family obstructs their active political participation.

The number of women members in political parties has increased steadily over the last couple of years, but their share in leadership positions has not. A suitable political participation of women can only be achieved if prejudice is dissolved and if parties develop a climate of openness which encourages women to play a more active role. Political equality of women, however, must not remain a matter for women alone but it has to become an issue for the party. Measures have to be devised and used in a more deliberate and controlled fashion. The organisational tiers of the party are called upon to develop new ways of involving larger circles of male and female citizens in the decisions and political activities of the party. In view of the growing number of politically minded women, the purpose of participation should be clearly defined and put into practice step by step.

Participation of women has to go well beyond the so-called alibi woman. The CDU calls on the federal government, the *Land* governments and the local councils to involve women more than in the past when appointing members of committees or when filling top positions. It is the joint task of men and women to abolish the gross discrepancy between women's party membership and their representation in parliaments and party offices. . . .

Citizens should be able to participate in their democracy. Therefore, party congress calls on the CDU/CSU parliamentary party and on the CDU parliamentary groups in the regions and in local assemblies to check . . . how the electoral legislation could be changed to provide voters with better chances of participation when casting their vote, in particular by enabling the voter to change the order of names on electoral lists in line with his or her preferences. Such changes in the electoral law will improve the electoral chances of female candidates.

(*Source: Essener Leitsätze*, ed. CDU Bundesgeschäftsstelle. Hauptabteilung Öffentlichkeitsarbeit, Bonn, 1985: 15–16.)

Index

Index

Index

Index

Potsdam Agreement, 24
primary sector
  decline of, 159
printing industry, 169
property rights, 49
Pross, Helge, 77
  study of housewives in 1970s, 86–7

qualifications
  gender gap in, 110, 113
  and interest in politics, 198–9
  university, 130–1
  vocational, 110–13
  and women's employment, 106–7, 264
quotas, women's, 233–4, 253
  and CDU, 240
  and Free Democratic Party, 234–5
  and Green Party, 234, 251, 252
  and Social Democratic Party, 235–8, 243–4, 246

refugees
  at end of Second World War, 24–5, 32, 34
Renger, Annemarie, 228, 231, 232

salaries, *see* pay
Schelsky, Helmut, 76
Schlei, Marie, 226–7, 228, 231
Schmidt, Helmut, 226, 227
Scholz-Klink, Gertrud, 17
schools
  hierarchy of, 104, 106
  types of, 102–4
Schumacher, Kurt, 231
secondary sector, 159
Selbert, Elisabeth, 45
self-development, 145, 148
self-employment, 83
service sector
  part-time employment in, 175
sexual experience, 91–2
single women, 24–5, 79–81
skill shortages, 174
Social Democratic Party (SPD)
  ASF women's organisation, 244, 246
  election to party executive in 1988, 238
  and enfranchisement of women, 9, 10
  and equality for women, 44, 45

  motivations for membership, 215
  move to centre, 203
  obstacles to women holding office in, 219
  recruitment of women in, 246
  women members, 209, 210, 212, 213, 267
  women members of Bundestag, 221–2
  women as parliamentary candidates, 224, 226, 236, 245
  women in parliamentary group, 231–2
  and women's movement, 66–7
  and women's quotas, 235–8, 243–4, 245, 246
  and women's vote, 201, 203–4, 206
  and working class, 200, 204
socialisation patterns
  gender differences in, 91–2
socialist women's movement, 9
social role of women
  changing conceptions of, 76–7, 93–5
Strauß, Franz Josef, 231
Süßmuth, Rita, 227–8, 248

teachers
  training of, 136, 138, 140
  unemployment among, 141–3, 144
teaching
  as career choice for women, 140, 141, 142
tertiary education
  examination performance of women in, 133–40
  number of students in, 129
  students with vocational training in, 130
  see also universities
tertiary sector
  part-time employment in, 173, 175, 179
  women employed in, 159–60, 172, 173
Timm, Helga, 231
trade unions, 63
training
  and Employment Promotion Act, 56–9
  in-service, 168
  and new technology, 167–74
  vocational, *see* vocational training